The Italian Letter

The Italian Letter

How the Bush Administration Used a Fake
Letter to Build the Case for War in Iraq

Peter Eisner and
Knut Royce

RODALE

Rodale books may be purchased for business or promotional use or for special sales. For information, please write to:
Special Markets Department, Rodale Inc., 733 Third Avenue, New York, NY 10017

Printed in the United States of America
Rodale Inc. makes every effort to use acid-free ∞, recycled paper ♻.

Library of Congress Cataloging-in-Publication Data

Eisner, Peter.
    The Italian letter : how the Bush administration used a fake letter to build the case for war in Iraq / Peter Eisner and Knut Royce.
       p.   cm.
    Includes bibliographical references.
    ISBN-13 978–1–59486–573–2   hardcover
    ISBN-10 1–59486–573–6   hardcover
    1. Iraq War, 2003—Causes.   2. United States—Politics and government—date
    3. United States—Foreign relations—date   4. Political corruption—United States.
    I. Royce, Knut.   II. Title.
DS79.76.E28 2007
956.7044'31—dc22   2007004529

Distributed to the trade by Holtzbrinck Publishers

2   4   6   8   10   9   7   5   3   1   hardcover

We inspire and enable people to improve their lives and the world around them

For more of our products visit **rodalestore.com** or call 800-848-4735

To Sunny, Momo and Bé

and to Lorraine Eisner

Contents

Characters

Their positions in 2003:

ACCAME, FALCO, retired Italian admiral

AL-SAHHAF, MOHAMMED SAEED, Iraqi information minister

AL-ZAHAWIE, WISSAM, Iraqi ambassador to the Vatican

BAUTE, JACQUES, head of the Iraq Nuclear Verification office at the International Atomic Energy Agency

BERLUSCONI, SILVIO, Italian prime minister

BLAIR, TONY, British prime minister

BLIX, HANS, chief UN weapons inspector in Iraq

BOLTON, JOHN, undersecretary of state, Arms Control and International Security

BURBA, ELISABETTA, Milan reporter at the weekly *Panorama* who was given the Italian letter

BUSH, GEORGE WALKER, 43rd president of the United States

CHALABI, AHMED, head of the Iraqi National Congress, based in London

CHENEY, RICHARD, 46th vice president of the United States

CHOUET, ALAIN, head of the French Security Intelligence Service

CLARKE, RICHARD, retired White House counterterrorism advisor

DEARLOVE, SIR RICHARD, head of British intelligence, MI6

DODGE, SIMON, nuclear weapons analyst, State Department Bureau of Intelligence and Research

ELBARADEI, MOHAMED, chief of the UN International Atomic Energy Agency

FEITH, DOUGLAS, undersecretary of defense, who established the Office of Special Plans

FOLEY, ALAN, director of the CIA's Center for Weapons Intelligence, Nonproliferation, and Arms Control

FORD JR., CARL, head of the State Department Bureau of Intelligence and Research

HADLEY, STEPHEN, deputy US national security advisor

HANNAH, JOHN, senior security advisor to Vice President Cheney

HASTERT, JOHN, 59th speaker of the House of Representatives

HUSSEIN, SADDAM, president of Iraq, overthrown in the 2003 US invasion of Iraq

IONTA, FRANCO, chief prosecutor in Rome

JONES, BRIAN, British defense ministry intelligence analyst

JOSEPH, ROBERT, staff member at the National Security Council

KWIATKOWSKI, KAREN, retired air force lieutenant colonel, who worked at the Pentagon

LEDEEN, MICHAEL, fellow at the American Enterprise Institute, specialist on Italy and the Middle East

LIBBY, I. LEWIS "SCOOTER," chief of staff for Vice President Cheney

LUTI, WILLIAM, Pentagon official in charge of the Near East and South Asia Affairs (NESA) Directorate

MAINASSARA, IBRAHIM BARE, late president of Niger, assassinated in 1999

MARTINO, ANTONIO, Italian defense minister

MARTINO, ROCCO, Italian intelligence operative who delivered the Italian letter to Burba

MAYAKI, IBRAHIM, former Nigerien foreign minister

MONTINI, LAURA, also known as "La Signora," employee at Nigerien embassy, Rome

MYLROIE, LAURIE, fellow at the American Enterprise Institute

NUCERA, ANTONIO, retired colonel at SISMI, the Italian military intelligence agency

OWENS-KIRKPATRICK, BARBRO, US ambassador to Niger

PILLAR, PAUL, CIA national intelligence officer for the Near East and South Asia Affairs Directorate

PLAME WILSON, VALERIE, an officer at the CIA's Counterproliferation Division

POLLARI, NICOLO, head of Italian military intelligence

POWELL, COLIN, US secretary of state

RICE, CONDOLEEZZA, national security adviser

ROSSELLA, CARLO, editor of *Panorama*

RUMSFELD, DONALD, secretary of defense

SEMBLER, MELVIN, US ambassador to Italy

SHULSKY, ABRAM, head of the Office of Special Plans

TANDJA, MAMADOU, president of Niger in 2000

TENET, GEORGE, director of Central Intelligence Agency

WILKERSON, LAWRENCE, chief of staff to Secretary of State Colin Powell

WILSON, JOSEPH, retired US ambassador, sent on fact-finding mission to Niger by the CIA

WOLFOWITZ, PAUL, deputy secretary of defense

WOOLSEY, JAMES, former director of Central Intelligence Agency

Acronyms

CIA—Central Intelligence Agency

COPACO—The Italian parliamentary committee that investigated the Niger case

DGSE—French intelligence agency, Direction Générale de la Sécurite Extérieure

DIA—Defense Intelligence Agency

IAEA—International Atomic Energy Agency

INR—Bureau of Intelligence and Research, State Department

MI6—British government intelligence service

NCIS—Naval Criminal Investigative Service

NESA—Near East and South Asia Affairs (NESA) Directorate, Pentagon

NIE—National Intelligence Estimate

NSC—National Security Council

OSCE—Organization for Security and Cooperation in Europe

OSP—Office of Special Plans

SISMI—Italian intelligence agency, Servizio per le Informazioni e la Sicurezza Militare

SSCI—Senate Select Committee on Intelligence

UNVIE—US Mission to International Organizations in Vienna

WHIG—White House Iraq Group

WINPAC—Center for Weapons Intelligence, Nonproliferation, and Arms Control, CIA

Chronology

1998

October: The International Atomic Energy Agency reports: "There are no indications that there remains in Iraq any physical capability for the production of amounts of weapon-usable nuclear material of any practical significance."

December 16: The United States, supported by Britain, launches four days of air attacks on Iraq.

1999

February 1: Niger's ambassador to Rome sends a telex addressed to the foreign minister in Niamey announcing the upcoming visit of Iraq's emissary to the Vatican, Wissam al-Zahawie.

February 5: Al-Zahawie visits Niger, seeking support from African countries to oppose UN sanctions. American embassy files report on the public visit, describing it as routine.

March/April: The CIA receives a report that a delegation of Iraqis, Iranians, and Libyans visited Somalia to discuss extracting uranium. But Iraq and Iran are sworn enemies; a US government inquiry (the Robb-Silberman Commission) later reports it was "not considered reliable by most analysts at the time."

Early summer: Ibrahim Mayaki, then prime minister of Niger, meets with an Iraqi official during a meeting of the Organization of African Unity in Algiers. He later told Ambassador Joseph Wilson that the official was Iraqi information minister Mohammed Saeed al-Sahhaf, who later became known as "Baghdad Bob." They did not discuss uranium.

November 12: Paul Sereno of the University of Chicago announces in the journal *Science* the discovery in Niger of *Jobaria*, a 20-ton, 70-foot-tall dinosaur that lived 135 million years ago.

2000

Antonio Nucera, a SISMI officer who headed the agency's counter-proliferation section in Rome, approaches Rocco Martino, a former Carabinieri policeman, asking if he is interested in earning some money. He introduces Martino to Laura Montini, who works at the Nigerien embassy in Rome, planted there by SISMI.

Montini gives Martino a series of documents, which he forwards to French intelligence agents. Some of the intelligence deals with Islamic fundamentalism and politics in the Balkans.

The State Department renews operational links to the Iraqi National Congress (INC) by paying the group $340,000 a month to gather intelligence on Iraq. It abandons this arrangement in 2002.

December 1: A substantial UK Joint Intelligence Committee assessment is published. "Unconfirmed intelligence indicates Iraqi interest in acquiring uranium."

2001

January 2: The Nigerien embassy in Rome reports a burglary in which letterhead stationery, documents, and official seals are stolen. No culprit is found.

January 20: George Walker Bush is inaugurated as the 43rd president of the United States.

April 2001: A meeting supposedly takes place in Prague between 9/11 hijacker Mohammed Atta and an Iraqi intelligence official. From December 2001 until the invasion, the Bush administration makes reference to the meeting. Czech investigators and the CIA later dismiss the claim, which was based on a single unreliable witness.

Summer: Rocco Martino assembles a dossier of information including the Italian letter, provided by SISMI operatives. It is a package of forged documents based on papers stolen from the Nigerien embassy, plus old material from SISMI files.

September 11: Al Qaeda hijackings and attacks in New York, Washington, DC, and Pennsylvania.

September 12: James Woolsey, former CIA director, says on a nationwide television cable program that "there could be some government action involved together with bin Laden or a major terrorist group. And one strong suspect there I think would be the government of Iraq."

Late September: Woolsey, supported by undersecretary of defense Paul Wolfowitz and Richard Perle, chairman of the Defense Policy Board, flies to London to gather information to support his suspicion. London is the home of Ahmed Chalabi, exiled leader of the US-backed Iraqi National Congress. The Senate Intelligence Committee later reports that Chalabi's INC "attempted to influence United States policy on Iraq by providing false information through defectors directed at convincing the United States that Iraq possessed weapons of mass destruction and had links to terrorists."

October 15: SISMI presents the CIA Rome station with the first report about the alleged Iraq–Niger uranium deal. The CIA Rome station reports to Washington, noting that the information is uncorroborated.

December: Michael Ledeen arranges a secret meeting attended by Italian military intelligence personnel, Pentagon officials, alleged Iranian intelligence agents, and noted Iranian intelligence fabricator Manucher Ghorbanifar.

2002

January 29: Bush in the State of the Union address describes Iraq, Iran, and North Korea as part of an "axis of evil."

February: Italian intelligence gives the CIA the verbatim text of one of the Martino documents. It contains numerous errors.

February 12: The Defense Intelligence Agency reports that Niger is supplying 500 tons of uranium a year to Iraq. Vice President Cheney asks the CIA to provide more information.

February 14: WINPAC at the CIA reports that the Italian intelligence claim about a Niger uranium sale lacks "crucial details."

February 26: Ambassador Joseph Wilson travels to Niger on a fact-finding mission for the CIA.

March 1: The State Department Bureau of Intelligence and Research reports that the Niger sale of uranium to Iraq is unlikely.

March 5: Wilson, back from Niger, is debriefed by two CIA agents and reports that there is no evidence of the sale.

March 24: Cheney says on *Late Edition with Wolf Blitzer* that Saddam Hussein is actively pursuing nuclear weapons at this time.

May 10: The CIA's Near East (NESA) office reports that "a foreign government service says Iraq was trying to acquire 500 tons of uranium from Niger." On August 1 the same office issues a report on Iraq, but does not mention Niger uranium.

June: The CIA, after an exhaustive investigation, dismisses the allegation that Mohammed Atta met with Iraqi agents in Prague.

July 23: Sir Richard Dearlove, the head of British intelligence, tells Prime Minister Tony Blair after a visit to CIA headquarters that war is inevitable and "the intelligence and facts were being fixed around the policy."

August 26: Cheney says in Nashville that Iraq poses a mortal threat.

Late summer: The White House Iraq Group is formed to run the public relations campaign to sell the war on Iraq.

September 8: Cheney on NBC's *Meet the Press* repeats the discredited Mohammed Atta charge. He said, "We have reporting that places [Mohammed Atta, the lead 9/11 hijacker] in Prague with a senior Iraqi intelligence official a few months before the attack."

September 8: Judith Miller and Michael Gordon of the *New York Times* report that Iraq purchased aluminum tubes to enrich uranium for a nuclear bomb.

September 24: Britain issues a report claiming that Iraq was seeking uranium from Africa and including a statement by Blair that Saddam Hussein could launch weapons of mass destruction with 45 minutes' notice.

September 25: President Bush and Condoleezza Rice, the national security advisor, both make claims about the link between al Qaeda and Iraq.

September 28: Bush repeats Blair's 45-minute claim.

October 1: The Intelligence Community publishes an NIE that claims Iraq is reconstituting its nuclear weapons program and includes SISMI's intelligence that Iraq has been shopping for uranium from Niger.

October 4: The CIA publishes an unclassified report but does not mention the Africa uranium purchase.

October 7: Bush delivers a speech in Cincinnati and, on the advice of CIA director George Tenet, does not mention the Iraq–Niger uranium connection.

Elisabetta Burba flies from Milan to Rome, where she receives the Italian letter and accompanying documents describing the Niger–Iraq deal from Rocco Martino.

October 9: Burba delivers the documents to the US embassy in Rome on the advice of her editor, Carlo Rossella, at *Panorama*.

October 10: The House gives Bush authorization to go to war, and the Senate quickly follows.

October 16: The documents delivered by Burba are distributed to members of the Intelligence Community in Washington.

Burba travels to Niger and, like Wilson, finds that the Niger–Iraq uranium sale is unlikely.

December 7: Iraq submits to the UN Security Council a 12,000-page report denying possession of weapons of mass destruction.

December 17: The CIA's WINPAC challenges the Iraq report in a classified report, complaining that Iraq did not acknowledge efforts to procure uranium from Niger.

December 18: The State Department rebuts the Iraq report and publicly mentions for the first time that Niger is the country in Africa where Iraq has been seeking uranium.

2003

January 13: Simon Dodge, a State Department nuclear weapons specialist, sends colleagues in the Intelligence Community an e-mail saying that the uranium story "probably is a hoax."

January 20: A White House report says Iraq's declaration to the UN is a shameless lie.

January 23: National Security Advisor Rice says in the *New York Times* that Iraq's declaration to the UN "fails to account for or explain Iraq's efforts to get uranium from abroad."

January 26: Secretary of State Colin Powell asks, "Why is Iraq still trying to procure uranium?"

January 27: The White House gives a draft of the State of the Union address to CIA director Tenet. Tenet gives it, apparently without reading it, to an assistant.

UN weapons inspectors in Iraq say they need more information from the United States to search for evidence.

January 28: President Bush delivers his State of the Union address, which includes the "16 words."

February 5: Secretary of State Colin Powell details US charges against Iraq before the UN Security Council, mentioning the aluminum tubes but not the Nigerien uranium. His speech convinces many, but, less than a year later, most of the claims are proven false.

February 10: Now-retired Iraq ambassador al-Zahawie is summoned to Baghdad for an interview with UN officials.

March 20: The "Coalition of the Willing" launches the invasion of Iraq.

May 1: Bush declares, "Major combat operations in Iraq have ended."

May 29: Cheney aide I. Lewis "Scooter" Libby asks Marc Grossman, undersecretary of state, for information about recent articles in the *New York Times, Washington Post*, and *New Republic* about Wilson's trip to Niger. Grossman asks Paul Pillar for a report.

June 23: Libby meets with Judith Miller of the *New York Times* and, according to her notes, tells her that "Mr. Wilson's wife might work for the CIA."

June 27: Libby tells Bob Woodward of the *Washington Post* that Iraq's effort to obtain uranium was "vigorous."

July 6: Wilson publishes a piece in the *New York Times*, "What I Didn't Find in Africa."

July 8: Bush administration officials leak information about Wilson to various news media.

July 16: Italian newspaper *La Repubblica* reveals a connection between the Italian letter and SISMI, Italian military intelligence.

July 18: David Kelly, Britain's top defense analyst on WMD, commits suicide. He had been quoted anonymously in BBC reports as saying that Britain had "sexed up" information in its September 24 white paper on Iraq.

July 19: Elisabetta Burba acknowledges in the Italian newspaper *Corriere della Sera* that she was the journalist who received the Niger documents.

July 24: Burba publishes her own report on the Niger fraud, "The Scoop That Wasn't."

July 30: The CIA tells the Justice Department that a crime might have been committed by disclosing Valerie Plame's name.

2004

July 7: The Senate Select Committee on Intelligence finds no fault with the Bush administration, but reports that the CIA suffers from "a broken corporate culture and poor management."

2005

March 31: The Robb-Silberman Commission issues a report on Iraq and also finds no fault with the Bush administration, saying that in "no instance did political pressure cause [analysts] to skew or alter any of their analytical judgments."

November 21: Vice President Cheney says the suggestion that prewar information was "distorted, hyped, or fabricated by the leader of the nation is utterly false."

Chapter 1

16 Words

"In world affairs . . . it was a minor plot. In the lives of the
American people it was the end of innocence."
BARBARA W. TUCHMAN, HISTORIAN,

IN HER BOOK *THE ZIMMERMANN TELEGRAM*

Washington, DC, January 28, 2003

The 43rd president of the United States, George Walker Bush, entered
the halls of the Capitol promptly at 9 p.m. Eastern Standard Time on
January 28, 2003, to speak before a joint session of the 108th Congress. It was a typical winter evening in Washington, DC, with the
temperature just above freezing. The president, led by a traditional
receiving committee, made his way up the center aisle. After receiving
several minutes of applause, Bush hopped jauntily up to the lectern
and gave copies of his speech to the men seated behind him: John

Dennis Hastert, a congressman from Illinois who was the 59th Speaker of the House, and Richard Bruce Cheney of Wyoming, the 46th vice president of the United States. All three men wore dark suits, Cheney and Hastert sported red ties, and Bush's tie was light blue.

President Bush acknowledged the applause and cheers once more and then began reading. The early portion of the 2003 State of the Union message focused on his domestic program, income tax reductions, Medicare reform, and faith-based volunteer programs for the disadvantaged. Among other proposals, he sought $15 billion to fight AIDS in Africa and the Caribbean.

But the heart of the speech was about foreign policy: This State of the Union message would solidify a new role for the United States in world politics. President Bush would assert the right to wage preemptive war. About forty minutes into the nationally televised address, President Bush spoke about terrorism. Step by step, he made the case for the invasion of Iraq, which he said posed a clear and present danger to the United States. It was his clearest statement of the evolving administration doctrine: the shift from deterrence to aggressive action, attacking enemies before they could strike.

The president raised the specter of the September 11, 2001, attacks on the World Trade Center and Pentagon and said that al Qaeda, the Islamic terror organization, had links to Saddam Hussein. He said that Hussein "aids and protects terrorists, including members of al Qaeda." He said that Hussein "could provide one of his hidden weapons to terrorists or help them develop their own."

Bush listed those hidden weapons: Iraq had material to produce 25,000 liters of anthrax, 38,000 liters of botulinum toxin, 500 tons of sarin, mustard gas, and VX nerve agent, all of which could kill millions of people. He said that Iraq was expanding an arsenal that could deliver the weapons. After listing the chemical and biological dangers, George Walker Bush turned to the most frightening prospect, declaring:

> The British government has learned that Saddam Hussein recently sought significant quantities of uranium from Africa.

The shocking sentence, which topped off a litany of evidence against Saddam Hussein, was central to the Bush administration's attempt to rally public support for the likely invasion of Iraq. But the statement that night was particularly surprising to many members of the American Intelligence Community, as Bush's assertion appeared to be based on information they had already dismissed as lacking credibility. Within hours, Bush's charge was questioned and criticized, and the statement became the single most controversial point in the State of the Union speech. After the March 20, 2003, invasion, pundits began to refer to the president's claim, in shorthand, as "the 16 words."

In fact, on the day before the State of the Union message, members of the UN Security Council had heard significant doubts expressed about the Bush administration's charge that Iraq was reviving its nuclear program. The director general of the International Atomic Energy Agency (IAEA), Mohamed ElBaradei, told them that his team of inspectors had to date "found no evidence that Iraq has revived its nuclear weapons programme since the elimination of the program in the 1990s." He pleaded for more time to continue searching for evidence, but to no avail. "With our verification system now in place, barring exceptional circumstances, and provided there is sustained proactive cooperation by Iraq, we should be able within the next few months to provide credible assurance that Iraq has no nuclear weapons program. These few months would be a valuable investment."

Though he attributed the intelligence to the British, Bush's declaration was based on a report about Iraq's purchase of uranium sent to the Central Intelligence Agency (CIA) fifteen months earlier, in October 2001, by the Italian Military Intelligence and Security Service, a government agency better known as SISMI. British and French intelligence agencies would also receive the same Italian intelligence.

About three months before Bush's address, a shady former member of the Italian national police had slipped a document to Elisabetta Burba, a Milan journalist, that appeared to confirm the Iraqi uranium purchase. The letter was written in French and was purported to be addressed to Saddam Hussein by Mamadou Tandja, who was president of Niger in 2000. It approved the sale to Iraq of 500 tons a year of pure uranium—*uranium pur* in French.

David Albright, a nuclear weapons specialist, and several intelligence officials said that the term probably referred to yellowcake, a lightly processed form of the ore more easily transportable than raw uranium ore. The 500 tons could produce ten bombs a year if refined to bomb-grade material. And that, if true, could be alarming.

Without turning over a copy of the letter, SISMI officials in late 2001 and early 2002 told the CIA that they had intelligence disclosing Niger's agreement to sell the material to Iraq. US intelligence officials confirmed that this letter, the only document detailing the amount of uranium to be delivered, was critical to the administration's successful public campaign warning Americans that Iraq was a nuclear threat.

Shortly after receiving the Italian letter, Burba handed it over to the US government with a package of supporting documents.

The Italian letter and accompanying dossier of forgeries comprised one of the most damaging frauds in US history. Yet the hoax should have unraveled in February 2002, when SISMI provided the CIA with the verbatim text of one of the documents. It contained numerous errors—dates were wrong, officials were misidentified and their positions outdated—easily detectable with a simple fact-check on Google.

Nevertheless, the Bush administration highlighted the flawed intelligence as compelling evidence to convince Congress and the American public that Iraq was hell-bent on acquiring nuclear weapons. On March 20, 2003, the United States invaded Iraq, toppled Saddam Hussein, and began the occupation. By the end of 2006, nearly 3,000 Americans had been killed and 22,000 were wounded; estimates of Iraqis killed in the four years of violence as the country disintegrated in civil war ranged from 50,000 to 600,000.

Rarely in the history of the United States has a fraudulent premise brought such wide-ranging consequences. The case rivals the explosion of the battleship *Maine* in 1898, which provoked the Spanish-American War, prompted by a report still disputed more than a century later that Spain had deliberately mined the US ship in Havana's harbor; or the passage of the Gulf of Tonkin resolution after the administration of President Lyndon Baines Johnson reported that North Vietnamese ships had attacked two US destroyers on August 4, 1964, directly leading to expanded US involvement in the Vietnam War.

Perhaps no single document has had such an impact on US policy and opinion since the detection of the Zimmermann Telegram in 1917, a secret communication from Germany to Mexico that helped draw the United States into World War I. But in that case, there was at least one fundamental difference: The Zimmermann Telegram, written by the German foreign minister, was intercepted by British intelligence. It was real. The Italian letter was an obvious fake.

President Bush already had substantial support for military action in Iraq, and his speech, detailing the nuclear threat, elicited strong public approval. Congress had authorized the war in October, more than three months before Bush's January 28 speech. But the president's assertions that Iraq supported al Qaeda and was an emerging nuclear menace served to counteract vocal criticism at home and abroad by establishing the ironclad justification for war: to halt Iraqi nuclear development before it was too late.

Many analysts at the CIA, Department of Defense, and other intelligence agencies in the United States were skeptical of reports of an Iraqi nuclear buildup. In fact, several months before Bush's State of the Union address, George Tenet, the director of Central Intelligence, had convinced the White House after days of discussions to eliminate from another Bush speech any reference to the African uranium. He told the National Security Council that it was based on weak intelligence. After that, Tenet and other top officials either didn't receive timely drafts of major statements or didn't get them at all. White House officials gave Tenet the draft of the State of the Union speech one day in advance. Tenet didn't normally read the drafts of speeches, preferring to pass them down to CIA specialists in the areas to be covered. This time the draft was hand-carried to the office of Jami Miscik, then the deputy director for intelligence—and apparently disappeared.

The nuclear card was introduced in the fall of 2002 after the administration had initially waged a very effective campaign to convince America that Hussein was somehow linked to the September 11 al Qaeda attacks. When Bush delivered his speech, it had been 504 days since the horrific attacks on the World Trade Center and Pentagon and the plunge of a fourth hijacked airliner into an empty field in Pennsylvania, all of which killed nearly 3,000 people. By the evening of the 2003 State of the Union message, a majority of Americans believed that Saddam Hussein was involved in those attacks, and many continued to believe so years afterward.

The deep wounds and damage inflicted on September 11 had not healed. Americans were frightened, and the administration said there was good reason to be. There are terrorists out there, the government said, still willing to kill Americans, and some of them have found safe harbor in Iraq. In fact, there was absolutely no convincing intelligence linking Iraq to al Qaeda, much less connecting Hussein to al Qaeda leader Osama bin Laden. On the contrary, analysts believed any such ties to be highly improbable, given that bin Laden considered Hussein to be an apostate—a Muslim worthy of death—and the secular Hussein, in turn, was a staunch opponent of Islamic fundamentalism.

But ultimately, none of the facts on the ground mattered. The seeds for the invasion had been planted long before the 2003 State of the Union message. Paul O'Neill, Bush's first secretary of the treasury, recalled that during the new administration's first National Security Council meeting in January 2001, the ouster of Hussein was near the top of the agenda. "From the start, we were building the case against Hussein and looking at how we could take him out. . . . It was all about finding a way to do it. . . . The president saying, 'Fine. Go find me a way to do it.'"

The push to invade took on fresh urgency as the Twin Towers lay smoldering and heroic New York City rescue workers combed the rubble for signs of survivors. According to notes taken on the day of the attacks by Stephen Carbone, a senior Pentagon official, then-Defense Secretary Donald Rumsfeld wanted the "best info fast. Judge whether good enough hit S. H. [Saddam Hussein] at the same time. Not only UBL [Osama bin Laden]. Go massive. Sweep it all up. Things related and not."

The next day Bush himself discussed a military campaign to over-throw Hussein and asked his counterterrorism chief, Richard Clarke, to find out if there was even a "shred" of intelligence indicating a Hussein link to the attacks.

Ardent neoconservative members of the Bush administration and their supporters had lobbied for years for US military action against Iraq. On September 12, 2001, one of them, James Woolsey, a former director of the Central Intelligence Agency, appeared on a nationwide cable television program and eagerly spread the message.

When I see bin Laden issuing fatwahs, religious edicts, putting out videotapes, issuing poems, having his subordinates talk about how they're taking part in terrorism against the United States, I begin to think that maybe we're supposed to focus solely on bin Laden. And there might be something else in training.

My suspicion—it's no more than that at this point—is that there could be some government action involved together with bin Laden or a major terrorist group. And one strong suspect there I think would be the government of Iraq.

Bush and Vice President Cheney initially distanced themselves from the claims of Woolsey and his fellow neoconservatives that Iraq sponsored international terrorism. Five days after the attacks, Cheney said that there was no evidence linking the hijackings to Iraq, adding, "Saddam Hussein is bottled up at this point." But the voice of reason would last only a few weeks.

In late September 2001, just days after the terrorist attacks, the deputy secretary of defense, Paul Dundes Wolfowitz, an unwavering advocate for war with Iraq, dispatched Woolsey to London, the home base of the Iraqi National Congress, then led by Ahmed Chalabi, an Iraqi expatriate who had nurtured close ties to both men and to other influential neoconservatives. Woolsey's mission was to gather proof of an Iraqi link to both the September 11 attacks and to the 1993 bombing of the World Trade Center, which killed six. Years earlier, the Federal Bureau of Investigation (FBI) had dismissed any Iraqi government connection to the 1993 bombing.

Throughout 2002, though never directly accusing Iraq of complicity in the September 11 attacks, Bush, Cheney, and war advocates like Woolsey implicitly linked Iraq to September 11, sometimes by merely mentioning Hussein and bin Laden in the same sentence.

On September 8, 2002, Cheney was asked on NBC's *Meet the Press* whether he still believed what he had declared on the same program a year earlier—that Saddam Hussein had no role in the 9/11 attacks. "I'm not here today to make a specific allegation that Iraq was somehow responsible for 9/11. I can't say that." Then he suggested that Iraq indeed might have had a role. He said, "We have reporting that places him [Mohammed Atta, the lead 9/11 hijacker] in Prague with a senior Iraqi intelligence official a few months before the attack." Asked by host Tim Russert about the CIA's assessment of the alleged event, Cheney said, "It's credible."

Three months earlier, the CIA, in an exhaustive analysis of possible links between al Qaeda and Iraq, had concluded that it was unlikely that Atta and the Iraqi intelligence operative, Ahmad Khalil Ibrahim Samir al-Ani, had ever met. The CIA said, "The most reliable reporting to date casts doubt on this possibility. . . . A CIA and FBI review of intelligence and open source reporting leads us to question the information."

Yet the administration's repeated suggestions of a possible connection between Iraq and 9/11 had the desired effect of selling the Iraq invasion. A *Washington Post* poll taken two years after the attacks found that seven out of ten Americans still believed that Iraq had a role in the September 11 attacks.

The chief al Qaeda–Iraq conspiracy theoretician was a Woolsey colleague at the neoconservative American Enterprise Institute, Laurie Mylroie, who claimed that the World Trade Center bombing in 1993, the 9/11 attacks, the bombings of the US embassies in Kenya and Tanzania, and even the 1995 destruction of the federal building in Oklahoma City were the handiwork of Saddam Hussein. Her book, written in 2000, *Study of Revenge: Saddam Hussein's Unfinished War Against America,* contended that the Iraqi leader was the hidden mastermind behind the first attack on the World Trade Center. Her claims were widely dismissed by the CIA, FBI, and others as fantasy-ridden and bad reporting. Peter Bergen, an al Qaeda specialist and a fellow at the New America Foundation, called her a "crackpot."

Woolsey, Cheney, Wolfowitz, and other members of the Bush

administration did not challenge these baseless charges. The neocon-servatives had gained a strong foothold under George W. Bush and had long advocated preemptive unilateral military action by the United States to promote pro-Western democracy in the Middle East.

Advocates of an invasion of Iraq knew that, for all the talk of Iraqi weapons of mass destruction, only the threat of nuclear weapons or a direct link to 9/11 would convince Americans that war with Iraq was necessary. There were substantial questions about the impetus biological weapons would provide, even if Iraq, which had had an active biological research program in the 1980s, had them. "Before the first Gulf War in 1991, Iraq had experimented with biological weapons. Nobody really took it all that seriously," said retired army colonel W. Patrick Lang, former head of the Defense Intelligence Agency's Middle East section. "Biological weapons are very hard to weaponize. Their effect on a battlefield, both on users and on those under attack, is unpredictable." Biological weapons had never been considered to be of battlefield use, so it would be hard to make the case that possessing them was a sufficient trigger for preemptive attacks. Chemical weapons would have to be churned out in such large quantities that their production would be very difficult to conceal. US war planners in the 1970s had calculated that thousands of tons would be needed to have a significant effect on a single massed Soviet division. The Intelligence Community had estimated in October 2002 that Iraq had between 100 and 500 metric tons of chemical warfare agents. The Bush administration knew full well that the only weapon of mass destruction was the nuclear bomb.

Yet intelligence about Saddam's imaginary nuclear program or ties to al Qaeda, flawed as it was, was not used by the Bush administration to craft policy or decide whether war was necessary. In a scathing 2006 essay in *Foreign Affairs*, Paul Pillar, who had been the CIA's top Middle East expert, provided this retrospective:

Intelligence on Iraqi weapons programs did not drive its decision to go to war. . . . [It] was the desire to shake up the sclerotic power structures in the Middle East and hasten the spread of more liberal politics and economics in the region. . . . What is most remarkable about prewar US intelligence on Iraq is not that it got things wrong and thereby misled policymakers; it is that it played so small a role in one of the most important US policy decisions in recent decades.

Pillar was in part wrong. Few Americans would be willing to spill the blood of their youth to spread "more liberal politics and economics" in any region of the world. But a war could be sold if the homeland was under threat of a nuclear or terrorist holocaust. That was where intelligence played a significant role. The administration cherry-picked the most alarming conclusions, embellished them, and used them to wage an enormously successful campaign to convince Congress and America that it was under imminent threat and going to war was the right thing to do.

In the summer of 2002, top officials established a special committee, the White House Iraq Group, or WHIG, at the White House, that was exclusively dedicated to the mission of selling America on the threat posed by Iraq. Its most resonant message was that Hussein, armed with a nuclear bomb, was a mortal danger to the United States, especially if he slipped one to his purported allies in al Qaeda. National Security Advisor Condoleezza Rice, Cheney, and others, as part of their organized campaign, began referring to "mushroom clouds" in their public pronouncements. They were able to fill out their exhortations to war thanks to the details of the Italian letter, whether or not intelligence agencies rejected the information, whether or not the document was a sham. The possibility that Iraq might have purchased uranium in a clandestine operation in West Africa added to the message of imminent danger and helped generate the fear necessary to offset doubts sowed by some Democrats, government critics, and anyone else supposedly soft on the war against terror.

President Bush laid out a case for action in his State of the Union speech that night in January 2003, casting the available intelligence, most of it out of date or largely uncorroborated, in the most menacing possible light. He said there was an urgent need to stop Iraq before Saddam Hussein could orchestrate an attack on the United States. George W. Bush recited data gleaned from international inspections in Iraq in the aftermath of the 1991 Gulf War, launched by his father, President George Herbert Walker Bush, neglecting to also say that Iraq's nuclear facilities had been destroyed after that war, and no resumption of the program had been detected. United Nations (UN) inspectors were back in Iraq examining records, scouring the countryside for nuclear, biological, and chemical programs, but were finding nothing. On the very day of the State of the Union message, January 28, 2003, frustrated UN weapons inspectors complained that the administration was holding back the intelligence they needed to do their job. US officials had claimed they were concerned that their most sensitive information might end up in the hands of Iraqi officials, who could then doctor or further hide the evidence.

"We know the Americans have concerns, but if they want to make their case . . . they should be more forthcoming with us," said one UN official involved in the inspections.

The president of the United States was not leaning toward international cooperation.

"We will consult, but let there be no misunderstanding: If Saddam Hussein does not fully disarm, for the safety of our people, and for the peace of the world, we will lead a coalition to disarm him," he said on that night.

With this, he was greeted by a standing ovation.

Little more than an hour after he had arrived in the halls of Congress to address the nation, George Walker Bush asked in somber tones, "God continue to bless the United States of America." He shook the hands of the assembled dignitaries closest to him and to sustained applause walked into the winter night.

The morning papers raised questions about Bush's claims about Iraq. "Critics will challenge some of the assertions Bush made last night," said the *Washington Post* in a story headlined, "One Topic Rules Bush's Thinking." "War Now Drives the Presidency," said the headline of an analysis in the *Los Angeles Times*, which noted that the Democratic response "offered no hint of dissent on Iraq."

Bush had taken a determined step toward the invasion of Iraq. During the seven weeks of war preparations that followed, his administration continued to trumpet this bogus intelligence based on the Italian letter and other fraudulent documents as a justification for attacking Iraq, even though neither the CIA nor other members of the Intelligence Community had found any evidence that Iraq was in fact an imminent nuclear threat. When it could, the CIA tried to moderate the content of speeches made by Cheney, Secretary of State Colin Powell, and Bush himself. Other than flawed intelligence reporting that Iraq had been buying aluminum tubes for centrifuges, very few of the raw bits of information that came into the intelligence hopper had been taken with particular concern. Even the information about the aluminum tubes was questionable—many analysts said the tubes could not be used for processing uranium in centrifuge cascades and were probably conventional short-range rocket casings instead. Word of Iraq's attempts to rebuild its nuclear capacity by shopping for uranium had come from an intelligence agency that was known to be one of the least reliable in Western Europe. CIA officials were immediately skeptical; they were well aware that Iraq already had a stockpile of uranium—it had its own domestic source and purchased tons of material from Brazil, Italy, Portugal, and Niger in the 1970s and

1980s—all of which was being closely monitored by the IAEA, a UN organization. Despite the administration's public claims, the UN program to search for illicit weapons was working.

After the US invasion, Bush and Cheney repeatedly predicted that illicit weapons would be found. When the last shred of hope was dashed more than a year later with an official declaration from the Iraq Survey Group that there were no such weapons, the White House had another explanation: Officials insisted that they had been victims of bad intelligence. That excuse might have been true if only those at the top had been naïve consumers of intelligence, not seasoned policy veterans with years of experience in reading intelligence products. Cheney, his staff, and members of President Bush's National Security Council all received specific warnings before the war from the CIA, from intelligence analysts at the State Department, and from the UN inspection teams that they were relying on questionable information.

Cheney was known as a voracious reader of such material. And the intelligence boiled down to "crap," in the word of Carl Ford Jr., a thirty-year veteran of the CIA who was in charge of the State Department's intelligence bureau during the prewar period. Ford had previously worked directly for Cheney and said that the vice president should have recognized that it was wrong to say that Iraq had reconstituted its nuclear program.

"Cheney's too smart. The fact is that he read the same things I did, and if he thought there were a lot of good things there, then he's not as smart as I thought he was."

It was 3 a.m. in Italy when Bush began reading his State of the Union address. Most Europeans probably didn't stay up to watch the speech, and Elisabetta Burba, an investigative reporter for the Italian newsweekly *Panorama*, was no exception. However, she began to develop an uncomfortable sensation in her stomach after reading newspaper accounts of the address and seeing news clips on television. How could the American president have mentioned the uranium sale from Africa? That was a story she'd had and hadn't written because she'd determined the information it was based on was bogus.

About three months earlier, Burba had been contacted by an old source, a n'er-do-well intelligence freelancer named Rocco Martino. Intelligence officers referred to Martino as a snitch, not an agent. Martino offered to sell her information suggesting that Iraq had purchased 500 tons of uranium from Niger, with accompanying documents. One of these even claimed that the material already had been shipped to Iraq, but Burba suspected the material immediately. It would make a great story if true, but it probably was not. At the time, her editor had asked her to take a copy of the Italian letter and dossier that Martino had given her to the US embassy in Rome for verification. It was a highly unusual thing to do, but to her lasting regret, she followed orders.

In sizing up President Bush's speech, Burba had two reactions: She was being scooped on her own story, a story she'd abandoned because she'd found the underlying information to be false. Burba also instantly recognized that what Bush was doing was laying the groundwork for an invasion of Iraq. She experienced a sinking feeling. "You know I feel bad about it," she told us, discussing her frustrations about the story and its aftermath. "You know the fact is that my documents, with the documents I brought to them, they justified the war."

Chapter 2

Selling the Story

The evidence indicates that Iraq is reconstituting its nuclear weapons program.

PRESIDENT GEORGE WALKER BUSH, CINCINNATI, OCTOBER 7, 2002

Rome, Tuesday, October 7, 2002

Until Elisabetta Burba received an unusual phone call in late September of 2002 that refocused the subject of her reporting, she was on a trip to the Balkans, working on a story about the Kosovo Liberation Army. During that time, Pino Buongiorno, a fellow reporter for *Panorama*, the Milan-based magazine Burba worked for, had published a story about Iraq, quoting intelligence sources who claimed Iraq had tried to purchase 500 tons of bomb-grade uranium from Nigeria via Jordan. Burba hadn't seen the report.

Buongiorno was well known for getting high-impact stories based on sometimes questionable Italian intelligence sources. It is easy to confuse the names Niger and Nigeria, although the countries are quite different. Niger is an impoverished country of about 12 million, a former French colony that had suffered through a series of military dictatorships. Like many other former French colonies, it had close economic ties with France, and the French government had significant influence in its political affairs. The major export, by far, was uranium oxide, also known as yellowcake. Yellowcake is a lightly processed form of uranium ore, a first step toward producing bomb-grade uranium. Mined uranium ore contains less than 1 percent of the fissionable isotope of uranium, uranium-235.

But now, back in Milan, Burba, 38 at the time and a veteran reporter, would soon be chasing after an Iraq story. A man had left an urgent message at her office. The message seemed important enough that the office secretary had felt she needed to track down Burba.

"Some guy called," the secretary told her. He didn't leave his name, just a number. "He said he needed to talk to you as soon as possible." Since she was winding up her Balkans reporting trip for the weekend, Burba waited until returning to Italy to call back. She was intrigued.

"Do you remember me?" the deep-timbered male voice said without identifying himself outright. It was Rocco Martino, an old source who was still playing a game of shadows and spy talk. Burba did remember him, though it had been a number of years.

Martino, a one-time Carabinieri and paid informant to Italian, French, and Egyptian intelligence services, had been hired to head the security operation at the Vatican during negotiations in 1995 about the future of Kosovo. He had contacted Burba to make a little money on the side. This was typical of how news and information was gathered in Italy. Unlike the news business in the United States, it was common for newspapers and magazines to pay their sources for information. Martino, while working in a sensitive security role and in a position of trust, had offered to sell her intelligence material connected to the Kosovo talks. When the material had been deemed accurate, Burba had published it in *Epoca*, the magazine she was working for at the time. Burba said the magazine paid Martino about $4,000 for the information.

Now, seven years later, he was once again trying to sell her information.

Martino spoke only in vague terms, asking if she knew anything about the sale of uranium from Africa.

Burba hadn't thought about that subject much. She did remember seeing a report from London some days earlier in the newspaper *Corriere della Sera* in which Prime Minister Tony Blair and the British government had charged that Iraq had tried to buy uranium from an unnamed African country.

Martino said he had some very interesting documents to show her, continuing to drop hints about a certain head of a Middle Eastern country who had bought uranium from a certain country. Could she fly down to Rome right away?

Paying sources for information was an unfortunate reality of Italian journalism. Burba didn't like it, but it was part of the system in which she operated. She had been in the United States, was familiar with American journalism, and had discussed journalistic integrity, independence, and responsibilities. She believed in those principles. But here she was dealing with a source offering potentially good information and expecting to sell it to the highest bidder. He was neither a whistleblower nor a noble source standing up for truth. Simply put, he was a merchant of information. Financial details had not yet been mentioned, but she had no doubt: Martino was in it for the money.

This was the media reality in Italy in 2002. Italian journalists could accept the rules of the game or not play. They also could criticize American journalism, which of course frowned upon the practice of paying sources of information but had its own problems in the Italian view—lacking critical analysis, lacking global context, and in its own way just as subservient and fawning to those in power. Italian prime minister Silvio Berlusconi was President George Walker Bush's best friend on the European mainland; he had made his fortune in the news business and was the preeminent owner of publications and radio and television networks throughout Italy, including *Panorama*, Burba's magazine. Berlusconi had shown that he was not interested in journalistic independence. He had used the news media to build his fortune—he was the richest man in Italy—and as a political force. *Panorama* was part of that system, and its editor, Carlo Rossella, was aligned politically with Berlusconi.

On Monday morning, Burba went into the *Panorama* offices and met with Giorgio Mulé, the deputy managing editor. She told him that an old source wanted to meet her in Rome, that he said he had something hot about Saddam Hussein and Iraq. He wouldn't be specific on the phone, Burba told him. Mulé had no objection.

Burba flew down to Rome on Monday, October 7, 2002. The flight from Milan was about 80 minutes long. Burba then took a cab from the airport and met Martino at the Bar Ungaro in central Rome.

Martino greeted her with characteristic grace. He was an older man with steel gray hair and a matching thick moustache. He was in his sixties and had a deeply lined, sun-baked face, with heavy pouches under both eyes. He was immaculately dressed as usual. Burba recognized his sophisticated style and his effort to impress. Martino was always trying to be suave with the ladies. Though he was a nice enough fellow, Burba had never been particularly charmed.

After ordering a cup of coffee, Martino suggested they have lunch at a Sicilian place he liked. They went to his car, an older model of a once-fashionable luxury car, which signified that perhaps the owner had once been better off than he now was.

Martino parked, and they entered the restaurant, one of those bistros that had a walk-down entrance, partly below street level. The subterranean atmosphere gave Martino a sense of security for discussing his business proposal.

He asked her, "Do you know anything about the country that has sold uranium to Iraq?"

"Niger," Martino answered his own question. He handed Burba a folder filled with documents, most of them in French. One had the mark of the government of Niger and the seal of the president of the country. It was addressed to the president of Iraq and confirmed a deal to sell 500 tons of pure uranium to Iraq annually. This was the Italian letter, the smoking gun in the package. It conveyed the formal approval of Niger's president to supply Saddam Hussein with a commodity that could only be used for a nuclear weapons program, because Iraq had no nuclear power plants.

Martino spread out the accompanying documents on the restaurant table and described what he was offering: proof, he said, that the government of Niger had sold the material; the addendum to that agreement; a list with dates, of confirmed contacts between the countries. Several of the documents referred to an Iraqi ambassador's trip to Niger, and one concerned a meeting of representatives from Iraq, North Korea, Syria, and Libya during a visit to Rome for a meeting of the UN's Food and Agriculture Organization.

Burba listened without saying much as she took a first look at the information. She recognized right away that the material was hot—if authentic. She also realized that confirming the origin of the documents could be difficult. Of course, it would have to be done. Burba didn't want to fall into a trap.

After this preliminary look at the documents, Burba and Martino ordered lunch. Eventually Martino, ever polite, came to the point. He wanted to sell the documents to *Panorama* for 20 million old liras—roughly $10,000 at the time, or about the same in euros. Italy had already switched to euros from its longtime currency, but Europeans often still calculated transactions in their now-retired monetary systems. It gave them a better idea of value.

"Where did you get the documents?" she asked.

"From a source," he said, nothing more.

"How do I know the material is legitimate?" Burba asked.

Martino said he was confident that it was.

Well, Burba said, if it checked out, they would talk about money. It would be a fine gentlemen's agreement, Burba said; and since this was a trusted relationship, she would take the dossier with her, to which Martino agreed.

After their meal, they took one more look at the documents. One was in a code consisting of groups of numbers in even rows with an embassy letterhead on top and a signature at the bottom, and Burba asked if Martino could decipher the document.

He said he could. He escorted her from the restaurant; they returned to his car and drove out of the center of town. Martino dropped her off at a gas station just outside the city and on the way to his house. He asked her to wait there while he fetched what he needed to decipher the information. About twenty minutes later, he returned and asked her to get in. They drove farther outside the city to a rest stop. Martino parked the car and pulled out a thick packet:

a photocopied Nigerien secret codebook, printed in 1967, which he claimed was used by that country's diplomats for secret transmissions.

The parking lot was not crowded, and Burba noted that Martino's usually cool demeanor betrayed signs of anxiety. He was shifting about nervously as he decoded numbers. There was probably reason to be worried: How would he explain being in possession of a codebook and a document mentioning uranium if a policeman happened by?

The coded document contained the letterhead of Niger's Ministry of Foreign Affairs and was dated August 9, 2001. Conveniently, the number groupings were broken by recognizable text, two instances of the designation "U 92"—that is, the chemical symbol and atomic number of uranium—and the word NITRA, the acronym of the shipping company Compagnie Nigerienne des Transports Aerien.

Martino froze when he saw a man drive up and park close to them. Martino looked at the driver and expressed concern, worrying that they had been followed. But the man drove away after a short time, and the incident appeared innocent. Martino turned back to the task. After a while, they decoded the message, which described an alleged deal between Niger and China, with no mention of Iraq.

Martino was not concerned and said he had many other documents to draw on.

He had also brought along evidence from home to show Burba that he had access to the Nigerien embassy in Rome. He said that his source was a woman at the embassy; the additional evidence was a letter from the Nigerien embassy in Beijing to the Nigerien embassy in Rome. As with the coded message, the letter, addressed from the Banco Nazionale de Lavora to the Nigerien embassy in Rome, gave no indication of an Iraqi deal. Martino said the material confirmed that he had access to documents produced and processed at the Nigerien embassy.

Burba told Martino she wanted to take the material with her and study it more. He agreed. She would speak to her editors and get back to him soon. Martino drove her back into town; she immediately hopped a taxi to the airport for a flight back to Milan.

That evening, Burba and her husband, Luigi, looked over the packet of documents. The centerpiece was the letter to Saddam Hussein: the Italian letter.

It was written in French, in all capital letters, in the form of an old telex before the days of computers and the Internet. It bore the letterhead of the Republic of Niger and was dated July 27, 2000, with an odd shield on the top, a shining sun surrounded by a horned animal head, a star, and a bird. The letter was stamped *Confidential* and *Urgent*.

MR. PRESIDENT.
   I HAVE THE HONOR OF REFERRING TO ACCORD NO. 381-NI 2000, CONCERNING THE PROVISION OF URANIUM, SIGNED IN NIAMEY ON THE SIXTH OF JULY 2000 BETWEEN THE GOVERNMENT OF THE REPUBLIC OF NIGER AND THE GOVERNMENT OF IRAQ BY THEIR RESPECTIVE OFFICIAL DELEGATED REPRESENTATIVES.
   SAID PROVISION EQUALING 500 TONS OF PURE URANIUM PER YEAR WILL BE DELIVERED IN 2 PHASES.
   HAVING SEEN AND EXAMINED THE SAID ACCORD, I APPROVE IT IN ALL AND EACH OF ITS REQUIREMENTS IN VIRTUE OF THE POWERS VESTING IN ME BY THE CONSTITUTION OF 12 MAY 1966.
   THEREFORE, I ASK THAT YOU CONSIDER THIS LETTER AS A FORMAL INSTRUMENT OF APPROVAL OF THIS ACCORD BY THE GOVERNMENT OF THE REPUBLIC OF NIGER WHICH THUS FINDS ITSELF DULY BOUND.
   I WOULD LIKE TO ADD, MR. PRESIDENT, ASSURANCES OF MY HIGHEST ESTEEM.

A seal at the bottom of the page read

The Office of the President of the Republic of Niger

Superimposed over the seal was a barely legible signature of the president of Niger, Mamadou Tandja.

Accompanying the Italian letter was another piece of correspondence, also in French, indicating that the yellowcake had been delivered. But that document, as with the coded material involving a Chinese sale, did not mention Iraq. This correspondence and the coded letter were allegedly written in August 2001 and were signed by a female official, Maiga Djibrilla Aminata, at the time the secretary general of Niger's foreign ministry. Aminata, who later married and used the last name Toure, became Niger's ambassador to Washington in 2006. At our request, she reviewed the two letters and acknowledged that her signatures and the letterheads were legitimate but that the contents were fabrications. She recalled having written the uncoded letter to a diplomat at Niger's Rome embassy approving his request for a vacation and wishing him a good holiday. As for the coded letter, she said she had never sent encrypted correspondence.

Burba and her husband wondered how Iraq, monitored by spy satellites, radar, and international monitors, could move 500 tons of uranium in hundreds of barrels across the desert, by ship across the Mediterranean, and then across its borders without detection.

Burba found a major flaw in the documentation after about fifteen minutes of browsing the Internet. A packet of five pages included a cover sheet from the Niger Foreign Ministry, which referred to a draft agreement between the government of Niger and the government of Iraq, "relating to the furnishing of uranium signed on July 5 and 6, 2000 in Niamey." The document was signed by Niger's foreign minister, Ailele Elhadj, but Elhadj had last served in that post in 1989 and was not employed in that capacity in 2000, when the document was dated. The document had also misspelled Elhadj's first name as Allele (the print was unclear and the capital I could have been a capital L). Meanwhile, a subsequent title page was printed with the word "ACCORD" in capital letters, but the text of the actual agreement was missing. Instead, the packet included two pages, listed as "Annex 1," providing some details of the presumed agreement. Burba's husband, Luigi, was a historian and observed that it was strange that the actual accord, or agreement, was missing. But there was no accord in the packet of forgeries. The annex was what SISMI, on February 5, 2002, had told the CIA was the accord itself. The Italian intelligence service had provided a "verbatim text," of the annex, but not the document itself. The annex claimed that a *"protocole d'accord,"* or draft agreement, between Iraq and Niger had been signed in Niamey on July 6, 2000. But the bogus package did not contain such a draft.

Nevertheless, the additional detail, especially the 500 tons referred to in the Italian letter, caught the attention of CIA Defense Intelligence Agency (DIA) analysts, who had been generally skeptical of SISMI's initial information the previous fall. It prompted the DIA a week later to issue a report that crossed Vice President Cheney's desk, triggering a sequence of events that eventually led to the 16 words in Bush's 2003 State of the Union speech.

In the course of a day, Burba had come away with substantial questions about the origin of the Italian letter, a full 100 days before Bush's State of the Union message.

The following morning, October 8, 2002, Elisabetta Burba was still unsure about Rocco Martino's dossier. She called Martino, telling him that she had looked more carefully at the Iraq–Niger documents and hadn't found them entirely convincing. Did he have more information that could make the case? He assured Burba that he had "a caseload of these documents," reiterated that the material was reliable, and promised to send further proof. After this exchange, Burba brought the story and her doubts to her bosses, Rossella and Mulé, who agreed with Burba that a lot of work had yet to be done, but that if the story were true, it was a great scoop. Or, as reporters say around the world, interesting—if true.

Burba told her editors she thought it would make sense to fly down to Niger and check around for confirmation. Rossella agreed, and Mulé went along with the idea but warned that it would be difficult to get corroboration in a place such as Niger, which had a closed government that would not be forthcoming on such a sensitive subject. Rossella then suggested that they simultaneously pursue another tack.

"Let's go to the Americans," he said, "because they are focused on looking for weapons of mass destruction more than anyone else. Let's see if they can authenticate the documents."

They went to work. Burba set about getting a visa and plane ticket to Niger. Rossella called the US embassy in Rome and alerted officials to expect a visit from Burba.

On Wednesday morning, October 9, Burba was en route to Rome again. She took a cab to the US embassy, which is housed at the old Palazzo Margherita, not far from the Porta Pinciana, on land once owned by the family of Julius Caesar. The embassy had leased the property, located on fashionable Via Veneto, since shortly after World War II. Access to the embassy compound was severely restricted, a reflection of the more modern era of international terrorism. Burba came to a security gate and walked through a magnetometer, where an Italian employee of the embassy press department came down to meet her.

After a few formalities, the Italian aide introduced her to Ian Kelly, the US embassy press spokesman. Kelly and Burba walked across the walled grounds of the embassy and sat down for a cup of coffee in the cafeteria. Burba told Kelly that she had some documents about Iraq and uranium shipments and needed help in confirming their authenticity and accuracy.

Kelly interrupted her, realizing he needed help. He made a phone call summoning someone else from his staff as well as a political officer. Burba recalled a third person being invited, possibly a US military attaché. She didn't get their names.

"Let's go to my office," Kelly said. They walked past antiquities, a tranquil fountain, steps, and pieces of marble, all set in a tree-lined patio garden.

It was unusual for outsiders to drop by with sensitive documents and strange for a reporter to be offering information. More commonly, reporters withheld documentation from officials and asked questions of them instead.

Actually, several officials at the embassy had been alerted to Burba's arrival, since her boss had contacted them the day before her visit. Rossella was considered a friend, a frequent social guest at the embassy, and a lover of all things American. He'd once been based in the United States. So Rossella's heads-up call to the US press office was as much the product of an ongoing relationship with the American diplomats as it was due to his role as an executive at the magazine.

One person who refused to meet with Burba (unbeknownst to Burba at the time) was the CIA chief of station, Jeff C., who operated under official cover. First of all, he had no interest in meeting with any reporter, especially a foreigner. Second, considering the culture of intelligence, Burba's visit was not the product of a clandestine operation. Overt meetings were not the stock and trade of the CIA station chief. In any case, he'd already heard more than he wanted to hear from Italian military intelligence, SISMI, about the alleged sale of uranium to Iraq. A year earlier, SISMI had given the CIA station a report about the alleged uranium sale.

First word had come days after the September 11 attacks in the United States that SISMI had received some information about a uranium deal involving Iraq. The CIA's Rome station asked for more. SISMI responded with a short summary of some of Martino's forged documents, without identifying him or providing details of the documents. The summary in Italian, with an English translation attached, claimed that Niger had wrapped up an agreement with Iraq to ship several tons of uranium. It said that the negotiations for the sale began in early 1999 and that President Mamadou Tandja had given it his stamp of approval, as had the State Court of Niger in late 2000. It also claimed that Foreign Minister Nassirou Sabo had cabled one of his ambassadors at an undisclosed European capital that the contract had been signed.

On October 15, the CIA reports officer at the embassy wrote a brief summary based on SISMI's intelligence, signed and dated it, and routed it to the Directorate of Operations (DO), Counterproliferation Division, at CIA headquarters in Langley, Virginia, with copies going to the DO's European and Near East Divisions. The reports officer was one of the most respected at the CIA, was fluent in Italian, and had established very good relations with Italian intelligence. She had limited the report's distribution because the intelligence was uncorroborated; she was aware of SISMI's questionable track record and did not believe the report merited wider dissemination. The DO then passed the raw intelligence to the Intelligence Directorate and to the CIA's sister agencies, including the DIA. A more polished document, called a Senior Executive Intelligence Brief, was written at Langley three days later in which the CIA mentioned the new intelligence but added important caveats. The classified document, whose distribution was limited to senior policymakers and the congressional intelligence committees, admitted that there was no corroboration and noted that Iraq had "no known facilities for processing or enriching the material."

For his part, Jeff C. had considered the report far-fetched, unconfirmed, and a waste of time. In any case, he and the CIA station wanted no part of meeting Burba or revisiting the Iraq–Niger report. Nor did he mention any of this to personnel outside the CIA station at the US embassy. So Kelly and his colleagues had no background on the material Burba was delivering.

The Italian journalist's chat with Kelly and his colleagues was brief. She told them Rossella had suggested she confer with them in order to try to substantiate the material she'd received, about which she had her doubts.

Kelly told her the embassy wasn't in a position to verify documents of this kind. It wasn't the business of an embassy—not the political section, which gathered information about Italian affairs and sent reports back to Washington, nor the commercial section, which handled business issues, nor cultural affairs, nor the press office, which provided news about the United States. All Kelly could do was make copies of the material and pass it along channels to see what the response might be. Burba said that was fine. Her boss, Rossella, had authorized her to leave copies so the material could be fully vetted.

The embassy officials pressed Burba for information about where she'd gotten the documents in the first place, but she refused to say more than what was already obvious: They had come from one of her sources. She would say no more, and soon the conversation was over. We'll be in touch, Kelly told her, somewhat unconvincingly. As she was guided out of the embassy complex, she felt a sense of doubt.

By the time she got to the airport, heading back to Milan once more, Burba was asking herself why Rossella had wanted to give the documents to the Americans in the first place. She had been the good soldier and had done what she was told in good faith. But why give the documents to the Americans or speak to them at all? She'd given up the exclusivity of her story, and perhaps now the Americans could undercut her story before she had a chance to do more reporting, or perhaps someone else would have a chance to make use of the documents before she was able to write about them.

She was happy at least that she hadn't handed over everything Martino had given her. She'd brought along a copy of the Italian letter, confirmation on the uranium deal from the president of Niger to Saddam Hussein. She also had given them a series of exchanges between the Iraqi embassy at the Vatican and the Nigerien embassy in Rome regarding a visa for Wissam al-Zahawie, Iraq's ambassador to the Vatican, as a presidential envoy. But she withheld the coded messages that Martino had given her when she asked him for more documentation to confirm the deal as well as the deciphered versions and a photocopy of a page from the Nigerien codebook.

Rossella had said the Americans were the obvious people to approach to seek confirmation about the documents. But was she likely to get an answer? Rossella was not naïve; he was a veteran reporter and had been a foreign correspondent based in the United States. How likely were the Americans to actually answer their question? Were these real documents? This was an intelligence matter, and the answer would probably be classified.

There was another question that came to mind: Was Rossella journalistically independent? Burba knew that her editor had good rapport with the Americans, and this made her uncomfortable. Rossella also was close to Berlusconi, and the prime minister was fawning in his support of the Bush administration.

Panorama had a reputation for publishing intelligence information such as Buongiorno's cover story a month earlier about Iraq's attempt to purchase uranium from Nigeria to be shipped via Jordan. Some reporters thought that the story was a plant by Italian intelligence operatives, and perhaps it was a first attempt to pass along the Niger–Iraq connection. Rossella defended the story and said it was an independent report, but it was never substantiated by the United

States or, apparently, anyone else. And Buongiorno had not been asked to go to the Americans for corroboration.

The magazine, like Rossella, supported US policy and the Bush administration. One prime example was evident that same week. Rossella had just contracted with a new columnist, Michael Arthur Ledeen, a prominent, controversial American neoconservative who, in turn, had been allegedly involved in Italian intelligence operations for decades.

Panorama published a question-and-answer interview with Ledeen in the October 3, 2002, edition of the magazine. The occasion was the publication of Ledeen's book, *The War Against the Terror Masters*. In the interview, published four days before Burba's first meeting with Rocco Martino, Ledeen echoed administration pabulum about Iraq and the "axis of evil" first declared by Bush in his January 29, 2002, State of the Union address. Ledeen said that US intervention was necessary in Iraq but only as part of a "war of liberation" to "free the Iranian, Iraqi, Syrian, and Saudi populations from the tyrants" that rule them.

Ledeen advocated US intervention in Iraq and elsewhere. He said: "This intervention is necessary. But my opinion is that it would be more effective to start with Iran, because that is the easiest country to liberate. There would not even be a need for military intervention: Our best weapon is the Iranians themselves, who hate the regime and who are prepared to face great risks to overthrow their tyrants."

Panorama published at least eighteen commentaries by Ledeen in 2002 and 2003. His columns also appeared regularly in the conservative *National Review* in the United States.

Ledeen also was a fellow at the neoconservative American Enterprise Institute, where he was an associate of James Woolsey, the former CIA director, as well as of other high-octane defense and intelligence veterans who supported and encouraged the Bush administration's drive toward Iraq. Twenty years earlier, Ledeen had worked with the Iran-Contra team that set up its "off-the-shelf" policy to support Nicaragua's right-wing contra rebels while participating in secret negotiations with Iran.

Because of his historical ties to Italy's power structure and to the Italian intelligence services, Ledeen was later mentioned by many conspiracy buffs as someone who might have had a hand in the Italian letter's evolution from forgery to intelligence. Ledeen denied any involvement, and no evidence was uncovered suggesting otherwise. "I was the target of lies," he said. "If you feel obliged to repeat those lies, then you will be putting yourself in the same category," he added with obvious indignation.

Rumors of Ledeen's involvement in the Niger uranium forgeries were fanned by disclosure in August 2003 that, with the assistance of SISMI, he had arranged for a hush-hush meeting involving Pentagon officials, alleged Iranian intelligence agents, and a noted Iranian intelligence fabricator, Manucher Ghorbanifar. The US ambassador to Italy, Melvin Sembler, had protested angrily when he discovered that Ledeen had set up the meeting in December 2001 without notifying him, as was required. He protested to Washington. "I don't know if he [Ledeen] was declared persona non grata, but the ambassador blew a gasket and demanded a guarantee that he would never conduct such an operation here again," said one embassy official.

Attending the three-day session were the alleged Iranian intelligence officials, described by one senior CIA official as imposters, Italian intelligence officials, Pentagon staffers Lawrence Franklin and Harold Rhode, and Ghorbanifar, the Iranian middleman involved in the Iran-Contra affair of the mid-1980s, in which the United States was to ship arms to Iran in return for the release of American hostages in Tehran. The CIA officially labeled Ghorbanifar an "intelligence fabricator and nuisance" after he failed four polygraph tests administered during the arms-for-hostages fiasco, and directed its officers never to deal with him. But Ledeen described him as "one of the most honest, educated, honorable men I have ever known."

There was no evidence that those present at the meeting discussed Iraq or yellowcake. Instead, it focused on alleged Iranian terrorism and rumors of dissent within the Iranian security services.

Despite his murky past, Ledeen continued to maintain high-level contacts in the White House, including the president's top political adviser, Karl Rove. David Kay, who led the CIA-directed postinvasion weapons of mass destruction (WMD) search team, the Iraq Survey Group, discovered that another of Ledeen's contacts was Vice President Cheney. At one point during the futile search for Saddam's weapons, Kay received a cable from the CIA telling him that Cheney wanted him to send someone to Switzerland to meet with Ghorbanifar. The never-say-die Iranian conman had a source who, for a mere $2 million (paid in advance), would provide intelligence on Iraq's nuclear weapons. Kay cabled back to the CIA saying he would not meet with the "known fabricator-peddler" unless ordered to do so. The order never came. Kay subsequently "discovered the latest Ghorbanifar stunt involved Michael Ledeen."

"Everyone tells me Michael Ledeen is not a stupid person," said Bill Murray, former CIA chief of station in Paris, where Ghorbanifar lived. "Then why does he persist in this [fronting for Ghorbanifar]?"

Murray, who spent countless hours in Paris in 2003 chasing down a phony tip provided by another Ghorbanifar frontman that Iraq had stashed enriched uranium inside Iran before the war, added, "The real danger with Ghorbanifar is that nobody has any idea of what his real motives are. Are they simply to make money? Are they to get back at the United States for having exposed him [as a fraud] in the past? Or are they because he's working for the Iranian government? . . . I think right now he's probably representing the Iranians.

They would love to see us make a huge tactical mistake. We already look so fucking stupid over Iraq."

Burba kept from Martino the fact that she was trying to confirm the reliability of the documents with the Americans, but she did tell him that she wanted to check things out in Niger before she would agree to pay him for the information. Martino wasn't happy; he wanted the money right away, but he could assume that *Panorama* would honor its agreement to pay him if they decided to go ahead and use the information.

Burba had the impression that Martino himself had no idea whether or not the documents were real. If anything, his demeanor persuaded her that Martino probably thought the dossier was legitimate.

Martino probably didn't care whether or not the documents were legitimate. He had laid hands on some of the documents in early 2000, when Antonio Nucera, a recently retired Italian intelligence officer still a consultant with the agency, had approached him with a business proposition. Would he like to make some money by working with a friendly contact he had at the Nigerien embassy?

Nucera said that the contact was a woman code-named "La Signora," and she would have valuable information that he could sell wherever he wanted. Martino had only one question: How much money is in it for me?

Nucera then introduced Martino to the woman, Laura Montini. They met at a restaurant in Rome, and Nucera left them to their own business. Montini was sixtyish, divorced or widowed with children. She was just a bit younger than Martino, who couldn't resist wooing her. The two traveled more than once to a beach resort, and friends were wondering what was up.

Whether or not there was romance, there certainly were prospects for business. Suggesting he had little trust in the people he dealt with, Martino routinely carried a hidden recorder to tape conversations. Montini began feeding her new suitor a series of documents; he, in turn, forwarded the material to French intelligence agents, who then paid Martino a stipend of $1,000 a month. Some of the intelligence dealt with Islamic fundamentalism, and other material involved politics in the Balkans.

Martino hoped the Italian letter would be his crown jewel and betrayed no concern if it and the accompanying documents were authentic; the bottom line was that, in any event, he could market them to various agencies. There was money for both of them. And if Montini or anyone else needed protection, there was a convenient alibi. The Nigerien embassy had reported a burglary on January 2, 2001, telling Rome police that letterhead stationery and consular stamps had been stolen from their flat. Italian police never found the perpetrators or reported any leads in the case.

Martino had not identified Montini by name but described what she looked like and referred to her as La Signora. Since Burba had decided to examine every facet of Martino's story, she wanted to check if La Signora existed in the first place. So rather than seeking the required visa for her trip to Niger in Milan, where the African country had an honorary consul, Burba flew back to Rome. A visa request made at the Nigerien embassy would give her an excuse to check the place out.

Meanwhile, she'd done some quick backgrounding on the country and collected information about plausible story ideas—one angle was writing about wood carvings, which Niger exported, or on recent dinosaur excavations by paleontologists. Experts told her not to expect an easy time in the West African country. Colleagues and friends told her the government was not open with reporters and that it was hard to negotiate the bureaucracy. Communication and transportation to

Niger were hard enough, and moving around once you got there was daunting and rudimentary.

Niger's embassy in Rome amounted to nothing more than an apartment on the fifth floor of a drab, middle-class residential building on Via Antonio Baiamonti, a few subway stops from central Rome and a short walk from the Piazza Mazzini. The embassy was easy to miss, marked only by a weatherworn three-colored flag dangling from a short pole mounted at an angle from the window frame.

Burba buzzed at the fifth-floor apartment. A middle-aged woman answered the door, and she certainly matched Rocco Martino's description of La Signora. Burba spoke quickly about her interest in traveling to Niger to do some research on dinosaurs for a story she was writing. The woman was cordial enough and gave her the necessary paperwork for a visa.

During the short visit to the embassy, Burba was careful to avoid arousing suspicion about her real motives. It was doubtful that La Signora would even know that Rocco Martino was trying to sell the documents to Burba and the magazine. In Martino's shady world, he wouldn't be giving details to La Signora about how he was going about his business. He was trying to sell the documents on his own.

But Burba did phone Martino, who was expecting an answer: He wanted his money. She said nothing about the visit to the Nigerien embassy nor her contacts with the American embassy. Burba told Martino the editors hadn't decided yet whether to use the documents and wanted more proof. Martino was impatient to collect his $10,000 fee, but she told him he would have to wait until she came back from her quick trip to Niger. She would check out the story in person and then get back to him. Martino didn't like it, but he had no recourse.

Burba decided to phone Ian Kelly, the press attaché at the US embassy, hoping that the Americans had come up with information on the documents she had left with them. If the documents turned out to be authentic, snooping around in Africa might prove difficult, even dangerous. But if the story were revealed to be untrue, the purpose of the trip would be to research an entirely different story, that of a hoax, and she would need to be able to explain to readers why it was so unlikely that Niger had secretly sold any uranium supplies to Iraq.

Kelly agreed to take her call. Since Burba's visit about a week earlier, he had made copies of the Italian letter and accompanying documentation and sent one batch down to C., the CIA station chief, and another to the State Department in Washington. C. recognized that the material was nothing new, a version of the same junk that Italian military intelligence had given him almost a year earlier. Associates said C. filed his stack in a drawer and didn't even bother to report receiving it to CIA headquarters. C. had concluded that the material was "the same bullshit he [and the CIA] already knew," according to a friend at the CIA, who said C.'s chief error was in not alerting officials at Langley that the documents had become available and that the embassy was shipping them to Washington. Another explanation, offered by a source familiar with the CIA's internal investigation into the matter, was that C. simply shrugged off the reports "because they were not obtained in a clandestine manner." C. declined requests through a CIA spokesman for an interview.

Kelly's role in the matter was essentially over once he'd sent the documents to Washington. He received instructions that the State Department had nothing to say publicly: Hold off Burba, tell her nothing, and make no promises.

"At this moment, we cannot tell you that these documents are reliable or that they are unreliable," Kelly told her. That was the extent of the conversation.

Burba recognized that the Americans were not going to be helpful. This was no surprise—she'd always had misgivings about bringing the material to the embassy to begin with and had done so only because she was following Rossella's orders. After hanging up with

Kelly, she called Rossella at the magazine office in Milan and told him that all was well but that the Americans weren't talking.

"Oh, you should not have been bothering the Americans," the managing editor said. "They would have called you when they were ready."

Rossella's deference to the Americans irritated her. How could calling the Americans be an imposition? After all, she was the one who had given them the documents.

Martino's approach to Burba with the Italian letter coincided with accelerating US preparations for war. On October 7, 2002, the same day that Martino had given Burba the Italian letter and the rest of the dossier, President Bush had launched a new hard-line PR campaign on Iraq. In a speech in Cincinnati, he declared that Iraq under Saddam Hussein was a "grave threat" to US national security.

"It possesses and produces chemical and biological weapons. It is seeking nuclear weapons," he said. Bush's increasingly bellicose line was a progression from Woolsey's early televised musing that Iraq could have been involved in the 9/11 attacks.

Woolsey and his colleagues at the American Enterprise Institute had repeatedly fanned the flames with claims that Iraq was a rogue state that would soon possess nuclear weapons. George Tenet became director of central intelligence in 1997, about a year and a half after Woolsey left that post. But Tenet had been able to convince the White House to drop one questionable claim from Bush's Cincinnati speech: that Iraq was seeking uranium in Africa. The information was too fishy, Tenet explained to the National Security Council and Bush's speechwriters.

Bush dropped the shopping-for-uranium claim but nevertheless ratcheted up the bomb threat. He said in Cincinnati that if Saddam Hussein obtained bomb-grade uranium the size of a softball, he would have a nuclear bomb within a year. This particular doomsday scenario had first been unveiled several weeks earlier, on August 26, by Vice President Dick Cheney. In a speech in Nashville to the 103rd national convention of the Veterans of Foreign Wars, he declared with no equivocation that Hussein had "resumed his effort to acquire nuclear weapons."

On October 16, as Burba was en route to Niger, copies of the Italian letter and the accompanying dossier were placed on the table at an interagency nuclear proliferation meeting hosted by the State Department's intelligence bureau. It was nine days after Bush's Cincinnati speech and seven days after Burba's delivery of the documents to the US embassy in Rome.

The Western Europe Division desk at the State Department (EURO/WE) received Burba's material and forwarded a copy to the department's Bureau of Intelligence and Research (INR). That was the relatively small bureau at the State Department whose job it was to analyze incoming intelligence for the department's top policymakers. Analysts there had a quick look and didn't bother to ask for an official translation from French.

"It was bullshit," said an INR analyst. "It was clear it was bullshit." Analysts at the research bureau were familiar with Niger and the former French colonies of Africa. At least one of them had been stationed in Niger. The sale of tons of uranium couldn't have happened, in their estimation. The analysts knew that a French state-owned company operated the Nigerien uranium mines and kept tight controls on the business. The transfer of tons of yellowcake to Iraq would have been a huge event—and hard to cover up. In any case, one analyst at the bureau asked, "Why would Iraq be looking for yellowcake?"

The INR had determined the documents were phony right away

and produced by far the most accurate assessment of Iraq's weapons program of the sixteen agencies that make up the Intelligence Community.

But the small intelligence unit operated in a bubble. Few administration officials—not even Secretary of State Powell—paid much attention to its analytical product, much of which clashed with the hawks' assumptions.

But there was little effort to alert the CIA that its original tip in the fall of 2001 was the product of a scam. One exception was an e-mail from Simon Dodge, an INR nuclear weapons analyst, to colleagues in other agencies on the same day his department received the documents. He alerted them that he had immediately detected a problem with one of the documents. "You'll note that it bears a funky 'emb. of Niger stamp' (to make it look official, I guess)." That telling clue that something was wrong did not register concern elsewhere.

The INR, nevertheless, shared the bogus documents with those intelligence operatives attending the October 16 meeting, including representatives of the Energy Department, National Security Agency, and Defense Intelligence Agency. Four CIA officials attended, but only one, a clandestine service officer, bothered to take a copy of the Italian letter. He returned to his office, filed the material in a safe, and forgot about it.

The Nigerien uranium matter was not uppermost in their minds. Some of the analysts—though perhaps none who attended the proliferation meeting—had to deal with the issue largely because Cheney, I. Lewis "Scooter" Libby, and the National Security Council had repeatedly demanded more information and more analysis.

Carl Ford Jr., the blunt Vietnam War veteran and career intelligence official who headed the State Department's Bureau of Intelligence and Research, criticized the process. "Anyone who tried to make a nuclear weapons reconstitution program out of this crap was either incompetent or had sort of seen the handwriting on the wall and thought, 'Maybe it's possible they [the policymakers] want to hear that.'"

Burba went to Niamey, Niger's capital, on October 17. The trip was difficult because a civil war in neighboring Ivory Coast had shut down some air routes. Burba worked carefully, making contact with friendly missionaries and members of nongovernmental organizations. They warned her to be alert, that journalists weren't welcome, and that pressure from Islamic groups in the northern part of the country sometimes made travel dangerous. She followed through on her subterfuge of saying she was tracking down information about dinosaurs and visited the National Museum to check out the artifacts.

She then began tracking down evidence on the Italian letter. Burba's investigation followed a series of similar but still secret inquiries by former ambassador Joseph Wilson on behalf of the CIA eight months earlier. Burba was not a trained intelligence operative, but it became clear that Niger was not capable—even if it had been interested in doing so—of secretly shipping yellowcake to Iraq or anywhere else.

She found that a French company controlled the uranium trade, and any shipment of uranium certainly would have been noticed. If a uranium sale had taken place, the logistics would have been daunting. Burba discovered that yellowcake was stored in 400-kilogram (880-pound) barrels, each filled only halfway, more or less 200 kilos for each barrel, to control weight and safety. With delivery in two shipments of 250 metric tons each, she estimated that each batch would have required a convoy of trucks; and since tractor-trailers are rarely seen in West Africa, "it would have meant an incredible amount of trucks," she said, describing her thought process. "They would have needed hundreds of trucks," a large percentage of all the trucks in Niger, something that would have been impossible to conceal.

Each truck would have had to travel hundreds of miles southwest from the desert mine sites in Niger to Cotonou, a major port city in neighboring Benin, where the uranium would have had to be loaded on ships. And all of that would have had to be done discreetly, beginning in a sleepy country where convoys of trucks kicking up dust and carrying barrels of uranium would have been noticed and likely reported by security teams patrolling the streets. "And the streets are dangerous. They would have needed a huge security apparatus. The streets are full of bandits. So somebody would have known."

The ship then would have had to sail, again unnoticed, along the west coast of Africa and into the Mediterranean, bound probably for a port in Turkey, secretly offloaded, and then transported by land once more, this time to Iraq, from its northern border in Kurdistan.

Then there was the political aspect of the story. A risky enterprise to sell uranium to Iraq would have been disastrous, if discovered, for an impoverished nation courting the United States and Europe for critical aid. "The government was pro-Western, depending on lots of aid from Europe, the European Union, and from the United States. . . . It wouldn't have made sense that they would have made such a deal."

The finances of paying for the deal were also questionable. The bank that allegedly had handled the financing had only one branch and would have been incapable of arranging such a complicated commercial transaction, because it did not have corresponding offices overseas that could have wired money undetected. The financial transaction would have required the small bank to contact larger international banking agents, which would be on the lookout under international banking rules for signs of illicit commercial dealings and, in turn, probably would have reported the money transfer as a violation of the US-led international economic boycott of Iraq.

After seven or eight days of meetings with officials, diplomats, and members of nongovernmental organizations, Burba decided there was no indication that Niger had shipped anything to Iraq and that an agreement to sell just didn't make sense. "You have to add that to all the doubts I had about the documents, those corrections, and names of the people which were wrong. Putting everything together, I came back convinced that those documents were really doubtful."

When she was finished, Burba's air connections made it impossible to take the additional step of visiting the port of Cotonou, but she had seen enough to be confident of her analysis. Instead, she flew back to Italy via Paris after about a week, longer than she needed to reach her conclusions. Back in Rome, she told her editors that the Niger story didn't check out and then called Rocco Martino, who continued to insist that the documents were real. Burba perceived a disconnect. She believed Martino was sincere, that he felt that he was providing real documents, and suspected that he too had been the victim of the forgeries.

After eight days, Burba returned to Milan and reported her findings to her bosses in detail. She didn't believe the evidence provided by Martino; it was impossible. Both Rosella and Mulé accepted her report and agreed: There was no story.

Next she called Martino. It was a brief conversation.

"I'm not going to use those documents because we consider them unreliable," she said. "That means we're not going to give you any money."

Martino was disturbed and insistent. "No, no, no," he said. "It is reliable, it is reliable."

Burba was surprised by Martino's protests and didn't know what to say. She had the feeling that he was not knowingly part of a scam and that there was more to the story. But there was nothing to be done at the moment. The magazine was dropping the story and that was final. Burba hung up the phone.

At Christmas 2002, Rocco Martino, always the gentleman, sent a text message to Burba, wishing her a happy holiday. Burba was fed up with him and his story, and so were her bosses. If she answered at all, it was a curt response that gave no sign that she was interested in doing any more business with him. The fiasco surrounding the Italian letter had been enough.

But the 2003 State of the Union address changed her mind.

Burba wanted to write about the Italian letter and the documents. She went to her editors and proposed a story that wouldn't cost them money. Look, she said, we agree that the source's story is false. But Bush's speech gives us an interesting angle; we have the opportunity to write a huge scoop. "We know what Bush is basing his claim on; what we know is that we received some documents about the uranium trafficking. And we left a copy of the documents with the American embassy."

The Italian letter had been the basis for Bush's 16 words; that was no small matter. "We know something: How did it happen? Let's look for the source of the documents. We have a story here," Burba said.

Even as she laid out her proposal, she had the feeling that no one was listening to her. The newsroom was not a happy place. She felt she was being treated rudely and unfairly for her honest work. Since she'd come back from Niger, Rossella had rarely spoken to her directly. After that, he wanted to hear nothing about the subject.

Rossella, for his part, was confused and dismayed. Burba's perception of trouble in the newsroom was accurate, even though they hadn't spoken about it. From Rossella's point of view, Burba was also acting strangely. She had refused to reveal her source to him.

It's one thing to respect a confidential source, but what happens when the source is lying? Do you still have to protect him on that basis? Her answer was no: for fake news, no protection.

But she still didn't want to reveal the source, perhaps because she felt sorry for Martino. At one point, Martino had called and said he had fled the country, fearing his life might be in danger. In one way, it was laughable, but yet how did she know the pressures he faced? He had asked her for help and advice: What did she think? Did she think someone would try to kill him?

Why, she wanted to know, was Martino afraid? What was the basis? "Who are you working for?" she asked him. "Are you working for someone else? Are you working for the Americans?"

"No, no, no!" Martino answered repeatedly. He had gotten the material from La Signora, and that was it.

Rossella didn't care about Burba's proposal for a story on the fraud. He felt that he had fulfilled his responsibilities by sending Burba to Niger to check the story out, and that was as far as it went. "I tried; I paid for the trip, and she couldn't prove the story. It was false, it was junk, it was rubbish," he said.

Rossella understood what it meant to protect sources. He was the editor, but he had been a longtime correspondent and investigative reporter himself. It was very odd, he said, that she wouldn't reveal the source. He could unravel the whole story himself if he had the name. What was worse, Burba had told Mulé who the source was, extracting a promise that Mulé not tell Rossella. It was equivalent to Bob Woodward refusing to give *Washington Post* editor Ben Bradley the name of Deep Throat during Watergate.

"For me she was not the most important reporter at the newspaper," Rossella said. "She was not even in the foreign affairs department; she was in the national department. There were three or four reporters who were more important."

Rossella said that he'd had misgivings about the story, and his concerns were amplified when Burba didn't offer up the source. "It was very strange from the beginning," Rossella said. "Perhaps she didn't trust me, or she didn't like me; I don't know."

Rossella turned down the story, even after others started picking up on the fraud. Not long after the invasion, other news media in Italy, elsewhere in Europe, and then in the United States reported that the source of the information had been a batch of bogus letters and other documents passed along several months earlier to an unnamed Italian reporter, who handed the information over to the United States. A Rome newspaper, *La Repubblica,* later received an abbreviated version of the package and was the first to disclose that SISMI had foisted the intelligence on the CIA.

"I felt I had been scooped by my own story," Burba said.

She was right. Bush's "16 words" had been lifted almost verbatim from a British dossier published on September 24, 2002, that cited a litany of "intelligence" showing that Iraq possessed a number of banned weapons and was developing a nuclear bomb. "There is intelligence that Iraq has sought the supply of significant quantities of uranium from Africa," the British document said. That claim was based on the same intelligence provided by SISMI to the CIA almost a year earlier. SISMI had passed the intelligence—but not the actual documents—along to the British a few months after sharing it with the United States. To no avail, the CIA had urged the British not to use the uranium claim in the dossier, asserting that it was highly questionable.

And Burba had the very documents that had originated the intelligence, including the Italian letter. But it wasn't until months after the invasion that her editors allowed her to write a story about the scoop she almost had.

Chapter 3

Special Plans

Air force lieutenant colonel Karen Unger Kwiatkowski was one of the estimated 62 million people who watched George Walker Bush's State of the Union speech live on television. She was one of perhaps thousands of members of the sixteen government agencies known collectively as the Intelligence Community, which includes, most notably, the Central Intelligence Agency, the Defense Intelligence Agency, the State Department's Bureau of Intelligence and Research, the National Security Agency (NSA), and the Federal Bureau of Investigation. Many other US government employees stationed overseas were given print and video copies of Bush's speech.

Kwiatkowski was from North Carolina and was a twenty-year US Air Force veteran who had been assigned to the supersecret NSA before being transferred to do regional policy analysis at the Pentagon, most recently at the Near East and South Asia (NESA) directorate. Before that she had been an analyst for the Sub-Saharan Africa desk, which included Niger. Her NESA bureau, bustling with activity prior to the anticipated war on Iraq, was sifting for evidence that Saddam Hussein had secreted away weapons of mass destruction.

Kwiatkowski, a slender woman with auburn hair, was a fast-talking critic of what she saw going on at the Pentagon. She obtained an ROTC scholarship in 1978 and entered the military as a second lieutenant after college. She had earned a variety of university degrees: a bachelor's at the University of Maryland, a master's at Harvard, and a PhD in world politics at the Catholic University of America in Washington, DC.

Kwiatkowski had been gung-ho on fighting the war on terrorism. She was among the more than 20,000 Pentagon employees at work on September 11, 2001, when a hijacked American Airlines Boeing 757 jet crashed into the West façade of the building at 9:38 a.m., killing the 64 passengers and crew and 125 people on the ground.

She described the scene in a television interview: "We saw the fireball. Didn't know where it came from, had no concept of—that something had actually hit much lower and exploded through four stories. . . . We stood on the grass on that beautiful day and saw the gash in that Pentagon. You know, just an amazing day.

"There was certainly a sense of shock and anger, a need to retaliate. . . ."

One month after the attacks, US and British troops stormed into Afghanistan and deposed the Taliban government. Osama bin Laden, the acknowledged mastermind of 9/11, was apparently trapped for a while in the mountains of Tora Bora, a remote mountainous region on the Pakistani border, but eventually escaped with his top lieutenants.

Kwiatkowski was an officer of senior rank with no command under her and had only a peripheral role in the war on terrorism. But as a citizen and a soldier, she applauded the invasion of Afghanistan and supported the president.

"It seemed to me very logical that our initial strike-back would be at Afghanistan," she told us. "I mean, they said Osama was there, the Taliban was being funded by Osama, they were harboring him. Made a lot of sense. I had no real problems with the thing on Afghanistan. It made sense to me, and I think it made a lot of sense to a lot of people."

Therefore, Kwiatkowski did not react with skepticism to Bush's State of the Union speech. She had worked on the Sub-Sahara desk until mid-2002 and had not seen any intelligence claiming that Niger (or any African state) might have been supplying Iraq with uranium, but she assumed new information had been uncovered.

"Oh my God," she had burst out with characteristic verve. "It's my old office."

She figured that her former colleagues would be celebrating their discovery at the African desk, a relative backwater in the Intelligence Community and low in importance at the Defense Department's policy planning section. If the president was now declaring that a uranium purchase had been detected in Africa, it would be her old office that would have been analyzing the information. Any such report that Iraq was hauling in new supplies of uranium would have passed through the Sub-Sahara desk for analysis and military policy implications.

The next morning, Kwiatkowski wanted to share the triumph with her colleagues and so went to the office of her former bureau to congratulate her friends. The policy planning section was located on the fourth floor of the Pentagon, one floor below the offices of Defense Secretary Rumsfeld and the other top brass. "Wow," she thought to herself, "the office has finally found something."

"Hey guys, you made the president's speech; you're somebody!" she said, bursting in.

She was greeted by blank stares and no signs of victory. Instead, people were scurrying around with their heads down, answering e-mails and phone inquiries.

Kwiatkowski corralled one of her friends to ask what was going on.

"We don't know where the hell that came from; we're in big trouble, phones are ringing, people are asking us if we did it, but we didn't do it. We had nothing, we had no knowledge of this, this is not anything we've ever seen before."

Then, suddenly, she understood that something was wrong.

The policy office should have been in the loop. The Pentagon, via the policy office, gathered a constant stream of intelligence from its own sources, from the CIA, the NSA. If her former colleagues hadn't received any information from the Intelligence Community about an alleged rogue operation in an African country, then the system was somehow broken. But she didn't at that point consider the possibility that the information was fake.

Ever since September 11, 2001, a number of analysts at the CIA, the State Department, and the Defense Department had been skeptical about Bush administration claims that Iraq maintained significant stockpiles of banned weapons or was aligned in any way with al Qaeda. Even more did not believe that Saddam Hussein was pursuing a nuclear bomb. And key analysts at the US Central Command—the military command responsible for preparing for and waging the Iraq war—were convinced before the invasion that they would find no banned weapons once they went in. The skeptics based their conclusions on the same raw data available to other analysts who made the opposite case, that Iraq was rearming with chemical and biological weapons, was allied with Osama bin Laden, and was developing a nuclear bomb. They were looking at the same material: the Italian information about Iraq and Niger and the intelligence about Iraq's purchase of aluminum tubes. State Department analysts, for example, immediately discounted the Niger claim, while analysts at the CIA's Directorate of Intelligence Center for Weapons Intelligence, Nonproliferation, and Arms Control (WINPAC) said it was possible. But the difference in opinion had more to do with politics than with analysis of the intelligence. Many officials at the CIA realized that the Bush administration wanted the intelligence about Iraq weapons to be reported as true, whether or not it really was. They also realized that the tide was going with the top leaders at the Pentagon, who had the ear of Vice President Cheney and Defense Secretary Rumsfeld.

Lawrence Wilkerson, Secretary of State Colin Powell's chief of staff during the months leading up to the war, also noticed something unusual going on. "There were people at the CIA, especially in WINPAC, who were—this is too strong a word but I'll use it anyway—in league with the vice president's office and [Defense undersecretary for policy] Douglas Feith," he said.

Civilian leaders at the Pentagon nurtured and rewarded those who went along with their policies. The overthrow of Saddam Hussein, whether by invasion or by nurturing an insurrection, had been a long-held objective of Deputy Defense Secretary Wolfowitz and Feith. Both men were members of the powerful neoconservative fraternity, which grew up in the United States in the late 1970s and began to mature during the Reagan administration. A number of prominent so-called neocons had served on the staff of the late Cold War senator Henry M. "Scoop" Jackson, a fervent anti-Communist who advocated the spread of US democracy around the world.

Feith had formed a small intelligence unit at the Pentagon that cherry-picked raw intelligence to portray Iraq as an imminent threat swarming with al Qaeda terrorists. He matched these analysts with policymakers who had little need for unbiased intelligence. They called themselves the Cabal and wielded enormous influence with Cheney. They developed an unofficial pipeline to Cheney and senior

National Security Council (NSC) officials, feeding the White House a steady stream of questionable intelligence on Iraq that was warmly received because it reinforced a decision that had already been made.

Wolfowitz, who worked closely with this operation, was born in 1943 and was a graduate of Cornell University and the University of Chicago. He had served under Cheney in the Defense Department during the first Gulf War. Before that, during the Reagan administration, Wolfowitz had been director of policy planning at the State Department, where he'd assembled a team of advisers who later had prominent roles in the second Iraq war. Among them was Scooter Libby, a student of Wolfowitz's when the latter taught at Yale and Cheney's chief of staff until he was forced to resign following federal indictment for allegedly lying to the FBI and a grand jury; Francis Fukuyama, who broke with the neoconservatives in 2006 over his disagreement with their promotion of the Iraq war; and Zalmay Khalilzad, the first US ambassador to Iraq to be appointed after the 2003 US invasion.

The neoconservatives formed a tightly knit fraternity of policy-makers who, under George W. Bush, wielded extraordinary unlimited power in the formulation and implementation of foreign policy. Until the arrival of Bush, they had served intermittently in earlier administrations, notably inside the Pentagon, and between Pentagon assignments were active in powerful Washington think tanks and lobbying organizations, including some sympathetic to Israel's ultraconservative Likud Party.

The most influential of all neoconservative think tanks was the American Enterprise Institute (AEI), a well-endowed organization that champions many conservative causes but also has a soft spot for the Likud and is more accepting of foreign military intervention than conservative purists. Dick Cheney once was a senior fellow at AEI, and his wife, Lynne, was a senior fellow there. Other alumni include former secretary of state George Shultz and Jeane Kirkpatrick, UN ambassador under former presidents Ronald Reagan and Gerald Ford. Among its more influential members were Michael Ledeen and Richard Perle, an assistant secretary of defense under Ronald Reagan and chairman of the Pentagon's powerful Defense Policy Board during the first two years of the Bush administration. Perle, who also served on "Scoop" Jackson's staff, was the mentor of Feith, the undersecretary of defense during the Iraq war, and was an early advocate for the invasion of Iraq, arguing that it could be done quickly and cheaply—with just 40,000 troops—and predicting that "some grand square in Baghdad" soon would be named after Bush.

In late 2001, during the Afghanistan bombing campaign, Wolfowitz asked his friend Christopher DeMuth, the president of the American Enterprise Institute, to put together a small team of scholars to assess the dynamics inside the Middle East that had produced the September 11 hijackers. The twelve-member team concluded, among other things, that removing Saddam Hussein from power was an imperative to transforming the region into a more stable and less threatening part of the world. Their report was delivered to top administration officials, including Rice, Cheney, and Bush himself. It deeply impressed the three.

Another organization that has also attracted neoconservatives over the years was the Jewish Institute for National Security Affairs (JINSA), which promotes strong military ties between Israel and the United States. Dick Cheney served on JINSA's advisory board, as did Kirkpatrick, Ledeen, Perle, and Woolsey. Feith was vice chairman of their advisory board in the early 1990s.

So these like-minded people held strong views, reinforced by years of fraternal groupings. Not surprisingly, civilian leadership at the Pentagon, led by Rumsfeld, Wolfowitz, and Feith, had little tolerance for dissent. The neoconservatives didn't hide their worldview, and they expected subordinates to follow their policies without questioning them.

People knew the attitude the powers that be had from the outset: "We know he has it [WMD]. If you can't find it, you're incompetent," said a Defense Intelligence Agency analyst at the time. "For an intelligence person, career civil servant, or even a military officer, that's a very difficult position to be put in. Even to come in with doubts was almost heresy."

The raw intelligence picked up after UN inspectors were pulled out of Iraq in 1998 was at best thin and often flatly wrong. Much of the Pentagon's intelligence was corrupted by the stable of Iraqi defectors sponsored by Ahmed Chalabi, a brilliant manipulator and businessman who had been convicted of bank fraud in Jordan in 1992. Feith and Wolfowitz hoped that Chalabi would preside over Iraq after the US invasion. Chalabi and his Iraqi National Congress (INC), based in London, were given more than $30 million by the Defense Department in the run-up to the Iraq invasion, payment in part for providing intelligence, most of which turned out to be worthless.

In a substantially declassified report, the Senate Intelligence Committee charged that Chalabi's INC "attempted to influence United States policy on Iraq by providing false information through defectors directed at convincing the United States that Iraq possessed weapons of mass destruction and had links to terrorists." Though Chalabi and the INC were considered with great skepticism by many people inside the Intelligence Community, the defectors' false accounts were nevertheless used to bolster key judgments about Iraq's nuclear and biological programs in an authoritative but fatally flawed October 2002 National Intelligence Estimate, viewed by Congress at the time as the most compelling reason for voting to authorize the invasion. Powell eventually would cite some of the INC intelligence—also bogus—in his February 2003 speech before the United Nations that laid out the administration's case for war.

INC defectors, for example, corroborated sensational intelligence about Iraqi mobile biological labs described by Powell in the speech. The original claim had come from an Iraqi fabricator, code-named Curveball, who was controlled by German intelligence. Without the INC seconding of that material, it was unlikely that Powell, who insisted on multiple sources for his long list of Iraqi transgressions, would have included the mobile lab claim in his speech.

The CIA had had a working relationship with Chalabi and the INC in the 1990s but abandoned all ties to the group following a catastrophic Chalabi-sponsored attempted insurrection against Saddam in 1995, which resulted in the rounding up and killing of scores of its plotters, including Iraqi soldiers and INC members. In 2000, the State Department, under instructions from Congress, renewed operational links to the INC by paying the group $340,000 a month to gather intelligence on Iraq. It, too, abandoned the INC in 2002. But Bush's National Security Council ordered the Pentagon to take over, and the Defense Intelligence Agency became the INC's new sponsor. The DIA knew it was inheriting a can of worms. "At the time it assumed responsibility for funding and managing the INC's collection effort in October 2002, the DIA cautioned that the INC was penetrated by hostile intelligence services [including Iran's] and would use the relationship to promote its own agenda." A similar warning came from the CIA, which had severed ties in 1996.

In late 2001, former CIA director Woolsey, an ally of Chalabi, introduced one of the INC-sponsored fabricators, Iraqi major Mohammed Harith, to the Pentagon. The DIA produced more than 250 intelligence reports based on this informant's claims. Three years later, the CIA conducted a review of Harith's intelligence and found that much of his WMD reporting "remains questionable" and that his description of an alleged nuclear facility was "demonstrably incorrect." A lie detector test showed that he "appeared deceptive" when asked whether the INC had coached him on what to tell his

American debriefers, including details about the alleged nuclear facility.

Even with the bogus and alarmist intelligence flowing from INC-sponsored Iraqi defectors, Feith and Wolfowitz believed that too many intelligence reports being generated by the DIA and CIA underestimated the threat of Hussein and consequently weakened the rationale for invasion.

So, with the approval of Defense Secretary Donald Rumsfeld, Feith and Wolfowitz decided shortly after September 11, 2001, to create their own supersecret intelligence analysis operation at the Pentagon, totally separate and unknown to the members of the Intelligence Community. The new shop, called Team B, opened unannounced with two desks and two computer terminals. The first two analysts occupying the new desks were David Wurmser, who later became Vice President Dick Cheney's Middle East advisor, and F. Michael Maloof, a longtime Pentagon aide who twice was stripped of his security clearances in 2001 for allegedly failing to report his contact with a woman he had met in the former Soviet Republic of Georgia. He subsequently married the woman. Losing security clearance is rare and can end the career of officials working on classified projects.

Maloof and Wurmser were longtime neoconservatives who shared the views that a preemptive invasion of Iraq was justified because Saddam Hussein was a danger to the United States and Israel and that his ouster would foster democracy in the Middle East. Their assignment was to track down evidence linking Iraq to the September 11, 2001, attacks—any footprint would be sufficient justification for invading Iraq. Only much later did intelligence officials discover what they were doing and described their work as cherry-picking the available intelligence from established spy agencies and open-source articles to "prove" that Osama bin Laden and Saddam Hussein were in cahoots.

The intelligence they gathered was neatly packaged in PowerPoint presentations and delivered directly to Cheney's chief of staff, I. Lewis Libby. Libby was the pointman in the administration for producing reports showing WMD and ties to al Qaeda. Cheney was suspicious of what he was being told by the Intelligence Community, according to Rand Beers, who at the time was the National Security Council's senior director for combatting terrorism. "He didn't trust it."

Cheney and Feith were delighted with the pseudo-intelligence they were receiving from Maloof and Wurmser. "They were simply providing information that those people already believed in," Beers told us. "They were providing them with the evidence that would allow them to make the arguments that they were making" about Saddam Hussein's unholy alliance with Osama bin Laden.

At the same time, Cheney and Rumsfeld led a verbal offensive, asserting that Hussein was partnering with terrorist groups, especially al Qaeda. The CIA had never said such a thing and CIA analysts didn't believe it was true. Only Douglas Feith's two-man personal intelligence unit at the Pentagon, Team B, was able to weave rumors into a conclusion that Hussein and bin Laden were soul mates. The two-man analytical team—which later expanded to fourteen—got its name from a conservative and hard-line commission of "outside experts" in the 1970s, which challenged the CIA's assessments of Soviet military might. President Gerald Ford created the commission at the urging of his chief of staff, Dick Cheney, and his defense secretary, Donald Rumsfeld.

Team B's conclusions about the Soviet Union's military prowess, later determined to have been mostly wrong, were far more alarming than the CIA's. But it had the desired effect of scaring many members of Congress, who became more generous with funding the Pentagon.

Ford named Paul Wolfowitz to Team B on the recommendation of Cheney and Rumsfeld.

The Bush administration's Team B, while more modest in size and scope, was driven by a similar motive: to scare Congress and all Americans by linking Iraq with al Qaeda. Cheney kept repeating one of Team B's urban legends: that Mohammed Atta had met with an Iraqi intelligence officer several months before the 9/11 attacks. He said so even after he was informed clearly by the CIA that the intelligence was suspect, at best.

As a result of the misinformation, at one point 70 percent of Americans said in opinion polls that Hussein had something to do with the toppling of the Twin Towers.

Feith's team sought to sell its analytical conclusions to CIA director George Tenet and his top aides. Tenet heard the evidence and was not impressed. As far back as 1998, the CIA and National Security Council had pored over the intelligence and could find no operational connection between al Qaeda and the Iraqi government. Under enormous pressure from the administration, the CIA tried again in 2002 to find such a connection but there was none.

Once convened, Team B became known as Douglas Feith's personal intelligence experiment and was adapted for a larger operation dedicated entirely to the coming war with Iraq. By late summer 2002, Feith's policy staff underwent a major expansion in preparation for war. William Luti, a retired navy captain who had moved from Cheney's office to the Pentagon, oversaw the NESA directorate, as well as the Sub-Saharan Africa desk and Team B, for Feith. That August, NESA's Iraq desk grew from four to eighteen staffers. It included a handful of professional analysts from the DIA and the military services, but others were unabashed hawks: They were outspoken advocates for invading Iraq. What had been the small Iraq desk under NESA morphed into the Office of Special Plans.

Special Plans was run by Abram Shulsky, a soft-spoken and very bright intelligence academic who had served under Assistant Secretary of Defense Richard Perle during the Reagan administration. But Shulsky, who also had been an aide on the Senate Intelligence Committee during the 1980s, did not have hands-on experience with the intelligence process. Colleagues said he fit in well with the agenda: He tended to accept intelligence only if it fit his predetermined ideological conclusions. As a result, he easily accepted the information cooked up by conmen like Chalabi.

The dominant view in the Intelligence Community had not changed. The Community scooped up and analyzed every possible source of intelligence, including the supersecret National Security Agency, which vacuums the airwaves for virtually all forms of electronic transmissions—from cell and landline phones, radios, the Internet, missile tests, diplomatic and military correspondence, encrypted or in microbursts, at home and abroad.

Professional intelligence analysts rely on inductive reasoning, or gathering relevant data first and then making assessments based on that data. Throughout the period of the run-up to the war, many were unconvinced that Iraq had resumed its nuclear weapons program, and most did not believe that Saddam Hussein was harboring al Qaeda terrorists. But the Office of Special Plans had already reached its own conclusions. Feith's team made square pegs fit into round holes and then briefed their "findings" to sympathetic policymakers, including Rumsfeld, Libby, and Steve Hadley, who at the time was number two at the National Security Council.

Lt. Col. Kwiatkowski, the officer assigned at the time to the Near East and South Asia desk, observed the creation and transformation of the Office of Special Plans. She thought it was unusual that superiors told NESA personnel to avoid using the title "Office of Special Plans" for the new Iraq initiative, even inside the Pentagon. Officials ordered them never to confirm that it was an expanded Iraq planning desk. Kwiatkowski and her colleagues were told, in fact, to keep the entire matter secret even from the Joint Chiefs of Staff. It was a strange directive, but there was a purpose behind the secrecy. Special Plans became a back-channel advisory team for Defense Secretary Rumsfeld on war preparations, according to retired army colonel Patrick Lang, former head of the human intelligence unit at the Defense Intelligence Agency and chief of the agency's Middle East division. The Joint Chiefs of Staff is the principal military adviser to the president. The secretary of defense, through the chairman of the Joint Chiefs, directed the commander of the US Central Command to prepare plans for the invasion. The Joint Staff would then approve or modify the Central Command's plans, in conjunction with the secretary. And Rumsfeld, in turn, relied heavily on input from Special Plans.

Other than its access to Rumsfeld, Special Plans had no direct input on invasion plans, but it did establish many critical support activities. It coordinated, for example, the Iraqi exile opposition under the leadership of Ahmed Chalabi. It organized military training courses in Hungary for the so-called Free Iraqi Forces, established and funded by the Bush administration. Perhaps most important, it did much of the planning for postwar Iraq, which even the dwindling supporters of the war admit has been an unmitigated disaster.

Ahmed Chalabi was a frequent visitor to the NESA and Special Plans offices at the Pentagon and often brought along Iraqi defectors well coached by the INC, which also prepped them on how to pass lie detector tests. When asked to comment on the numerous claims from within and outside of the administration that his INC was advising defectors on what to say, Chalabi was indignant. "Of course these are false charges. They are hyped up by people, journalists with an agenda who have tried to do blame shifting." The DIA had responsibility for culling information provided by Chalabi's agents. A DIA report later concluded that the information had been virtually worthless.

The Iraqi expatriate opposition forces, including the Free Iraqi Forces, became major irritants to US and British commanders after the March 20, 2003, invasion. "There were a lot of the opposition forces who kept getting in the way," said Lang. "They were uncontrollable and undisciplined." Chalabi's stock fell after the invasion, when news accounts disclosed that his intelligence chief was a long-time senior officer in Iran's espionage service. US authorities, meanwhile, investigated Chalabi for allegedly passing secrets to Iran.

One Special Plans mission was to produce propaganda casting Saddam Hussein as a mortal threat to the United States. The office generated talking points on Iraq for the Pentagon policy staff, which in turn prepared briefings for guests or anyone who requested them. Such briefings included assertions that were often unsubstantiated and even out-and-out false. According to Kwiatkowski, Special Plans staffers declared that Hussein "had harbored al Qaeda operatives and offered and probably provided them with training facilities." Another claim was that Hussein "was pursuing and had WMD of the type that could be used by him, in conjunction with al Qaeda and other terrorists, to attack and damage American interests, Americans, and America . . . [Saddam Hussein] was plotting to hurt America and support anti-American activities, in part through terrorists."

The Office of Special Plans also produced what in the trade is called "alternative" analysis, assessments at variance with the cautious and often irritatingly nuanced conclusions emanating from the Intelligence Community. Much of the analytical product of Special Plans was transmitted up the Pentagon's civilian chain to Feith, Wolfowitz, and finally to Defense Secretary Rumsfeld.

But Special Plans enjoyed extraordinary privilege and power that belied its relatively small staff because it had direct access to Vice President Cheney's office. Critics have described this access as a stovepipe, a direct channel that eliminated filtering or analysis from other intelligence services. The stovepipe delivered information, very often raw and wrong, to Cheney and other policymakers to stoke their prowar enthusiasm. Some of the intelligence that flowed to Cheney via Luti's office came from Chalabi's INC fabricators. The INC had its own lobbyists in Washington. One, Entifadh Qunbar, boasted in a memo in June 2002 to the Senate Appropriations Committee that INC intelligence reports on Iraq's alleged WMDs and ties to terrorism were being delivered directly to John Hannah, a senior national security aide to Cheney as well as to Luti. Another INC lobbyist, Francis Brooke, admitted he routinely discussed similar INC-generated Iraq intelligence with Hannah, Luti, and Libby.

Kwiatkowski recalled the first time she heard of Libby. It was when her boss, Luti, barked out an order: "Scooter needs this right away!"

"Who is this 'Scooter'?" Kwiatkowski remembered wondering. Cheney's Defense Department liaison officer was a regular courier between Luti and the vice president's office. He was a well-known figure around Special Plans and came and went frequently, wearing civilian clothes. "He was a very personable, good-looking guy, typical of what you get to work on these high-visibility jobs. You get the good-looking, nice, cookie-cutter officers, very confident, very articulate. And that's what he was, a good, good guy."

Kwiatkowski did not, on the other hand, recall ever seeing a military aide assigned to President Bush show up, which also would have been strange. "I don't even know who the frickin' White House military rep was," she told us.

The link between Cheney's office and the Pentagon circumvented the traditional interagency process—a bureaucratic and often cumbersome deliberation protocol involving senior members of relevant federal agencies. The process was intended to safeguard against unilateral decisions that could lead to devastating results.

It was, in the view of some administration officials, an indication of Cheney's seemingly boundless authority and interest in controlling information. The Pentagon was a focal point.

Retired army colonel Lawrence Wilkerson, Colin Powell's chief of staff at the time, observed the process. "Wolfowitz and Feith had a vision. They were ruthless in implementing that vision, and therefore they were always ahead of everybody else. They brooked no opposition. They knew what was going on, and they had the vice president to back them up."

The vice president, of course, knew intimately how the Pentagon and the White House worked. He had been the secretary of defense under Bush's father, George Herbert Walker Bush, during the Gulf War in 1991 and chief of staff for President Gerald Ford in the mid-1970s.

Cheney's power was boundless. Wilkerson observed that there had been only one period since the 1947 passing of the National Security Act when nearly as much power had been concentrated in one person other than the president of the United States. That was during the Watergate scandal in the early 1970s, when Henry Kissinger served simultaneously as both national security adviser and secretary of state. At the time, President Richard Nixon was embroiled in the controversy that would lead to his resignation, and Kissinger had wide authority. "It was incredible, even the part where Kissinger goes to Moscow on one occasion and reverses the president's instructions to him and in effect becomes the president of the United States. Nixon's so engulfed in Watergate at this point that he doesn't realize what Henry's doing to him. So if you want to see a template of similar concentration of power, then you go back to that time and look at it to try to figure out what's going on now. The difference being, of course, that it's now far more life-threatening."

The civilian policymakers at the Pentagon had constitutional authority over the uniformed officers. Cheney, Rumsfeld, Wolfowitz, and Feith represented the president, the commander in chief under the Constitution. In 2006, a number of uniformed officers who had recently retired publicly criticized their civilian bosses. One, marine lieutenant general Greg Newbold, said in a *Time* magazine essay in April 2006 that he regretted that he hadn't pushed harder against the civilian leadership for what he said was their misuse of intelligence that was taking the United States to war.

Newbold, who retired as the Pentagon's top operations officer four months before the invasion, said his decision to leave in part was a result of his "opposition to those who had used 9/11's tragedy to hijack" national security policy. He thought the Iraq invasion was "an unnecessary war" and that the "zealots' rationale for war made no sense." Among the many failures, he wrote, was "the distortion of intelligence in the buildup to war."

"The commitment of our forces to this fight was done with a casualness and swagger that are the special provinces of those who have never had to execute those missions—or bury the results."

Chapter 4

An Order That Could Not Be Refused

Washington, DC, February 12, 2002

About two weeks after Bush's 2002 State of the Union address, perhaps best remembered for his declaration that Iran, North Korea, and
Iraq constituted an "axis of evil," Cheney issued an order that would
transform an insignificant bit of intelligence into a powerful symbol
of Iraq's nuclear ambitions. On Tuesday, February 12, 2002, Cheney
demanded that the CIA, the nation's preeminent spy service, take a
hard look at an item that had just crossed his desk claiming that Iraq
was shopping for uranium.

It was a Defense Intelligence Agency report, designated as NMJIC
Executive Highlight, Vol. 028-02, February 12, 2002, which asserted
that Iraq was shopping for uranium from Niger.

The initial tip for the information had come to the CIA from SISMI, the Italian intelligence service, several days after the September 11, 2001, terrorist attacks. The CIA Rome station, headed by Jeff C., asked SISMI for details and then produced its first report on the subject, sending it to Washington on October 15, 2001. This first report was based on a summary of intelligence provided by Italian intelligence and did not include the actual forged documents that Rocco Martino eventually handed over to Elisabetta Burba. On the contrary, the first report was thin gruel and did not, for example, even include the amount of uranium Iraq allegedly was seeking. CIA officers and analysts throughout the Intelligence Community greeted the report with much skepticism, according to a Senate Intelligence Committee report.

"At the time [late 2001], all [Intelligence Community] analysts interviewed by Committee staff considered this initial report to be very limited and lacking needed detail. CIA, Defense Intelligence Agency, and Department of Energy analysts considered the reporting to be 'possible' while the Department of State's Bureau of Intelligence and Research regarded the report as 'highly suspect.'" In fact, a number of CIA officers and managers treated the intelligence with skepticism right from the beginning. One reason was that the CIA, which has had long experience with SISMI, viewed the agency with professional contempt. "Italian [intelligence] reporting is never that credible," said a senior DO officer who knew SISMI well. "If the [global] Intelligence Community has a clown act, it's the Italians." Retired CIA officers who served in Rome agreed, and some said the DO officer's description was too kind.

Unfortunately, the DO did not share with analysts the source of the reporting, only that the information had come from a foreign government service. Even if the intelligence was trustworthy, it lacked urgency. "How important can yellowcake be when you're talking about the imminence of a nuclear program?" asked Richard Kerr, the former CIA deputy director for intelligence who led an in-house team that studied the Iraq intelligence failures. "I'm interested in fabrication, whether they're doing high enrichment tests." In other words, did Iraq have the industrial capability to turn the yellowcake into bombs? And the CIA's intelligence on that question, though more disturbing than the facts on the ground, still amounted to a resounding no.

Paul Pillar, who, as national intelligence officer for the Near East and South Asia, was responsible for evaluating intelligence about Iraq, said there was another reason no alarm was sounded. Iraq already had a large amount—550 tons—of yellowcake in storage, stockpiled under IAEA seal, but the UN inspectors only checked it once a year. It also had its own uranium mines, which had not been in use since Iraq ended its nuclear program at the end of Operation Desert Storm in 1991.

"One of the reasons it didn't make any sense was that access to uranium ore wasn't the short pole in the Iraqi tent as far as nuclear weapons were concerned," he said. "They had no need. They had the stuff."

The intelligence was so suspect that the CIA kept it out of a public white paper on Iraq's alleged weapons of mass destruction arsenal that the agency published in October 2002. It also tried unsuccessfully to convince the British government to drop it from a controversial dossier the United Kingdom published in September 2002.

The Rome station continued to gather information from SISMI and produced a second report on February 5, 2002. Unlike the initial report, this one offered some details of the alleged deal, including critical information culled from the Italian letter: The amount of uranium to be delivered was 500 tons a year, to be shipped twice a year. But again SISMI gave no copies of documents to the CIA. SISMI this time did provide what it said was a "verbatim text" of the alleged accord between Iraq and Niger.

The verbatim text was not of an accord or contract, but of a document labeled as an annex. The annex was one of the bogus documents that Rocco Martino eventually gave to Elisabetta Burba.

And the verbatim text was legal mumbo jumbo purporting to reflect the deliberation and final approval of the uranium deal by Niger's highest court, which it said was the State Court. There were major flaws, none of which, apparently, was caught by the CIA or DIA analysts. For example, the title given for the Niger court was outdated. The State Court (Cour d'Etat) had been renamed the Supreme Court (Cour Suprême) in 1990. The court's ratification of the Iraq deal was said to have occurred on Wednesday, July 7, 2000. That day fell on a Friday. The five officers of the court cited at the bottom of the annex served together in that capacity only between February and May of 1989. And one of them, Bandiaire Ali, was described as Iraq's attorney general. He was Niger's attorney general in 1989.

The errors were so egregious, according to Vincent Cannistraro, a retired senior CIA officer who was posted for many years in Italy, that it should have been immediately obvious that Niger officials or diplomats were unlikely to have produced such documents.

The DIA report that landed on Cheney's desk that Tuesday winter morning was largely based on the CIA Rome station's February 5 report and, unlike the CIA version, DIA had juiced up the language, and it did sound the alarm. It said that Iraq "probably" was "searching abroad for natural uranium to assist in its nuclear weapons program." The title of the DIA report was even more conclusive: "Niamey signed an agreement to sell 500 tons of uranium a year to Baghdad." Niamey is the capital of Niger.

This second report, replete with flaws, jump-started a new round of intelligence gathering, and what had been a moribund morsel of questionable information catapulted to center stage. Nevertheless,

CIA and DIA analysts should have been able to flag the faults right away with minimal effort. A fifteen-minute Google search would have caught the mistakes—in fact, Elisabetta Burba ended up doing just that on her own.

Melvin Goodman, a twenty-five-year veteran of the CIA's Intelligence Directorate, said that the failure to catch obvious errors reflected a systemic problem in the Intelligence Community. Analysts, he said, "don't do that kind of fact-checking. They're not skeptical enough of sources they do get. They make intuitive judgments: 'This is good; this is crap.'"

"The problem is you don't always have the right people looking at the right documents at the right time," said an intelligence official familiar with the dissemination of the Niger documents. "If you had the right people looking at these documents, they would have said, 'Gee, these terms are hosed up, they're out of date.'"

"This gets to one of the maxims of this profession," the intelligence official said. "From small details, large conclusions can result." And from small erroneous details, disastrous conclusions can result.

It was not just the first cluster of analysts at the CIA who failed to recognize the errors in SISMI's intelligence. The intelligence wound its way through numerous desks in the Intelligence Community and no questions were raised. Only one agency, the State Department's small intelligence bureau, smelled a rat right from the beginning and dismissed the reports as inaccurate if not outright bogus.

The DIA's ominous report certainly caught Cheney's attention. Within four days, he declared that Iraq had developed a "robust set of programs to develop their own weapons of mass destruction." With scant information to back up the charges, the vice president was early out of the gate in becoming the administration's most hyperbolic voice in casting Iraq as a global menace. And now he had a secret report backing up what he had already been claiming.

So on that February 12, the vice president demanded that the CIA gather more information: If the DIA could produce such a report, he wanted more data from the CIA as well. Since he was the administration's lead foreign policymaker, this was no small request; his power was manifest. Cheney was a long-term player in US foreign policy and often a critic of intelligence agencies. He had served as President Gerald Ford's chief of staff from 1975 through 1977 and as defense secretary under President George Herbert Walker Bush, helping orchestrate the US invasion of Panama in 1989 and the ouster of Iraq from Kuwait in the 1991 Gulf War. During that war, he had heard frequent complaints from Colin Powell, then the chairman of the Joint Chiefs of Staff, and from then–army general Norman Schwarzkopf, commander of the coalition forces, that the CIA's intelligence in support of the war effort was worthless. As a congressman from Wyoming between two stints in Republican administrations, he had been a probing and occasionally acerbic overseer of intelligence agencies while sitting on the House Intelligence Committee.

Cheney knew the Intelligence Community's weak points and where to apply pressure. In the case of the Iraqi intelligence reports, much of the pressure involved badgering analysts into producing assessments that it made clear Iraq was in league with al Qaeda.

It is a rare analyst who will admit to altering conclusions because of pressure from his superiors. Unfortunately, it is not that rare for an analyst, especially one overly eager to advance his career, to produce a report consciously or unconsciously tailored to please his boss. The result is what is called the politicization of intelligence. "Politicization is never an issue of somebody telling you to write something or changing your judgment," said John Gannon, a respected former deputy director for intelligence. It is more subtle than that. During the run-up to war, he said, policymakers, including Cheney or Libby, routinely challenged the analysts, who were working with questionable intelligence to begin with, to reassess their conclusions until it matched what the policymakers themselves believed. "The bias of power [as with Cheney] tends to trump the bias of analytical objectivity," Gannon said.

The vice president and his staff berated analysts, sometimes in person at CIA headquarters in Langley, Virginia, when they received reports diverging from administration assumptions. "They were hammering the CIA over and over," recalled Melvin Goodman, a retired thirty-year veteran of CIA analysis. "They just wouldn't let go."

Cheney's involvement was unprecedented. Presidents and vice presidents rarely if ever had gone to CIA headquarters other than for ceremonial events. Not even George Herbert Walker Bush, who had been CIA director under President Gerald Ford, went to the CIA campus very much when he was vice president under Ronald Reagan or as the 41st president of the United States. CIA headquarters was named for the former president in 1999.

Cheney crossed the Potomac to visit the CIA at least six times, mostly to challenge analysts who were skeptical that Saddam Hussein was harboring al Qaeda terrorists. But Cheney and his aides also railed about the weak analysis and insufficient reporting on Iraq's weapons of mass destruction. "When the vice president goes over and sits down with the analysts for chats, that's highly irregular, highly unusual," said Wayne White, a veteran intelligence officer and deputy director of the State Department's Bureau of Intelligence and Research. "It means those people are being pressured."

Paul Pillar, a veteran CIA official, had been the national intelligence officer for the Near East and South Asia and was responsible for evaluating intelligence about Iraq. He said Cheney and the Bush administration "repeatedly" pushed the Intelligence Community "to uncover more material that would contribute to the case for war." He said intelligence about Iraq was not used to craft policy decisions but to "justify decisions already made."

A top-ranking former deputy director of the CIA, Richard Kerr, described the pressure as pervasive. "There was a lot of pressure, no question," said Kerr. "The White House, State, Defense, were raising questions, heavily on WMD and the issue of terrorism. Why did you select this information rather than that? Why have you downplayed this particular thing? . . . Sure, I heard that some of the analysts felt there was pressure. We heard about it from friends. There are always some people in the agency who will say, 'We've been pushed too hard.' Analysts will say, 'You're trying to politicize it.' There were people who felt there was too much pressure. Not that they were being asked to change their judgments, but they were being asked again and again to restate their judgments—do another paper on this, repetitive pressures. Do it again."

The CIA was not alone in feeling the heat. A veteran DIA analyst sympathized with the civilian intelligence agency and said Defense Department officers were also pressured. I. Lewis Libby, Cheney's chief of staff, publicly berated generals when they questioned administration assumptions about Iraq. All the while, many defense analysts said they had no credible information to corroborate the claim that Iraq had resumed its nuclear program.

One DIA officer assigned to the Joint Chiefs of Staff said that much of the intelligence material coming in was raw, questionable at best, and almost never confirmed. Intelligence officers were under pressure and predisposed to offer answers that made Cheney happy, so reliable material was not separated from debris. "The human intelligence was so bad, so horrendous," said the DIA officer, referring to information from the INC and others. "It seems like a big disinformation campaign. The sources were so bad. It's almost like making pudding. Once you make it and it's blended in, you can't sort out the good from the bad."

Not everyone in the Intelligence Community was persuaded by the critical second report from SISMI. Analysts from the State Department's intelligence bureau still believed that Niger would be "unwilling and unable" to carry out a deal to sell 500 tons of uranium to Iraq, and that Iraqi officials were unlikely to risk such a transaction because they were "bound to be caught." Among other things, Iraq was subject to an international embargo, and the shipment would be large and easily detected. CIA officers in Rome asked their Italian counterparts for more information and asked if SISMI would submit its source to a lie detector test. The Italian service refused to do so, saying only that the information came from "a very credible source."

The source SISMI was referring to was Laura Montini—La Signora—an employee of the Nigerien embassy who had been on the SISMI payroll for many years. Her job was to steal documents from the embassy files and provide them to operatives at SISMI.

The identities of the current and former SISMI officers who actually fabricated the documents remain a mystery—perhaps even to top officials at SISMI.

A former top CIA official with numerous contacts inside SISMI said that the agency's top officers, including its chief at the time, Nicolo Pollari, appeared to have been unaware of the forgery operation. A strong indication that they were kept in the dark was the aggressive investigation into the affair that they ordered after learning that the intelligence they had provided the CIA was based on fraudulent documents. The investigation was not made public, but several senior SISMI officers, including some of the CIA official's contacts, were targeted for prosecution. They were not officially charged. As is typical of the numerous scandals that have beset SISMI over the years, everything was swept under the rug, and it remained unclear whether any careers were terminated. Pollari himself was subsequently fired and faced criminal charges in an unrelated case.

Analysts in Washington, meanwhile, dug into dusty files and pulled up some obscure reporting about a visit to Niger in 1999 by an Iraqi ambassador, Wissam al-Zahawie. There had been claims that Zahawie, Iraq's ambassador to the Vatican, was shopping for uranium on that trip. The tips had been considered plausible because there was no other obvious commercial interest in Niger, a leading world supplier of uranium.

At the same time, the US embassy in Niger, notified of the new intelligence from SISMI, cabled Washington that Ambassador Barbro Owens-Kirkpatrick had recently met with Serge Martinez, the managing director of the French mining consortium that ran the Niger uranium operation. Martinez told her "there was no possibility" that any of the annual production of 3,000 tons of uranium could have been diverted.

On February 14, or forty-eight hours after Cheney had ordered more information on the uranium intelligence, the CIA responded with a formal document known as a Senior Publish When Ready report, a finished intelligence product with limited distribution. The CIA document cautioned that the information Cheney had picked up from the DIA report lacked "crucial details," had come from a single foreign government service, and contradicted the reporting from the US ambassador on the scene, Owens-Kirkpatrick. The report had been prepared by the largest division at the CIA, WINPAC. A version of the CIA document circulated beyond Cheney and was sent to other senior intelligence consumers, but only Cheney's version included an additional nugget: The Italian military intelligence agency, SISMI, had provided the original information. This would have been a built-in warning to almost anyone who read it, because SISMI's lack of reliability was notorious.

The CIA's Counterproliferation Division also went to work immediately to satisfy Cheney's demand for quick information. The division is a clandestine department inside the Directorate of Operations that conducts covert operations to foil the global trafficking in illicit weapons. Officers there, including Valerie Plame, a fifteen-year veteran of the clandestine service, huddled over what they could do to satisfy Cheney. They asked the CIA station in Paris to check with the agency's French counterpart, the General Directorate for External Security, the DGSE, which had good coverage in Niger, its former French colony. A top DGSE officer, Alain Chouet, griped about the American demands but dispatched a small team of covert operatives who spent a few days in Niger. The French officers found nothing.

Because speed was essential, the Counterproliferation Division decided to send an envoy to Niger for a firsthand assessment. Plame's husband, former ambassador Joseph Wilson, was a logical choice. In a memo to her boss, Plame wrote, "My husband has good relations with both the PM and the former Minister of Mines (not to mention lots of French contacts), both of whom could possibly shed light on this sort of activity." She wrote the memo at the request of her boss. A senior CIA official confirmed that Plame had not volunteered her husband's name and that her division colleagues were fully aware of who he was.

Wilson was a retired career diplomat who had been ambassador to the West African nation of Gabon and was fluent in French. One of his first assignments had been to the American embassy in Niger in the late 1970s. He had been deputy chief of mission in Baghdad in the late 1980s and acting ambassador during Operation Desert Shield in

1990, when he negotiated for the release of several hundred hostages. He was the last American official to meet with Saddam Hussein before the United States attacked Iraqi forces occupying Kuwait at the start of the Gulf War in 1991. Most important, he had conducted an earlier secret mission in Niger for the CIA's Counterproliferation Division shortly after a brief visit to that country by Abdul Qadeer Khan, the father of Pakistan's nuclear program. Khan and his nuclear team had traveled to Niamey and to Sudan's capital, Khartoum, in February 1999, according to the 2000 memoir of one of Khan's business associates, A. M. Siddiqui. Khan's visit did not result in any uranium deals with Niger, Wilson "did not uncover any information," and the Counterproliferation Division did not distribute an intelligence report on Wilson's trip.

The Counterproliferation Division summoned Wilson on Tuesday, February 19, for a meeting at CIA headquarters. It was a dank winter morning, one week after Cheney forced the issue on alleged connections between Iraq and Niger. CIA case officers and analysts, as well as a representative from the INR, discussed the merits of dispatching Wilson—or anyone else—to Niger. Plame introduced her husband, then left after a few minutes. The questions at hand went back to the beginning: Was it plausible that Niger could be selling clandestine uranium supplies to Iraq? Would it be worthwhile to have someone go to Africa to check it out? Some said it was not necessary to send an investigator. The INR analyst said the US embassy in Niger had good contacts and could get to the bottom of the allegations without outside interference. The analyst reminded those attending that France controlled mining, milling, and transporting of uranium in Niger and certainly would not allow sales to Iraq.

A WINPAC analyst said that, given the political winds in Washington, even if they did send a well-placed envoy, higher-ups in the administration would not accept the results as being authoritative.

"The results from this source will be suspect at best, and not believable under most scenarios."

Wilson, for his part, was skeptical about finding proof of a uranium deal, although he hadn't seen any of the intelligence reports. He knew how Niger operated, and it would be hard to conceal such an ambitious and tricky enterprise. But he said his contacts among Nigerien officials would make it easy for him to get around in the country and gather information quickly. If called upon, Wilson said, he was willing to go.

After about two hours of meetings, the CIA officials thanked Wilson and said they would have an answer for him as soon as they could. The final decision was based on the perspective of the counterproliferation officers. They heard the expressions of skepticism but concluded they had no other option. Another possibility would have been to set up a time-consuming clandestine operation, but there was no time. The vice president demanded quick answers. He was in the process of assembling talking points for his upcoming tour of friendly Middle Eastern leaders, during which he intended to press the US case for action against Iraq.

The agency called Wilson and asked him to embark as soon as he could; he obtained a visa and set off for Niger a week later. Landing in the capital, Niamey, on February 26, he looked down on the city of 750,000 and realized how little had changed since he'd been a junior officer there a quarter of a century earlier. He saw camel caravans, dust, and the ruins of a cargo jet that had crashed short of the runway in 1977 when he lived there.

He met first with Barbro Owens-Kirkpatrick, the US ambassador. She was happy to receive her colleague but confused about why the government was sending someone else to examine the baseless rumors of a uranium deal, a claim she thought had been laid to rest. Washington had already sent in a military envoy, marine general Carleton Fulford. Fulford and the ambassador had just completed their own yellowcake investigation and were filing reports debunking the Iraq–Niger connection. Nevertheless, Wilson set out to gather information, agreeing to Owens-Kirkpatrick's request that he only meet with former Nigerien officials for fear he might spoil her relationship with current leaders. Wilson had no problem with that because most of his contacts had been made years earlier, and these people were out of the government.

Wilson's sources, former ministers and bureaucrats he had known for more than twenty years, told him that Niger's government was focused on maintaining good relations with the United States and would not risk breaking the Iraqi economic embargo, even if it could. The French government-run mining consortium, COGEMA, controlled every aspect of the uranium business in Niger and any diversion of uranium ore would be detected. The country's estimated yearly production of 3,000 metric tons of uranium was shipped exclusively to the consortium partners, France, Spain, Germany, and Japan, which processed it for electrical power plant generation. The evidence added up to a firm conclusion: "There was nothing to support allegations either that Iraq had tried to obtain or had succeeded in purchasing uranium from Niger."

Wilson stayed in Niger for eight days, longer than he needed to complete his investigation, but the air connections made it too difficult to leave any sooner. He returned to Washington on March 5; two CIA case officers came to his house and debriefed him one hour later.

The Bush administration and the Intelligence Community paid virtually no attention to the substance of Wilson's report, in part because the former ambassador did not substantiate what the administration wanted to hear. Analysts at CIA headquarters concluded that the report on Wilson's debriefing was of marginal value because "no one believed it added a great deal of new information to the Niger–Iraq uranium story."

As agreed by the CIA and Wilson, the debriefing report did not identify Wilson by name or describe him as a former ambassador. But the report went further, saying that while the source had "excellent access," he was someone "who does not have an established reporting record." This source description may well have undermined the gravitas of Wilson's findings in the eyes of other analysts. The CIA report neglected the fact that Wilson had written thousands of reports as a diplomat. Among those reports were "hundreds of cables during the period of the first Gulf War, many of which were read by very senior people in the national security establishment, including some significant reports of my meetings with Saddam Hussein."

As a matter of routine, the report on Wilson's trip was distributed throughout the Intelligence Community, but not routed directly to policymakers, including Cheney, although he had made clear he was interested in the subject. The reason was that "CIA analysts did not believe that the report added any new information to clarify the issue," the Senate Intelligence Committee observed.

The report on Wilson's trip may not have added new information, but it was accurate. A number of other intelligence reports about Iraq's alleged shopping for uranium also received wide circulation, including going to top policymakers, but they were all false.

One was related to a fax from late 2001 found in the possession of a Somali businessman. It described arrangements for shipping about 500 tons of unidentified commodities. The fax made no mention of uranium, Niger, or Iraq, but 500 was the number of tons named in the forged Italian letter. The shipment could have been for anything, bound for anywhere.

Another bad piece of information suffered from poor intelligence tradecraft and took some time to kill. It started with a telephone tip in November 2002 from an apparently well-intentioned businessman to a Naval Criminal Investigative Service (NCIS) agent posted in the French port of Marseille. The businessman claimed that Niger had sent yellowcake destined for Iraq to the port of Cotonou in Benin. That's where most of Niger's uranium is loaded onto ocean vessels. When DIA officers finally arrived at the Cotonou warehouses three weeks later, they found only bales of cotton.

The Marseille tip offered a classic illustration of how agencies fail to share information, dismiss intelligence not produced in their own service, and often neglect to check their own files.

The NCIS agent in Marseille was not an intelligence officer. He did not follow through with the source, who claimed to be a West African businessman brokering uranium deals. The tipster had provided his name and phone number. The NCIS agent, responsible for criminal investigations and protecting the US fleet when it visits Marseille, wrote up a brief report on November 25.

The agent did not contact the CIA station in Paris. A retired CIA officer said the agent "should never have originated the report without checking with the [CIA] chief of station in Paris. He's not there to do intelligence reporting. . . . All these guys think they're spooks."

The Marseille report landed at DIA headquarters, where officials "ran it all over Washington by hand, suggesting it was really sexy intelligence. . . . They do this all the time."

"That organization is hopeless. . . . When it comes to the humint [human intelligence] world they should not come out and play. . . . Over and over again, when they get into humint, they fuck it up." That, not surprisingly, was the view of a CIA man.

The feeling was mutual. "The Department of Defense despises the CIA," said Col. Wilkerson, who had served Powell as chief of staff at the State Department and also as his aide at the Pentagon when Powell was chairman of the Joint Chiefs of Staff.

The CIA Directorate of Operations asked the French to check on the Marseille report. A CIA officer complained in an internal memo that the DIA inspection team had not determined whether uranium was hidden in the cotton bales. The memo noted that the DIA inspectors did not use radiation detectors when inspecting the bales.

On the eve of President George Walker Bush's January 28 State of the Union address, the CIA drafted an intelligence report on the Benin warehouse story. It said a foreign government service disclosed that there indeed had been uranium in storage in Cotonou when the West African tipster called in Marseille, but that it had been a normal shipment bound for France, Niger's principal customer for yellowcake, not Iraq. The unidentified foreign government service was in a position to know; it was France's foreign intelligence agency, the DGSE.

On February 10, two months after its agents inspected the Cotonou warehouses, the DIA finally wrote a report admitting that only cotton had been found. The agency had waited that long to report its finding because the official assigned to the case, the defense attaché in the Ivory Coast, had been preoccupied with a coup in that country and a civil war in nearby Liberia.

On March 8 the DIA wrote a classified report to Secretary Rumsfeld downplaying the IAEA's conclusion that the Niger documents were forgeries. Other intelligence, the report said, indicated that the uranium intelligence claims were valid. The report's author had not looked in the DIA's own files because he included among the "other intelligence" the tip from Marseille—which had led to cotton bales.

Telling policymakers what they wanted to hear was common practice at the Pentagon.

Chapter 5

The Opera Lover and Baghdad Bob

"It was nonsensical . . . why in the world would Iraq
be looking for yellowcake?"
CARL FORD JR., DIRECTOR OF THE STATE DEPARTMENT
BUREAU OF INTELLIGENCE AND RESEARCH

No one in the high reaches of the Bush administration paid attention to—or was even aware of—Ambassador Joseph Wilson's anonymous debriefing report after his return from Niger in the winter of 2002. The CIA's reporting had downplayed Wilson's credentials and the value of what he had learned. His rejection of the Niger uranium connection did not advance the favored notion that Saddam Hussein had gone shopping for uranium.

But a CIA officer later told the Senate Intelligence Committee that one morsel in Wilson's debriefing—unsubstantiated third-hand speculation by the former Nigerien prime minister—had been deemed significant and served to confirm the argument that the Nigerien uranium purchase was plausible.

That detail was based on Wilson's reference, in his effort to give a full account of his CIA-sponsored trip, to an idle conversation he had had during the trip with the former prime minister of Niger, Ibrahim Mayaki.

Mayaki had told Wilson that he was unaware of any yellowcake deal with Iraq or any other rogue state while he served first as foreign minister in 1996 and 1997 and then as prime minister from 1997 through 1999. But, in an aside, Mayaki recalled an encounter with a businessman at an Organization of African Unity meeting in Algiers during the early summer of 1999. Mayaki didn't remember the name or nationality of the businessman but said the man had asked him to meet with an Iraqi official to discuss "expanding commercial relations." Mayaki, aware of the UN sanctions against Iraq, met briefly with the Iraqi official but didn't remember that person's name either.

The subject of yellowcake never came up during that short meeting between the two officials, nor did the word *uranium* ever pass their lips. Yet Mayaki told Wilson that it was possible that the Iraqi "might" have wanted to talk about uranium, even if he didn't actually do it.

Wilson's mention of Mayaki's comment eventually helped keep the Niger story alive. The mere speculation that an Iraqi official might have been thinking about uranium was hardly a fiber of evidence, but proponents of the war used it to justify the Bush administration's suspicion that Iraq was shopping for uranium.

Some intelligence operatives, keen to win approval by feeding the policymakers damning evidence, were able to blend Wilson's third-party speculation with news reports that did show that two Iraqi diplomats had in fact visited Africa in 1999.

One of the Iraqis was Ambassador Wissam al-Zahawie, an opera-loving, self-acknowledged outsider in the eyes of the Iraqi government, a career diplomat with no clout at the foreign ministry who, more importantly, had never been close to Saddam Hussein. The other official was Zahawie's boss for a time, Mohammed Saeed al-Sahhaf, who served as foreign minister of Iraq from 1992 to 2001.

Each visited Africa in 1999 as part of an accelerated effort by Saddam Hussein's government to break UN sanctions on Iraq after a punishing US-led bombing campaign. In four nights of air attacks against Baghdad and other parts of Iraq in December of that year, the Clinton administration, joined by Great Britain, had targeted military command and control centers, intending to disperse Hussein's Republican Guard and encourage mutiny among Iraqi forces. Iraqi officials protested that innocent civilians had been killed and took journalists to see a hospital filled with patients who had burns and shrapnel wounds. Three members of the UN Security Council—France, China, and Russia—criticized the bombings and called for an end to sanctions.

As a result of the Iraqi policy to win Third World support at the UN after the bombing, Zahawie was instructed to make two trips to Africa, one in February 1999 and another with his boss, al-Sahhaf, in June. It was reminiscent of a strategy that Libya's Muammar Gadhafi had successfully used in the 1990s to chip away at the US international embargo against his country.

Zahawie was suddenly ordered by Baghdad, he assumed, to travel to Africa as a last-minute replacement for al-Sahhaf and personally extend Saddam Hussein's invitation to visit Iraq to the presidents of Niger and three other West African countries, Burkina Faso, Benin, and Congo/Brazzaville (now Republic of the Congo).

Zahawie viewed the trip, then, as an attempt by officials in Baghdad to win sympathy among African countries at the UN. He knew next to nothing about Africa. Iraq, like most countries, did not have resident ambassadors in every world capital, so ambassadors were tasked from time to time to travel to other countries. But Zahawie had never been involved in missions involving bilateral relations in Africa, and he was content to stay put in Europe. His previous trips to Africa had been to attend international conferences. The ambassador figured that the directive from Baghdad was a cost and time-saving move to avoid paying airfares from Iraq to Paris and then down to Africa.

The urbane diplomat had no time to read up on the countries he was visiting on his sudden trip that February, and he told us that he didn't even know at the time that Niger was a source of uranium, because the matter didn't come up. "It never occurred to me that a country as poor as Niger could have anything of value to export, and the nature of my assignment—extending an invitation—did not require me to make a study of the political or economic policies of the four countries I was to visit at short notice."

Zahawie, a fluent English speaker with a refined British accent, was well known in diplomatic circles for his courtly manner and was not considered an insider in the Hussein government. He had joined the Iraqi Foreign Service in 1955, during the period of the monarchy that lasted until a military coup in 1958. Zahawie ascribed his long career to a combination of luck and staying mostly out of the public eye. He was proud to say that he was a member of no political party, and specifically not a member of the Baath Party, ruled and controlled by Hussein and his closest allies and family. Nor did he want to be.

He did everything he could in his diplomatic career to separate himself from politics and intrigue. He knew that he would never be given any central job that involved policymaking or brought close to Saddam Hussein's inner circle. Zahawie had the reputation of being a persuasive Iraqi nationalist, but he was never considered so trustworthy, he said, as to be "accredited as ambassador to any country where

[Iraq] may have had clandestine political, military, or economic contacts or operations."

Zahawie did make some well-publicized appearances, such as a protest before the United Nations in 1981 after Israeli jets bombed and destroyed Iraq's French-built Osirak nuclear reactor, south of Baghdad. This was not a bold or unusual stance: He was hardly alone in condemning the Israeli attack.

Citing that appearance at the UN, some analysts came to describe Zahawie as an expert on nuclear issues. Far from being designated as a nuclear specialist at the UN meeting, Zahawie said he was the last-minute substitute for Mohammed Saeed al-Sahhaf on that occasion as well. Neither was Sahhaf an expert on nuclear weapons issues. Zahawie also attended a 1995 UN conference reviewing the nuclear nonproliferation treaty and complained that Israel's open secret of having nuclear weapons represented a double standard, a position commonly taken in international forums.

Zahawie did not aspire to a higher diplomatic stature. While he had appeared at the United Nations, he never sought to be the permanent Iraqi ambassador to that body. Zahawie twice turned down an offer to serve in the prestigious post. "I did not want to put myself in that particular hot spot and under constant international exposure and not knowing what Baghdad was really up to," he wrote in the *Sunday Times*. Postings at the UN in New York, under the guise of diplomacy, he said, were typically "used as a cover for intelligence operatives acting upon direct instruction from Baghdad without the knowledge of a nonparty head of mission."

Instead, Zahawie actively sought and won the job as Vatican ambassador precisely because of his reputation as a diplomat who avoided intrigue and espionage. He told the foreign minister at the time, Tariq Aziz, that he would be the perfect choice for the Vatican job "because it had none of the activities usually associated with other embassies around the world." Zahawie had served at the foreign ministry in Baghdad, focusing on international organizations, and never in posts involving espionage or arms trafficking. He argued that it would be a mistake to appoint to the Vatican a diplomat who might be involved in such activities. It might "even ruin our good relations with the Vatican. The contacts and movements of the agent would immediately draw attention to the fact that he was in contact with parties that had nothing to do with the Vatican."

Zahawie's job representing Iraq at the Vatican was not heavy lifting, and it was also a solitary job—he was the only diplomat. His embassy staff was one locally hired secretary. The light duty gave him a chance to pursue his interests: European art, music, and fine food.

Stirring briefly from his quiet life, he flew down to Niger from Rome on February 5, 1999, and, following through as instructed, promptly met with President Ibrahim Bare Mainassara, who accepted Hussein's invitation to visit Iraq. Mainassara never had the chance to follow through; he was assassinated in April in a palace coup, and no Niger official traveled to Baghdad in that period.

Zahawie's Africa tour, which was reported openly by the local media, continued with visits to the other African countries. Later in the year, he returned briefly to Africa again, joining Sahhaf at a meeting of the Organization of African Unity in Algiers. He did not remember meeting with officials from Niger at the time, nor did he discuss business or commercial dealings with anyone.

Zahawie stayed on in Rome as the Iraqi ambassador to the Vatican for two more years, until August 2000. He then retired and took up residence in Amman, Jordan.

He was in Jordan when he read about Bush's 2003 State of the Union message and had no reason to connect Bush's reference to Africa to his 1999 trip to Niger. If Iraq had sought uranium in Africa, he figured, it would have been somewhere other than Niger. And even when he heard news reports that Niger was the country in question, he assumed that a more highly placed Iraqi insider must have made some other visit there at some other time.

On February 10, 2003, about two weeks after Bush's State of the Union speech and almost exactly four years after his trip to Niger, Zahawie received an urgent call from the Iraqi embassy in Amman. The foreign ministry was summoning him urgently and unusually back to Baghdad. He arrived the following day, not knowing what to expect and certainly not anticipating the interrogation that was about to take place.

Iraqi officials ordered him to appear before a team of five inspectors from the UN's International Atomic Energy Agency to answer questions about Iraqi uranium purchases in Niger.

In the years after Zahawie's visit to Niger, some American and British intelligence analysts had come to believe that the trip might have been connected to uranium. What else did Niger have besides uranium and dinosaur bones? Why would Iraq bother sending diplomats to Niger? the analysts asked. Iraq must have been looking for yellowcake.

That assumption was bolstered by several documents in the dossier of files that Rocco Martino handed over to Elisabetta Burba with the Italian letter. The files included Zahawie's request for a visa to Niger in 1999 and a copy of a telegram from the Nigerien embassy in Rome saying he was en route. By February 2003, both British and American intelligence agencies had copies of the letters.

The IAEA had been skeptical about claims that Iraq had embarked on a uranium-buying campaign. However, officials at the UN agency felt obliged to check out the story, including the Zahawie trip, because the questionable intelligence came from the United States, France, and Britain.

So the IAEA asked Iraqi authorities for access to Zahawie, and permission was readily granted. Five inspectors sat down with him in a rather gruff, hours-long interview. The questioning was conducted by only two of the five, a Briton and a Canadian. No Iraqi official was present, and Zahawie recorded the session on his own tape recorder.

Was Zahawie aware, one of the questioners asked, of any meetings between Iraqi and Nigerien officials?

"Of course," he replied, confirming that he had traveled to Niger in 1999. He noted that it was not a secret mission and at the time was openly reported in the news.

Did he receive anything from officials in Niger?

"Well, yes," Zahawie replied. The president of Niger gave him a camel saddle, known as a *howdah*, although he tried to turn it down, saying that it was too large for his travels on commercial flights across the African continent.

This was not the kind of detail the UN officials were interested in.

"Nevertheless," Zahawie continued, "when I got back to the government guesthouse [in Niger], the *howdah* was there, looking like a small four-poster bed all wrapped up in gift paper.

"But I still had to leave it behind. I think what my interrogators had in mind was more like some samples of uranium—to promote the sale of Niger's valuable natural resources."

The questioners dropped that line of inquiry and changed the subject.

Had Zahawie discussed uranium with anyone in Niger?

"No," said Zahawie.

Had he made any veiled reference to uranium, any hint about uranium? one of the inquisitors asked.

"No," Zahawie replied. He told the inspectors that he didn't know at the time that Niger even produced or exported uranium.

Zahawie was dismissed. The UN team said in a subsequent report that, according to their judgment, he had been truthful and not deceptive in his answers.

State Department diplomats, who had gotten to know Zahawie over the years, also thought his participation in a uranium deal was implausible. Analysts also did not think that the Iraqi government would trust Zahawie or his boss, Sahhaf, to conduct sensitive negotiations. Zahawie was a Turkoman from the north. Sahhaf was a Shiite Muslim, one of the few outsiders in the Sunni-dominated government. Shopping for uranium would have been entrusted only to those closest to Hussein, and most officials close to Saddam Hussein were family members, members of the governing Baath Party, or friends from Hussein's hometown of Tikrit.

Hussein's two sons, Udai and Qusai, would have been more likely candidates to conduct a high-risk secret mission to find uranium in Africa, according to a Senate Defense Subcommittee staff member who closely monitored prewar Iraq. Even a shopping trip by one of Hussein's closest relatives would have been implausible, the staffer said. Iraq already had 550 metric tons of yellowcake under IAEA seal, and Hussein easily could have seized that material if he believed a resulting confrontation with the United States or the UN Security Council was worth the risk. Furthermore, the CIA knew that Iraq didn't have the massive industrial infrastructure required to convert yellowcake into bomb-grade uranium—though the CIA did wrongly believe that Iraq had some dual-use equipment that could be used if it decided to restart its nuclear program.

As the nonexistence of an Iraqi nuclear weapons program became more and more clear after the 2003 Iraqi invasion, defenders of the Bush administration argued that Zahawie was guilty anyway. It was a key posture for the Bush administration, because if there were no evidence at all, officials would be open to the charge that they had fabricated the story in the first place.

Fervent Bush supporters used Zahawie to argue that even without evidence, the administration had a plausible reason to believe Saddam Hussein had been pursuing nuclear weapons.

Christopher Hitchens, for example, a hard-line supporter of Bush's Iraq policy, published an unusual running debate with Zahawie, asserting that the Iraqi diplomat was a nuclear specialist who indeed had gone to Niger shopping for uranium in 1999. The British-born journalist also charged that Zahawie was a well-known anti-Semite and was perfectly capable of carrying out a risky mission on behalf of Saddam Hussein. Hitchens, who wielded a witty, acerbic pen, had shifted from championing causes identified with the political left to frequently supporting the neoconservative view in Washington.

After Joseph Wilson published an op-ed piece in the *New York Times* on July 6, 2003, revealing details of his fact-finding trip to Niger—"What I Didn't Find in Africa"—Hitchens blamed Wilson for originally giving credence to the idea that Iraq was shopping for uranium. After all, Hitchens said, Wilson had told the CIA that one of his sources speculated that an Iraqi official might have wanted to discuss uranium during an official visit to Africa.

Hitchens's argument, in effect, resurrected Wilson's offhand reference to Mayaki, the former Nigerien prime minister, and his speculation about a conversation that hadn't taken place. The problem was that Zahawie was not the Iraqi official in question.

Though Mayaki at the time of his conversation with Wilson had forgotten the identity of the Iraqi representative, he told Wilson after the invasion of Iraq that his memory had been refreshed by watching television. The Iraqi official he had met, he now was certain, was Mohammed Saeed al-Sahhaf, the one-time foreign minister.

Having been demoted to the post of Iraqi information minister, Sahhaf became an international laughingstock on television during the 2003 US invasion for making delusional Orwellian remarks as US forces charged through the gates of the Iraqi capital.

> They are not near Baghdad. Don't believe them. . . . They said they entered with . . . tanks in the middle of the capital. . . . There is no . . . any existence to the American troops or for the troops in Baghdad at all.

The news media nicknamed him "Baghdad Bob," and US intelligence analysts did not think he would have been entrusted with such a sensitive task as seeking nuclear weapons.

Hitchens, parroting the arguments of Bush administration officials, said that Wilson had somehow promoted the view that Zahawie must have been looking for uranium.

Hitchens wrote: "In order to take the Joseph Wilson view of this Baathist ambassadorial initiative, you have to be able to believe that Saddam Hussein's long-term main man on nuclear issues was in Niger to talk about something other than the obvious."

Wilson knew Zahawie well and scoffed at Hitchens's description of the Iraqi envoy as a Baathist or as Hussein's "long-term main man on nuclear issues." Wilson knew Zahawie was nothing of the kind.

But Hitchens's charges, in turn, angered Zahawie, and the men engaged in a public dialogue. Zahawie, who prided himself on being an accomplished diplomat who had weathered several regime upheavals in Baghdad, was particularly incensed when Hitchens declared that he was an anti-Semite based on the fact that he had once spoken against Israel at the United Nations and that he had a love for Wagnerian opera.

"The charge that I was a man much given to anti-Jewish tirades is a libelous fabrication," Zahawie told us. "I have been, in my UN statements, highly critical of Israeli and Zionist policies. Obviously,

Hitchens is promoting the Zionist campaign that would have the world believe that any such criticism is tantamount to being anti-Jewish and anti-Semitic. To confirm this insinuation, he informs his readers that I have 'a standing ticket for Wagner performances at Bayreuth' [actually, as a fan of *Das Rheingold* and *Götterdämmerung* in particular]. Just in case the reader still did not get the hint that I am anti-Semitic, Hitchens evokes the name of Hitler as another frequent visitor to Bayreuth. I wish I could be in a position to be able to afford such extravagance. In fact, I have been to Bayreuth only once, courtesy of the German government when Iraq and Germany were both members of the Security Council—in 1975. The German representative, Ambassador von Wechmar, invited a number of opera lovers to Munich and Bayreuth. We heard *Tristan, Parsifal,* and *Die Meistersinger*—but none of the *Ring* opera which are considered to reflect Wagner's anti-Semitism."

Some analysts also had given a measure of credibility to the uranium story and the Zahawie trip to Niger because they had concluded, wrongly, that Iraq was buying aluminum tubes intended for use in gas centrifuges to enrich uranium. Analysts at WINPAC, the CIA's Center for Weapons Intelligence, Nonproliferation, and Arms Control, briefly considered the possibility that the tubes might be for something else, perhaps even rocket casings, overlooking the fact that the tubes were exactly like those the Italian military had bought as casings for Medusa 81 rockets. Iraq in the 1980s had purchased those rockets from Italy and reverse-engineered them for domestic production during the embargo of the 1990s.

But respected senior engineers at America's nuclear weapons labs had told CIA and DIA analysts in 2001 and 2002 that the tubes ordered in multiple lots by Saddam Hussein were not sufficient or adequate for the up to 100,000 inner casings required for gas centrifuges to spin uranium hexafluoride for bomb-grade material.

State Department intelligence analysts also had this part of the story right, in the analysis of the centrifuges by Wayne White, the State Department official in charge of Iraq analysis at the INR:

> We captured one of the shipments. Those things were tested, they were woefully short of what was needed for a centrifuge system, the quality as well as the quantity showed they were about missiles. The moment I saw the info, I said of course, yeah sure, they're ordering a ton of these for artillery rocket shells. Other people would argue these are much better tubes than you need for a BM21 [a surface-to-air rocket originally designed by the Soviet Union]. If you're ordering things like this illegally, from Oil for Food, sometimes you have to buy things that aren't exactly appropriate to your needs. Maybe the firm that had cheaper tubes wouldn't deal with you. I just chalked it up to Iraq being unable to get material from companies that could sell cheaper tubes.

White also heard arguments that the tubes could still be reengineered, sawed down from 900 millimeters to a more standard size, usually no more than 600 millimeters, with 60,000 300-millimeter pieces of tubing left over. They would also have to be honed down to a more standard thickness, from 3 millimeters to 1 millimeter—an enormous task.

Before and after the invasion, David Albright of the Institute for Science and International Security, a nuclear weapons expert who assisted the IAEA inspectors in Iraq in the 1990s, provided detailed analysis of the tubes and struck down the claim. "The administration has refused to acknowledge that the tubes that Iraq was trying to order would be used in rockets," he wrote. "By failing to acknowledge this point, they are implying that Iraq sought all the tubes for centrifuges and planned to build over 100,000 centrifuges, a massive program for a country like Iraq. On its face, this claim is preposterous."

There was no other credible intelligence on Iraq's nuclear ambitions. British officials claimed they had additional intelligence reports, separate from Zahawie's 1999 trip, that brought them to the conclusion that Iraq had been seeking uranium in Africa. The British government, led by Prime Minister Tony Blair, clung to the claim even years afterward, insisting that it had had other information not shared with the CIA. It invoked an unusually strict interpretation of the so-called third-party rule, the practice among intelligence services of not revealing the identity of the originating intelligence agency—though most of the time they share the intelligence itself. As a result, Britain declined to reveal its so-called secret information even to the IAEA, although required by treaty to do so.

The British claim of independent information was shot down categorically when previously secret testimony was revealed in December 2006 by Carne Ross, who was a key British diplomat at the United Nations from December 1997 to June 2002. The testimony before a government inquest had been suppressed under the British official secrets act. "During my post, at no time did Her Majesty's Government assess that Iraq's WMD [or any other capability] pose a threat to the UK or its interests. On the contrary, it was the commonly held view among the officials dealing with Iraq that any threat had been effectively contained."

In retrospect, Wilson deeply regretted having had a small role unwittingly feeding the flames. He wished he hadn't mentioned the speculative remark about an inconsequential meeting that the former Nigerien prime minister had had with Baghdad Bob. "It was a meeting in which the subject of uranium was never raised," Wilson told us.

"Got to love it," Wilson said ruefully. "Based on that, we go to war."

Wilson was no more to blame for providing shreds of evidence in good faith that were later manipulated to sell the war than was Elisabetta Burba for handing over the Italian letter to US officials. Bush administration officials were engaged in their own sales campaign to promote the war, whether or not the evidence was compelling. Reality was not an obstacle.

Chapter 6

October Surprises

In August 2002, ever media conscious and playing to ratings, top members of the Bush administration were revving up an offensive to win over the hearts and minds of Americans and especially those in Congress who were still unconvinced about the need to invade Iraq. Just as the Pentagon had created the Office of Special Plans, which was assigned to customize intelligence that proved the case for war, the executive branch also set up a new propaganda arm—the White House Iraq Group, known as the WHIG, whose job it was to market the war.

The WHIG team was assembled by Andrew J. Card Jr., the White House chief of staff, and included, among others, Karl Rove, the president's director of political affairs; National Security Adviser Condoleezza Rice; Stephen J. Hadley, deputy national security adviser; and

I. Lewis "Scooter" Libby, Vice President Cheney's chief of staff. They held weekly meetings in the White House's Situation Room, a windowless, relatively austere room in the West Wing. It is the only room with secure videoconferencing equipment linking the White House with other agencies, such as the Pentagon and the State Department.

Before the creation of the WHIG, top officials had been talking about Saddam Hussein as a bad guy who invaded neighbors and killed members of the Kurdish and Shiite Iraqi population. They also painted Hussein as an ally of al Qaeda, a distortion of intelligence that was effective with the public but less so with Congress, which had access to conflicting information.

Wolfowitz, in an interview with *Vanity Fair* shortly after the invasion, was quite frank about why the administration settled on weapons of mass destruction as the key rationale for war. Hussein's brutality against his own people, he said, was "not a reason to put American kids' lives at risk." As for Iraq's links to terrorism, this was an issue "about which there's the most disagreement within the bureaucracy." Something else was needed, something that would clinch the case for war.

And the weapon of mass destruction that evoked the most fear was the nuclear bomb.

"The WMD that really had traction with the public was the nuclear threat," said Greg Thielmann, at the time a senior INR analyst. "It was the mushroom cloud. You can't lure people into panic on anything else."

The WHIG's plan was to organize a news media blitz surrounding the first anniversary of the September 11 attacks. It would be an aggressive and highly disciplined campaign to convince America that Iraq was a danger to the world, with the nuclear bombshell as the centerpiece. Part of the campaign was to coordinate intensified coverage the week before the September 11 observance, priming public opinion just before President Bush's trip to New York, which would include a visit to the World Trade Center site and a speech at the United Nations. Vice President Cheney, the ultimate administration hawk, hinted at what was to come when he told a friendly audience at the Veterans of Foreign Wars convention on August 26 in Nashville that Iraq posed a "mortal threat" that could "subject the United States or any other nation to nuclear blackmail."

But the White House waited until September to launch its endeavor. Andrew Card was candid about the decision on the timing in an interview with the *New York Times*. He said that the White House intended to make a deliberate pitch to the American people and figured it was a good idea to wait until after Labor Day, when people were back from their vacations. "From a marketing point of view, you don't introduce new products in August," Card told the *New York Times* on September 6.

Symbols and subliminal fear would drive home the danger of seeing the "mushroom cloud" if Americans didn't act, along with the reminder that the United States had discovered a "smoking gun."

On Sunday, September 8, 2002, the WHIG kicked off its media blitz in conjunction with a front-page story in the *New York Times*. The story had all the earmarks of what is known in the trade as a policy leak. Policymakers used such leaks to influence an agenda—in this case to prep America for war. The story even included what would become administration "talking points"—a package of words or phrases intended to be repeated by select officials to reinforce a message. The story, for instance, quoted administration "hard-liners" as saying they did not want to wait for a "mushroom cloud" to be the "first sign of a smoking gun." Those metaphors became administration clichés. Michael Gerson, Bush's chief speechwriter, was the author.

The *New York Times*'s ominous story had the headline "Threats and Responses: The Iraqis; US Says Hussein Intensifies Quest for A-Bomb Parts." The exquisitely leaked and quite startling report detailed how the government knew Saddam Hussein was building the Bomb:

> More than a decade after Saddam Hussein agreed to give up weapons of mass destruction, Iraq has stepped up its quest for nuclear weapons and has embarked on a worldwide hunt for materials to make an atomic bomb, Bush administration officials said today.
>
> In the last 14 months, Iraq has sought to buy thousands of specially designed aluminum tubes, which American officials believe were intended as components of centrifuges to enrich uranium.

The authors, Judith Miller and Michael Gordon, had inadvertently helped launch the massive White House PR campaign. Gordon, a respected national security reporter, had picked up the intelligence on the aluminum tubes and was told the United States had acquired and tested some of them. Miller worked her sources in the administration. Their exposé about the aluminum tubes was the administration's first public disclosure of intelligence purporting to show that Hussein was pursuing nuclear weapons. Not by accident, the article laid out in considerable detail what would become the WHIG's mantra for the next several months.

The *Times* story did not mention dissent among analysts, although top nuclear scientists at the Energy Department and INR analysts thought the tubes were poorly suited for centrifuges.

Aside from the aluminum tubes, the Intelligence Community had not received any significant new information suggesting that Iraq was reconstituting its nuclear program since UN inspectors were pulled out of Iraq in 1998. Most analysts treated the Nigerien uranium claim with skepticism. They realized that even in the unlikely case that the intelligence was true, it meant that Iraq was several years away from actually building a bomb.

But the administration was opening a back-to-school push for making the case for war.

"'The jewel in the crown is nuclear,'" a senior administration official said in the *Times* story. "'The closer he [Saddam] gets to a nuclear capability, the more credible is his threat to use chemical or biological weapons. Nuclear weapons are his hole card.'

"'The question is not, why now?' the official added, referring to a potential military campaign to oust Mr. Hussein. 'The question is why waiting is better. The closer Saddam Hussein gets to a nuclear weapon, the harder he will be to deal with.'"

Rice, Cheney, and other top officials used the same language that day on the talk shows.

A duty officer at the Pentagon's National Military Joint Intelligence Center described his experience in responding to the White House demand for information to prepare for the media blitz. He was working the late shift at the Joint Intelligence Center, a tiny division of the Defense Intelligence Agency that monitors global developments twenty-four hours a day. A sudden phone call from a White House staffer broke the monotony—it was from the office of Condoleezza Rice, at the time the president's national security advisor.

Rice, it turned out, was making the rounds of the weekend news shows, the White House aide said. *She would greatly appreciate your help,* the staffer said, in sending over a quick rundown on the status of Iraq's nuclear program and its weapons of mass destruction—text, along with photos and line drawings.

The navy officer, a respected professional who had been reactivated during the Iraq crisis, was levelheaded and courteous. He agreed to take care of it, but after hanging up the phone, he complained bitterly to one of his colleagues: "How many times do we have to say there is no such program?"

Nevertheless, the staff at the Joint Intelligence Center put together what it had—very little—and wrapped it up in caveats and doubts.

"We put something together . . . probably not exactly what they wanted," he said.

Whether or not Rice saw that Pentagon report, she adopted an assertive tone that Sunday, adding gravitas to the *New York Times* report.

"There is *no doubt* that Saddam Hussein's regime is a danger to the United States and to its allies, to our interests," she said on Cable News Network's *Late Edition*. "We *know* that there have been shipments going . . . into Iraq, for instance, of aluminum tubes that really are *only suited* . . . for nuclear weapons." While there always would be "uncertainty about how quickly [Hussein] can acquire nuclear weapons . . . We don't want the smoking gun to be a mushroom cloud."

Other key administration officials did the same; for one weekend, the *New York Times*, the whipping boy of the neoconservatives, had a wonderful scoop, which the Bush administration could wholeheartedly confirm.

Cheney, for instance, spoke on *Meet the Press* and pointed to the specialized "aluminum tubes," saying that "there's a story in the *New York Times* this morning," a reference to the *Times*'s description of the aluminum tubes that Iraq was buying.

The United States "may well become the target," Cheney said. Saddam Hussein "is, *in fact,* actively and aggressively seeking to acquire nuclear weapons. . . . If we have reason to believe someone is preparing an attack against the US, has developed that capability, harbors those aspirations, then I think the United States is justified in dealing with that, if necessary, by military force."

Four days after the *New York Times* exposé and the synchronized appearance on the networks by top administration officials, George

Bush followed through on the public relations effort. He spoke at the UN General Assembly on the first anniversary of the attacks on the Twin Towers and the Pentagon and made the linkage between Iraq and September 11 implicit. He warned of consequences if Iraq did not comply with demands it could not meet. "Resolutions ordering Iraqi disarmament and other UN demands," Bush said, "will be enforced—or action will be unavoidable."

The British government also played a part in the campaign. On September 24, Prime Minister Blair's government published a dossier that claimed that Iraq was seeking uranium from Africa. That specific claim was included despite the fact that senior CIA officials, particularly at the Near East and South Asia office, had been cautioning their counterparts at the British Secret Intelligence Service (MI6) for several days that the Africa information might be a sham and should not be used in a public document. It was not a unanimous view. At the CIA's WINPAC, some analysts believed Iraq had indeed been seeking uranium, if not from Niger then from elsewhere in Africa.

The White House moved quickly to publicize the British report. Bush's spokesman, Ari Fleischer, told reporters that the dossier contained "new information about Saddam Hussein's efforts to obtain uranium from African nations." He did not say and possibly did not know that the CIA had unsuccessfully tried to impress on the British that the information was too shaky to be included in such a public report.

"Our guys weren't able to persuade the Brits that this was too fishy for anyone to use," said Paul Pillar, the national intelligence officer for the Middle East, who himself tried to convince the British to drop the reference.

Also on September 24, the same day the British dossier was issued, Tenet gave a top-secret briefing to both the Senate Foreign Relations and Intelligence Committees. Congress was considering a resolution to give Bush the authority to wage war on Iraq, and the president was trying to muster enough votes to claim consensus. The Intelligence Community, meanwhile, was preparing the last drafts of a National Intelligence Estimate on Iraq's alleged banned weapons. Tenet told the intelligence committee about the claims that Iraq was seeking uranium from Niger, but said that questions had been raised about the evidence. To the foreign relations panel, he repeated earlier testimony that Iraq was buying the high-strength aluminum tubes. He left this meeting early, but one of the senators asked Robert Walpole, the CIA's top weapons expert, about Britain's claim that Iraq was seeking uranium in Africa. Walpole said the yellowcake evidence was thin and that the British dossier's claim was an "exaggeration."

On October 4, responding to a request from the White House, the CIA published an unclassified report that paralleled many of the claims made in the British dossier. As with the British report, this one was later criticized for being too alarmist about Iraq's alleged weapons. It contained no caveats suggesting that any of the intelligence could be questionable. But unlike the British report, the CIA document did not include the Africa uranium story.

The CIA's vacillation in assessing the Nigerien uranium intelligence illustrates the internal tug-of-war among analysts torn between wanting to be intellectually honest and those wanting to please the bosses. Officials at WINPAC tended to be the most sycophantic, according to the Robb-Silberman Commission, a presidential panel charged with investigating the intelligence failures that had plagued the community in recent years. "In the case of prewar assessments of Iraqi WMD, working-level WINPAC analysts described an environment in which managers rewarded judgments that fit the consensus view that Iraq had active WMD programs and discouraged those that did not," the commission concluded.

But even the more skeptical Middle East analysis shop, the Near

East and South Asia section, waffled on the Niger intelligence during the months preceding the invasion. CIA director Tenet later conceded to Senator Carl Levin of Michigan that the CIA's accounts of the Niger story had been "wildly inconsistent" in reports to policymakers in 2002 and 2003.

For instance, on May 10, 2002, NESA prepared a briefing book for senior policymakers updating the status of Hussein's weapons. This document reported: "A foreign government service says Iraq was trying to acquire 500 tons of uranium from Niger." Then on August 1, NESA published a paper on Iraq's weapons of mass destruction that did not mention the Nigerien uranium.

All of the public relations activity—the *New York Times* report and the television backup, followed by the British dossier—mounted in a crescendo toward a major policy speech by Bush scheduled in Cincinnati on October 7, 2002. Coincidentally, it was the same day that Rocco Martino handed over the fake Nigerien documents to Elisabetta Burba. Bush's speech, drafted as usual by Michael Gerson, was intended to home in once more on the primal fear planted by the White House Iraq Group—the specter of a mushroom cloud.

Bush had been warming up for the Cincinnati trip with a weekend campaign swing through New England, where he augmented his monumental reelection coffers, which had reached more than $130 million at the time. Meanwhile, Gerson, Bush's chief speechwriter, and other presidential aides worked on the Cincinnati speech. Gerson and Deputy National Security Adviser Stephen Hadley wanted to use the speech to alert Americans that Iraq "has been caught" trying to buy "up to 500 tons of uranium oxide from Africa—an essential ingredient in the enrichment process."

Over the weekend, the White House staff sent the sixth draft of the Cincinnati speech to the CIA, which was routine in terms of the typical administration vetting and confirmation process for such speeches. The CIA assembled a team of experts to review the draft. The agency normally takes great care in vetting presidential speeches, not only to ensure that the facts are reliable but also to prevent any damaging disclosure that could betray sources or methods of gathering intelligence.

The CIA response was a faxed three-and-a-half-page single-spaced memo to Hadley and Gerson. An analyst at the CIA's Near East office raised concerns about the credibility of the Niger claim. The memo urged the White House to "remove the [Niger reference] sentence because the amount [500 tons] is in dispute and it is debatable whether it can be acquired from the source. We told Congress that the Brits have exaggerated this issue. Finally, the Iraqis already have 550 metric tons of uranium oxide in their inventory."

National Security Council staff members were unimpressed and did not remove the offending passage. They prepared a new, seventh draft and made slight changes that didn't ease the CIA concerns. "The [Iraqi] regime," the NSC speechwriters wrote, "has been caught attempting to purchase substantial amounts of uranium oxide from sources in Africa."

When they received the seventh draft, the CIA vetting team realized that the White House was adamant about using the uranium intelligence, however questionable it might be. So they kicked the matter up to Tenet, who contacted Hadley and Rice directly and told them that the CIA had a problem with Bush's speech. The intelligence, Tenet said, was too weak and the president "should not be a fact witness on this issue."

Even after Tenet's direct intervention, the members of the CIA review team decided to repeat their concerns in another fax to Hadley and Rice. This memo repeated the concerns in more detail about using the Niger intelligence.

The Intelligence Community did not know yet that the material was based on forgeries, but the CIA memo made clear why it lacked credibility: "Three points: (1) The evidence is weak. One of the two mines cited by the source as the location of the uranium oxide is flooded. The other mine cited by the source is under the control of the French authorities. (2) The procurement is not particularly significant to Iraq's nuclear ambitions because the Iraqis already have a large stock of uranium oxide in their inventory. And (3) we have shared points one and two with Congress, telling them that the Africa story is overblown and telling them this is one of the two issues where we differed with the British." The other issue involved the aluminum tubes. The British dossier said the intelligence was questionable, while the United States insisted it was solid.

Tenet and his staff finally won out over Hadley and his reluctant staff, but it was a protracted struggle.

A senior CIA operations officer described the give-and-take between the agency and the White House. "I didn't even focus on this [the Niger story] until it was brought up in the fall, in the Cincinnati speech, because they [CIA managers] said this line from Rome had to be dropped out of the Cincinnati speech. And I said, 'What line from Rome?' Then they told me the story. So now we got this bullshit report from Rome and they [the White House] tried to put it into the speech."

The White House public relations machine faltered prior to the Cincinnati speech. Staffers neglected to specifically ask the major US television networks to block off time for the speech, which was customary when the president planned a major address. But the speech had been scheduled to begin at exactly 8:01 p.m. Eastern Time, a signal that they were leaving time for television anchors to introduce Bush at the top of the hour.

In any case, the three major broadcast networks, ABC, CBS, and NBC, elected ahead of time not to carry Bush's speech live. Fox Television, MSNBC, and CNN did carry the speech, but Bush spoke to a diminished national audience.

He delivered his twenty-nine-minute address at Cincinnati's Union Station, standing before the photogenic backdrop of a mosaic depicting Cincinnati industry and commerce, part of a series designed for the building by artist Winold Reiss.

Even without the line about African yellowcake, Bush conjured visions of a more proximate nuclear hell. He said that Iraq was reconstituting its nuclear program and that Saddam Hussein would be able to produce a nuclear weapon within a year if he succeeded in purchasing bomb-grade uranium. If Hussein were to "buy or steal an amount of highly enriched uranium a little larger than a single softball, he would have a nuclear weapon in less than a year," he warned. "He would be in a position to threaten America. He would be in a position to pass nuclear technology to terrorists." This hyperbolic declaration went beyond the equivocal claim of purchasing yellowcake; it would have taken years to process the yellowcake into bomb-grade material, assuming Iraq had sufficient centrifuges to do it.

The president portrayed Iraq's leader as a "homicidal dictator who is addicted to weapons of mass destruction." He also repeated the language created by the White House Iraq Group. "Facing clear evidence of peril, we cannot wait for the final proof—the smoking gun—that could come in the form of a mushroom cloud."

Bush went further, claiming that Jordanian terrorist Abu Musab al-Zarqawi had been hosted by the Iraqi government in 2001, when he allegedly received medical treatment in Iraq. But the *Washington Post,* citing intelligence officials, wrote several days later that there had been "no hard evidence Hussein's government knew he was there or had contact with him." In the same speech, Bush asserted that the United States had "learned that Iraq has trained al Qaeda members in . . . poisons and deadly gases." Three days later, *Newsday* quoted an intelligence official as acknowledging that there was only a "possibility" that Iraq had provided such training and said the intelligence had come from a single untested al Qaeda source. The intelligence was later dismissed as a fabrication. Evidence later gathered by the Iraq Study Group showed that Saddam Hussein had even sought to have Zarqawi arrested.

From Cincinnati, Bush moved on to Tennessee, where he attended a fund-raiser the next day and repeated the same Iraq themes before returning to Washington. The fear-mongering about mushroom clouds and al Qaeda terrorists had a powerful effect on members of Congress. Few of the lawmakers had bothered to look at the classified intelligence. Republicans took their cue from the White House and voted overwhelmingly in favor of war. Democrats, who were relatively politically insignificant at the time and either opposing the resolution or worried about the upcoming midterm elections, voted for it out of fear of being seen as weak on terrorism and nuclear bombs, or took the intelligence on Saddam and WMD at face value. On October 11, the House authorized Bush to go to war by a vote of 296 to 133, and the Senate quickly followed with a vote of 77 in favor to 23 opposed.

Congress had given Bush the power to "use the armed forces of the United States as he determines to be necessary and appropriate in order to defend the national security of the United States against the continuing threat posed by Iraq." With the congressional resolution in hand and the disturbing warnings from the former generals effectively muted by the invocation of the mushroom cloud, WHIG could celebrate its victory.

But the administration could not afford to relax the drumbeat; the American public needed the constant reminder that Iraq was a national security threat and that the Bomb would soon be armed for use.

Chapter 7

Selling the War . . . Again

As 2002 drew to an end, the White House war planners were worried that congressional and public support was slipping. American saber rattling was having an effect—the Iraqi government, not wanting an invasion, allowed UN inspectors, who had been pulled out in 1998, to return to the country. Worse for those promoting the war, the Iraqis had begun to cooperate fully with the inspectors. Since November, the UN inspectors had examined about eighty sites that the CIA had identified as suspicious. The inspectors found nothing.

A growing number of lawmakers, mostly Democrats, were introducing resolutions urging Bush to give the United Nations more time. Antiwar protests in Europe and America were making news.

And as early as August, a parade of respected former generals, including retired marine general Anthony Zinni, former head of Central Command for US forces in the Middle East, and Brent Scowcroft, a retired lieutenant general in the air force and national security adviser to Bush's father, urged caution before plunging into war. They warned that an invasion would not be as easy as some in the administration were predicting.

Finally, on December 7, 2002, Iraq submitted a formal, 12,000-page declaration to the UN Security Council that it possessed no banned weapons, complying with Security Council Declaration 1441; Saddam Hussein's government was telling the truth. The Iraqi government said it had no weapons of mass destruction—and made no reference, of course, to the alleged purchase of yellowcake. But the Bush administration rejected the Iraqi documentation and launched a new propaganda campaign to mute voices of dissent at home and abroad over the growing inevitability of war. For the first time, the United States publicly pinpointed Niger as a possible source of uranium for Iraq.

Cheney, Rice, and other members of the White House Iraq Group had all been parroting the alarming phrase about a mushroom cloud. They also had declared that Iraq's purchase of aluminum tubes was for centrifuges for its nuclear program—avoiding all mention of dissenting views among nuclear experts.

Now they turned to a reformulated PR campaign that focused on a single issue that was easier for most Americans to understand than centrifuge cascades—they said Iraq had been seeking uranium and had no civilian use for it. Elements of the CIA and the State Department were playing along.

On December 17, the CIA's WINPAC produced a classified report challenging Iraq's official denial to the Security Council that it had any proscribed weapons and complained that Iraq did "not acknowledge efforts to procure uranium from Niger."

On December 19, the State Department issued a one-page fact

sheet rebutting Iraq's 12,000-page declaration that it had no weapons of mass destruction. The title was: "Illustrative Examples of Omissions from the Iraqi Declaration to the United Nations Security Council."

Under orders from John Robert Bolton, the State Department's undersecretary for arms control and international security, the Bureau of Nonproliferation, which fell under his jurisdiction, produced the fact sheet in a single day. Bolton, an unabashed neoconservative, was a staunch supporter of war with Iraq—and was considered by many in the department to be its most undiplomatic diplomat. He was an ally of Cheney and a friend of Alan Foley, WINPAC's director, as well as of Robert G. Joseph at the National Security Council. Joseph was also a committed neoconservative who worked closely with like-minded hawks in the administration.

The fact sheet specifically mentioned Niger and said that Iraq's declaration "ignores efforts to procure uranium from Niger." The fact sheet had been developed from the draft of a speech UN ambassador John Negroponte was to deliver on December 20 to the Security Council. The draft speech also mentioned Niger by name.

Foley approved the reference to Niger in the fact sheet, even though he had recommended that Negroponte's speech refer more generally to Africa instead of Niger. Analysts at the State Department noted the inconsistency, but it was too late to change the text. When analysts at the State's Bureau of Intelligence and Research saw the fact sheet, they sent an e-mail to the nonproliferation bureau with the reminder that their group "assesses this reporting [of Niger yellow-cake] as dubious." And if the line were to be used, it urged that the word "reported" be added. It would be a quite different statement to say, "Iraq ignores *reported* efforts to procure uranium from Niger." The nonproliferation bureau did nothing about the recommended change, and the Niger claim remained as it was.

The WHIG campaign began gearing up for the next main event—a direct charge about Iraqi uranium shopping would be included in

President Bush's State of the Union message. Starting on January 20, 2003, eight days before Bush's address, top officials referred to Iraq's alleged search for uranium as a centerpiece in convincing the world that a madman had to be removed from office lest the rest of the world glow in the dark after a nuclear attack. Iraq, after all, had no nuclear power plants for electricity, so what else could the uranium be used for?

The White House issued a report to Congress on January 20 that denounced Iraq's declaration to the UN as a shameless lie. The declaration, it said, "failed to deal with issues which have arisen since 1998 [when UN inspectors were removed], including . . . attempts to acquire uranium."

Three days later, on January 23, Rice authored an opinion piece in the *New York Times* charging that Saddam Hussein had "fail[ed] to account for or explain Iraq's efforts to get uranium from abroad." The same day, the White House issued another report titled "What Does Disarmament Look Like?" that claimed the Iraq declaration "ignores efforts to procure uranium from abroad."

Powell addressed a World Economic Forum audience in Davos, Switzerland, on January 26. "Why is Iraq still trying to procure uranium and the special equipment to transform it into material for nuclear weapons?" he asked.

On January 29, Rumsfeld spoke to reporters at a news conference in the company of Gen. Richard Myers, the newly appointed chairman of the Joint Chiefs of Staff. He said Saddam Hussein's "regime . . . recently was discovered seeking significant quantities of uranium from Africa."

The White House had stopped asking the CIA to review reports or speeches. This seems to have been by design. Rice and Hadley were both members of the WHIG, whose mission was to sell the war. The CIA's objections could make the pitch more difficult.

But the sudden rush of claims about uranium caught the attention of Carl Levin, the Democratic senator from Michigan who sat on the intelligence and defense committees. He recalled clearly that CIA briefings to his committees and intelligence reports he had seen had rated the uranium story as suspect at best. He asked Tenet whether the Intelligence Community had vetted any of six recent administration reports or speeches, including the examples cited. The list did not include the State of the Union address.

Such clearances are critical, because the change of even one word in a sentence can reflect new intelligence. Powell's speech, for example, said that in January 2003 Saddam Hussein was *still* looking for uranium—a claim never made by intelligence officials. And Rumsfeld's assertion that Iraq had been "recently discovered" attempting to buy uranium was based on SISMI's intelligence, based in turn on the Italian letter and accompanying documents, which had been reported to the CIA fifteen months earlier.

Tenet told Levin that only one of the six speeches or reports had been sent to the CIA for clearance. It was a White House publication on January 23 that claimed that Iraq's declaration to the Security Council "ignores efforts to procure uranium from abroad."

All the while, Michael Gerson and his speechwriting staff at the White House were drafting the State of the Union message, and Bush was rehearsing the delivery. The State of the Union address did not receive the same careful vetting from CIA officials as the October Cincinnati speech, when the African uranium line was dropped. Hadley, who had been told by Tenet in October that the Niger story was suspect, was the senior White House official in charge of clearing national security issues in the State of the Union speech. He later said he forgot Tenet's warning. Gerson, who also had been warned by the CIA in preparation for the Cincinnati speech that the uranium claim was based on flimsy intelligence, also said he forgot.

White House aides did give a draft of the State of the Union message to Tenet, who had been attending an NSC meeting, on January 27, the day before the address. He was unusually busy that day, a top aide recalled. Tenet did not normally read administration speeches himself but would arrange for CIA specialists to clear them. When he returned to his office, he turned over the draft to one of his executive assistants, who hand-carried it to the office of Jami Miscik, the deputy director for intelligence. There, he gave it to one of her assistants. At that point, the draft disappeared. No one in Miscik's office could recall if it ever was assigned to anyone for review coordination. Several months after Bush's State of the Union address, WINPAC director Alan Foley found a draft of the speech in his division's files.

There was little need for vetting intelligence for precision in the shaping of Iraq policy. Key members of the government had signed off on the war long before. In an influential essay in *Foreign Affairs* magazine, Paul Pillar said that had the administration taken the intelligence to heart, it might well have concluded that war was unnecessary. "A view broadly held in the United States and even more so overseas was that deterrence of Iraq was working, that Saddam was being kept 'in his box,' and that the best way to deal with the weapons problem was through an aggressive inspections program to supplement the sanctions already in place. . . . If the entire body of official intelligence analysis on Iraq had a policy implication, it was to avoid war—or if war was going to be launched, to prepare for a messy aftermath." The WHIG manipulated the information to sell the war not only to the public but also to Congress.

After the Senate Intelligence Committee published its report on the Intelligence Community's woeful performance on Iraq, the committee chairman, Kansas Republican Pat Roberts, said Congress might not have approved the war had it known the intelligence was so weak. "I doubt if the votes would have been there," he said.

Meanwhile, the White House staff had cultivated allies throughout the system to propel the march toward war.

Chapter 8

At the CIA

"What the hell, give him what he wants."
ALAN FOLEY, DIRECTOR OF WINPAC

Though the White House received no formal clearance from the CIA to go ahead with the State of the Union speech, it did get back-channel approval from one of its allies within the CIA for the use of a critical line in the speech.

The okay came from Alan Foley, a savvy veteran of CIA internal politics. The red-haired, bespectacled Foley was the ultimate careerist, and in the twilight of his long career, he knew when to fight and when to go with the flow. He had been converted into joining the prowar camp, where true believers were not interested in the facts.

Tenet had appointed Foley as director of WINPAC when it was created in 2001 with the merging of the old Nonproliferation Center, the Arms Control Intelligence staff, which Foley had headed, and the Weapons Intelligence Staff in the Office of Transnational Issues. "When he became chief, his empire doubled or tripled overnight," said a senior CIA officer who saw him in Vienna after a "very happy" Foley was promoted.

One day in December 2002, Foley called his senior production managers to his office. He had a clear message for the men and women who controlled the output of the center's analysts: "If the president wants to go to war, our job is to find the intelligence to allow him to do so." The directive was not quite an order to cook the books, but it was a strong suggestion that cherry-picking and slanting not only would be tolerated, but might even be rewarded.

"Forget the stuff that they [policymakers] aren't interested in," said Melvin Goodman, a retired CIA analyst who had known Foley for more than twenty years, in explaining Foley's directive. If the intelligence "doesn't agree with the thesis, you let it slide by [to] support the argument that the administration is trying to make."

"That, to me, has always been classic politicization of intelligence," Goodman said. Goodman had testified against Robert Gates during Gates's contentious confirmation hearings to be CIA director in 1991 because, he said, Gates had fostered politicization as a deputy under the late director William Casey, who viewed the Soviet Union as more demonic and aggressive than the evidence supported. Gates replaced Rumsfeld as Bush's secretary of defense in late 2006. Goodman said that the politicization seen during the Bush administration had been more insidious because, during the Casey years, the pressure to slant analysis came from within the CIA, and analysts at that time at least had opportunities to confront their managers with dissenting views. "This is different," Goodman said. "What do you do when Cheney comes out to CIA headquarters or tells his CIA daily briefer, 'I don't want you briefing me anymore. I want somebody else.'"

Former CIA analyst Ray McGovern, who spent the Reagan years

toiling on Soviet issues, agreed that analysts in those years could challenge their managers. "But it didn't do any good," he said. He thought Foley, also assigned to the Soviet Division, was an "ambitious, highly qualified" analyst who had "good schooling and good credentials . . . He performed well the first couple of years."

After that, McGovern said, Foley "sold himself, big time." Asked to describe Foley's virtues, he said, "He baked good chocolate cakes."

The State Department's Carl Ford had a different take on Foley. He said that Foley was a poor manager who failed to run a disciplined shop—with hundreds of analysts and support staff, it is the largest in the Directorate of Intelligence. "I think it was people below him that were really sort of running amok," self-promoting by going over Foley's head with juicy, yet questionable, reports. He said Foley should have confronted Tenet and told him, "I don't care what these guys are telling you, Mr. Director. I've been here a lot longer than they, and this is bullshit."

Confronting Tenet would have been awkward, but Foley showed no sign of trying to do so. Whether or not he had sold out to his bosses or couldn't control his underlings, Foley was preaching to the choir when he ordered the WINPAC staff that December to give the president what he wanted. WINPAC had already displayed an unwillingness to listen to outside experts who disagreed and did not tolerate dissent from within. The Robb-Silberman Commission observed that a "culture of enforced consensus has infected WINPAC as an organization."

A senior CIA official who retired after the Iraq invasion began said that young, self-promoting, narcissistic, and very naïve analysts populated WINPAC. He described the staff as a "bunch of very eager, extremely ambitious, extremely opinionated [analysts]." If asked, he said, they would portray themselves as "I am beautiful, I am gorgeous, I am the smartest thing that was ever born—I don't need to know anything about the past."

Goodman said that the youth and relative inexperience of WINPAC analysts reflected the fast pace of hiring at the CIA over the past decade. "I've seen the demographic work. Very few have been at the agency for more than five years working on analytical issues and very few had more than three years in their field of expertise," he said.

With Foley's state approval, the sycophantic WINPAC staff fed the Bush administration's war plan. That was the subtext, for example, of WINPAC's response to the Iraqi declaration of December 7 at the United Nations. The response, written for the National Security Council, criticized Iraq for not having mentioned its purchase of the aluminum tubes and complained that the declaration also did not "acknowledge efforts to procure uranium from Niger."

The WINPAC position blatantly disregarded repeated warnings from skilled analysts at the Energy Department and the State Department's Bureau of Intelligence and Research that the uranium charge was weak and that the aluminum tubes were not part of a nuclear program. Simon Dodge, the nuclear analyst at the State Department, e-mailed a colleague at the Energy Department and complained that the WINPAC report to the National Security Council had not included his bureau's position—that the tubes were not suited for a nuclear program and that it was highly improbable that Iraq had shopped for uranium. The analyst from the Energy Department, which had correctly discerned that the tubes were for rockets, not uranium enrichment, replied that he found it "most disturbing that WINPAC is essentially directing foreign policy on this matter. . . . When individuals attempt to convert those 'strong statements' into the 'knock-out' punch, the administration will ultimately look foolish—i.e., the tubes and Niger."

Top scientists and engineers at the Energy Department's own nuclear facilities, including the Oak Ridge National Laboratory and the Lawrence Livermore National Laboratory, repeatedly told WINPAC that the tubes were unsuited for centrifuge rotors. They were too narrow, long, and thick-walled to fit in any known centrifuge. In addition, aluminum had not been used for centrifuge rotors since the pioneering years of uranium enrichment.

The specifications for the tubes, which Iraq had been buying fairly openly and from several suppliers, matched exactly those used in its variant of the Italian Medusa rocket, which it called the Nasser 81. The zinc-aluminum alloy tubing, designated as 7075-T6, is used in the rocket motor chambers of the US Navy's Mark 66 helicopter rocket. The tubing was also used in rockets manufactured by at least fourteen other countries, including Russia and Switzerland. In addition, the tubes had anodized coatings that would have had to be removed for use in centrifuges but were exactly what Iraq needed for its rockets because corrosion had ruined much of its existing supply.

WINPAC did not heed the warnings. All of that detailed analysis by America's top atomic scientists at the Department of Energy's nuclear labs was trumped by one hard-charging WINPAC engineer and analyst, Joe Turner. In sometimes-heated internal Intelligence Community deliberations and before highly skeptical IAEA scientists, Turner almost single-handedly championed the winning—and wrong—conclusion that was transmitted to the White House: that the tubes were intended for a nuclear centrifuge. He had an imaginative explanation for why the specifications for the tubes made them unlikely candidates for centrifuges: It was obviously Iraqi concealment of their true intent.

Simon Dodge and others had also told WINPAC, along with the rest of the Intelligence Community, that they had grave doubts about the Iraq–Niger connection. Foley and WINPAC could have figured this out for themselves had they examined copies of the Niger documents, which were handed over by Elisabetta Burba on October 9 and made available to the CIA on October 16.

On January 13, 2003—three months after the forgeries were made available—Dodge e-mailed colleagues in the Intelligence Community explaining why he had concluded that the uranium story "probably is a hoax."

He wrote that one of the documents received from Rome purported to reflect an agreement by the ambassadors to Italy of five Islamic countries, including Iraq and Iran, to mount a military campaign against Western powers. The notion of a united jihad directed by five diplomats representing nations inimical to each other was so ridiculous, he wrote, that this document, at least, was "clearly a forgery." Dodge then noted that the official stamps on this document were similar to those on the documents claimed to be uranium sales agreements and concluded, "The uranium purchase agreement probably is a forgery."

Some of the WINPAC analysts later admitted to the Senate committee's investigators that they had contorted the Niger intelligence and even flimsier reports that Iraq had tried to buy uranium from Somalia and from the Democratic Republic of the Congo because it made for a more compelling case that Iraq was pursuing nuclear weapons.

The Somalia and Congo claims had come from informants and stretched credulity. The CIA, for example, received a couple of intelligence reports in 1999 that a delegation of Iraqis, Iranians, and Libyans had arrived in Somalia to discuss extracting uranium. But Iraq and Iran were sworn enemies, and it was highly improbable that they would have joined hands in a nuclear program that might have resulted in mutual annihilation. The Robb-Silberman Commission noted that these reports of other alleged African uranium suppliers were "not considered reliable by most analysts at the time" and were "subsequently judged not credible and recalled."

Though thin gruel, those wisps of intelligence were all WINPAC needed to support the case that Iraq was seeking to make nuclear bombs. "WINPAC analysts told committee staff that by January [2003] they had come to believe that if Iraq was in fact attempting to acquire uranium from Africa, it would bolster their argument that Iraq was reconstituting its nuclear weapons program because Iraq had no other use for the uranium," the Senate committee's report said. One of the analysts even admitted that he had "ratcheted down" analytical standards by accepting the African intelligence because there was little else to support a conclusion that Iraq was seeking to become a nuclear state.

One day in January 2003, Alan Foley, now fully on board with the White House's war plan for Iraq, had a brief conversation over a secure phone line with Robert Joseph at the National Security Council. The phone call gave White House staffers the approval they wanted to let them mention uranium in the State of the Union message.

At the time, Joseph was the National Security Council's special assistant to the president for nonproliferation. Iraq was one of his accounts. He was very bright and very passionate, one of the early advocates of the doctrine of preemptive first strikes. Wilkerson, Colin Powell's chief of staff, described Joseph as one of Cheney's numerous "spies" planted throughout the bureaucracy, in this case on the staff of the National Security Council.

Sometime in January—it is unclear when—Foley and Joseph had a brief and amiable chat over a secure phone line. The two men, who were friends and spoke often, didn't recall who initiated the call. Joseph needed the CIA's approval to include the Nigerien uranium intelligence in the upcoming State of the Union speech.

The reason for asking Foley for permission was obvious, a senior CIA official told us. The White House certainly wasn't going to ask Tenet to approve the language—it was the same material he had rejected three months earlier in Bush's Cincinnati speech. "The strongest supporter of the neoconservatives and hard-liners within the agency was WINPAC, as opposed to the Counterproliferation Division and others. Which is why they went to Alan Foley at WINPAC to get their buyoff in the State of the Union. While he [Foley] quibbled about the language, he eventually agreed to the formulation which became part of the speech."

Foley and Joseph did not discuss the credibility of the information in what would become known as Bush's 16 words. As a career CIA official, Foley was deeply concerned about the rules for classification of intelligence information, and he only had a minor question about attribution for the intelligence on uranium purchases. The US intelligence, obtained from SISMI, was still classified, he said. No problem, Joseph replied. The White House speechwriters would be happy to use Britain's September 24 white paper as the source for Iraq's uranium shopping in Africa. Foley accepted that idea because the British report was not classified.

And so, with agreement from Foley, Bush's speechwriters jotted down the 16 words: "The British government has learned that Saddam Hussein recently sought significant quantities of uranium from Africa."

There were strong indications that Foley all along was toeing a line he did not believe. Several days after Bush's State of the Union speech, Foley briefed student officers at the National Defense University at Fort McNair in Washington, DC. After the briefing, Melvin Goodman, who had retired from the CIA and was then on the university's faculty, brought Foley into the secure communications area of the Fort McNair compound. Goodman thanked Foley for addressing the students and asked him what weapons of mass destruction he believed would be found after the invasion. "Not much, if anything," Goodman recalled that Foley responded. Foley declined to be interviewed for this book.

Nevertheless, Foley and WINPAC continued to march in lockstep with the administration about Iraq's nuclear program, even as evidence increasingly showed that Iraq had no such plan. The division's final report before the March 20 US invasion reported: "All intelligence experts agree that Iraq is seeking nuclear weapons" and warned that Baghdad could produce a bomb within a year if it got its hands on weapons-grade material.

The declaration did not fit the known facts. Carl Ford said, "There was no new evidence coming in when the Intelligence Community changed its view to say, 'Well, guess what, they're reconstituting their nuclear weapons program.'"

Moreover, said Ford, no significant information had been received since the United Nations determined in 1998 that the Iraqi nuclear program had been dismantled.

Yet despite the lack of new evidence, Iraq's threat of building a nuclear bomb "changed after this administration came to power," Ford said. "For several years up till then, if . . . the Intelligence Community would be asked the question 'Have they reconstituted a nuclear weapons program?' our answer would be 'No, we don't think so. We don't see the evidence.'"

Alan Foley retired from the CIA in 2003, a few months after the Iraq invasion. Robert Joseph attended Foley's retirement party, and Foley singled out Joseph in his farewell speech, "thanking him for showing up," according to a senior CIA official who attended the function. Some of those who saw Foley at the small retirement affair described him as having changed physically, that his once cherublike face was drawn and wan. Foley told colleagues that he was exhausted.

Chapter 9

Mother Teresa

Foggy Bottom, January 28, 2003

Lawrence Wilkerson was at his State Department office in Washington's Foggy Bottom neighborhood during the State of the Union message on January 28, 2003. He was only half-listening. He had been a close aide and confidante of Colin Powell for a long time, having served with Powell at the Pentagon in 1989 when Powell was named chairman of the Joint Chiefs of Staff. Wilkerson hadn't seen an advance version of the State of the Union address—the Bush White House did not routinely share in-advance speeches relating to foreign policy with Powell, the nation's highest-ranking diplomat, and when they did, it was at the last minute and the secretary had little time to vet the speech within the department (the White House would change this policy after the 2003 State of the Union address and allow

Wilkerson several days to vet speeches with departmental experts). Wilkerson did not immediately register the substance of the 16 words, which had been especially jarring to members of the State Department's Bureau of Intelligence and Research. He did note one irritating portion of the speech that would cause him problems.

> The United States will ask the UN Security Council to convene on February 5 to consider the facts of Iraq's ongoing defiance of the world. Secretary of State Powell will present information and intelligence about Iraq's illegal weapons programs; its attempt to hide those weapons from inspectors; and its links to terrorist groups.

That meant that Wilkerson and his staff would have to kick into high gear to produce the consummate version of US charges against Iraq. Powell's major address on a world stage would have to be assembled and written in a week. Wilkerson had expressed mixed feelings about the administration's policy on Iraq up to that point. He assumed that the intelligence on weapons of mass destruction was generally correct, even if it was sometimes politicized and exaggerated.

But Wilkerson, out to protect his boss, had vague concerns about the direction and content of the rhetoric he heard and the consequences for Powell. The secretary of state had made increasingly hawkish statements about Iraq after having long supported international, UN-based action. In the last month, his tone had shifted closer to that of Bush and Cheney. Wilkerson had discussed the issue in so many words with Powell, who had not been able to put the brakes on the Bush administration's juggernaut toward war.

Wilkerson considered Powell to be a devotee of the system, and both men knew that a neoconservative tide was driving Iraq policy. Powell's style was to argue with his superiors as best he could until decisions were made. But after that, with more than a hint of the military man's outlook, Powell adopted those decisions as his own. He had, in Wilkerson's assessment, "tremendous deference toward the president as an elected official of the American people."

Powell didn't return to the State Department office after attending the State of the Union message, so Wilkerson didn't see him until the next morning. He knew Powell would brief him on the speech, and they'd then talk about the impending trip to New York and the speech before the United Nations.

That night Wilkerson wondered why Powell was the one going to New York. He speculated that UN ambassador John Negroponte could do the briefing, just as Adlai Stevenson had done the Cuban Missile Crisis briefing for President John F. Kennedy in October 1962, when the Soviets had tried to install nuclear missiles in Cuba. Kennedy's secretary of state, Dean Rusk, had not given the briefing—and that crisis was far more serious than the Iraq crisis. So why was Powell at the UN this time? But Wilkerson did not speculate for long. He knew why the administration had selected Powell. His boss was the only member of the administration with poll ratings in the stratosphere. Powell had once said to him that the only one higher in the polls than he was Mother Teresa.

The morning after the State of the Union address, Powell walked through the door that adjoined his and Wilkerson's offices. The secretary handed his chief of staff a forty-eight-page document. "This is the script for my presentation at the United Nations in a few days," he told Wilkerson. "Form a task force and move out to CIA headquarters and put it together. Will Toby from the NSC and John Hanna from the vice president's office will help you." So Wilkerson put together a small task force, moved out to Langley, and began putting together the case for war.

Powell and Wilkerson held marathon meetings with CIA officials and with their own staffs to assemble the case for war. Their "guidance" was a forty-eight-page draft of a recommended speech prepared by Hannah and Libby in Cheney's office. It was full of thinly sourced allegations, a number of them coming from Chalabi's network of defectors. Powell and Wilkerson would have none of it. "I suggested we go to the October 2002 NIE [National Intelligence

Estimate] . . . and we threw the forty-eight-page script out. And John Hannah sat there looking like he was a wounded dog for about five minutes," Wilkerson recalled.

One immediate decision was made—Powell did not want to mention President Bush's allegations about Iraqi uranium purchases in Africa. He was listening to his intelligence staff, who were the strongest dissenters in the Intelligence Community on the subject of the alleged Iraqi nuclear program. "The SISMI report was blown out of the water," said Wilkerson. Powell said Niger wasn't on his radar screen. But that didn't matter. Cheney and the White House Iraq Group had the Niger story working for them and could still talk about the threat of mushroom clouds, regardless of what intelligence officers told them.

Despite the high-level talks leading up to Powell's speech, doubts did not always filter in. The CIA mindset remained the same: Tenet and his staff were operating on the assumption that war was inevitable and played along with the administration to curry favor and protect their jobs. On February 4, 2003, the day before Powell made his compelling and ultimately deeply flawed presentation on the Iraqi threat to the Security Council, a senior CIA official gave this response to an urgent e-mail disclosing that the key source behind a claim that Hussein had mobile biological labs was a fabricator: "Let's keep in mind the fact that this war's going to happen regardless of what [the source] said or didn't say, and the Powers That Be probably aren't terribly interested in whether [the source] knows what he's talking about."

Powell and Wilkerson held detailed sessions with George Tenet and his deputy, John McLaughlin, at CIA headquarters while preparing for the UN speech. Powell demanded multiple sourcing on the assertions he was going to make. His requirement prompted numerous arguments.

"The secretary of state and I sat at the CIA and listened day and night to the DCI [Director of Central Intelligence]—Tenet—and the DDCI [Deputy Director of Central Intelligence]—McLaughlin," preparing for the UN speech. On several occasions, Powell stared down

Tenet and demanded proof. "Tenet never blinked. He said, 'You can count on that.'"

These were often all-night sessions: writing, honing, adding and subtracting points, raising questions about information on mobile biological laboratories, on human intelligence about hiding weapons systems. There was little sleep. Audiovisual specialists with Hollywood experience put together sophisticated displays, photographs, and audiotapes to accompany the UN speech. Analysts said that the array of information was one of the greatest disclosures of US human and signal intelligence ever seen.

Powell's arrival at UN headquarters in New York marked a defining moment that was compared to Adlai Stevenson's appearance before the Security Council during the 1962 Cuban Missile Crisis. He launched into an eighty-minute speech, the payoff for those sleepless nights presided over by Wilkerson.

While he avoided the substance of the Italian letter, Powell raised the specter of nuclear weapons in a backhanded fashion, saying that "we have no indication that Saddam Hussein has ever abandoned his nuclear weapons program."

He said that what had blocked Hussein's nuclear ambitions had been his inability to obtain bomb-grade uranium or plutonium and Iraq's lack of the industrial infrastructure required to produce the bomb-grade material. "Since 1998," Powell said, "his efforts to reconstitute his nuclear program have been focused on acquiring the third and last component, sufficient fissile material to produce a nuclear explosion. To make the fissile material, he needs to develop an ability to enrich uranium."

Powell also gave special attention to scientists who had the expertise to develop nuclear weapons. He described the purchase of aluminum tubes that had long been debated in the Intelligence Community, and which his own INR analysts had generally rejected as being for use in producing processed uranium. He said, "By now, just about everyone has heard of these tubes, and we all know that there are differences of opinion. There is controversy about what these tubes are for. Most US experts think they are intended to serve as rotors in centrifuges used to enrich uranium. Other experts, and the Iraqis themselves, argue that they are really to produce the rocket bodies for a conventional weapon, a multiple rocket launcher."

Powell's litany of charges included voice intercepts of men speaking in Arabic about "forbidden ammo" and "nerve agents," and about classified documents found at a nuclear scientist's home in Baghdad. The words may have been spoken and the documents recovered, but they evidently had nothing to do with weapons of mass destruction.

The majority of the charges would prove in less than a year to be false, misleading, and outdated. The speech generated unprecedented support for the US war effort, mostly, in Wilkerson's view, because of the person delivering the speech rather than the substance of what he said. "Mostly, when you put it in the mouth of Colin Powell, it works," he said.

Wilkerson afterward regretted that he hadn't taken Carl Ford along with him to the meetings at the CIA. Ford was himself a veteran CIA analyst and was up to speed on the intelligence about Iraq. He prided himself on getting it right.

Powell heard plaudits from the White House and was bathed with positive reviews. Longtime opponents of the war were persuaded by the secretary of state; it was seen as a turning point in the White House's promotion of the war, perhaps more successful than Bush himself and the WHIG propaganda effort.

"Colin Powell did more than present the world with a convincing and detailed X-ray of Iraq's secret weapons and terrorism programs yesterday," wrote Jim Hoagland, associate editor and a columnist at the *Washington Post*. "He also exposed the enduring bad faith of several key members of the UN Security Council when it comes to Iraq and its 'web of lies,' in Powell's phrase."

Nicholas D. Kristof wrote in the *New York Times*: "President

Bush and Colin Powell have adroitly shown that Iraq is hiding weapons, that Saddam Hussein is a lying scoundrel, and that Iraqi officials should be less chatty on the telephone."

Wilkerson, however, was dissatisfied. In the course of assembling the speech, he'd never focused on its overall impression. When Powell spoke at the UN Security Council, he was compelled to do so as he sat just off the Security Council floor and watched. "I finally concentrated on the screen and the secretary's words. When I watched it, I was depressed. I didn't think it was very effective at all."

Nevertheless, Wilkerson's public response was supportive. He praised the secretary of state and sought awards for the hardworking staff members who had produced the speech under extraordinary time pressure.

And then Powell penned another commendation, this one a very personal note recognizing Wilkerson for his efforts to produce and manage the speech.

Wilkerson received the note. He took it home, tore it up, and threw it away. He said, "I didn't think we'd done a very good job."

Powell had known that the Bush administration could use the goodwill and trust associated with his name to dissolve opposition to the war. One month later, as invasion appeared inevitable, another man came before the same Security Council forum at the United Nations and desperately argued for peace. It was Mohamed ElBaradei, the director general of the International Atomic Energy Agency, who had last reported to the Security Council the day before the State of the Union address, saying that his agency had found no information to substantiate US charges about a revived Iraqi nuclear program.

ElBaradei did not have Powell's star status, but he made one last effort to stop the impending invasion: an astounding, detailed refutation of US claims about Iraq. Routinely criticized by neoconservatives and hard-liners in the Bush administration, ElBaradei spoke the truth, but his pleas went unheeded.

Chapter 10

Vienna = Spy Central

On March 7, 2003, about two weeks before the US invasion of Iraq, Mohamed ElBaradei declared before the Security Council of the United Nations that the Niger intelligence was based on forged documents and that Iraq was not building a nuclear bomb.

ElBaradei's declaration was a last attempt to avert the US invasion of Iraq and also represented the culmination of his long-standing antagonism with the Bush administration's disdain for international cooperation. His report to a session of the Security Council, delivered in the presence of Secretary of State Colin Powell and Jack Straw, the British foreign secretary, pushed many Bush administration hawks over the edge.

With the US invasion of Iraq looming, ElBaradei was seeking more time for inspections. "After three months of intrusive inspections," he said, "we to date found no evidence or plausible indication of the revival of a nuclear weapons program in Iraq." A little more time, he said, "should enable us in the near future to provide the Security Council with an objective and thorough assessment of Iraq's nuclear capabilities."

About two-thirds of the way through his speech, he made the defining statement about the Italian letter and the Nigerien uranium claims: "Based on thorough analysis, the IAEA has concluded, with the concurrence of outside experts, that these documents—which formed the basis for the reports of recent uranium transactions between Iraq and Niger—are in fact not authentic. We have therefore concluded that these specific allegations are unfounded."

He was equally categorical on the main topics raised by President Bush in his State of the Union message and point by point knocked down the claims made by Powell before the Security Council in February. ElBaradei's dramatic declaration was crisp in its presentation and to the point—the US charges about weapons of mass destruction were false or unproven. It was historic in its import—a gambit to hold back the US invasion forces while the United Nations did its inspection work.

"I am able to report today that, in the area of nuclear weapons— the most lethal weapons of mass destruction—inspections in Iraq are moving forward," ElBaradei said.

> Since the resumption of inspections a little over three months ago— and particularly during the three weeks since my last oral report to the Council—the IAEA has made important progress in identifying what nuclear-related capabilities remain in Iraq, and in its assessment of whether Iraq has made any efforts to revive its past nuclear program during the intervening four years since inspections were brought to a halt. At this stage, the following can be stated:
>
> One, there is no indication of resumed nuclear activities in those buildings that were identified through the use of satellite imagery as

being reconstructed or newly erected since 1998, nor any indication of nuclear-related prohibited activities at any inspected sites.

Second, there is no indication that Iraq has attempted to import uranium since 1990.

Third, there is no indication that Iraq has attempted to import aluminum tubes for use in centrifuge enrichment. Moreover, even had Iraq pursued such a plan, it would have encountered practical difficulties in manufacturing centrifuges out of the aluminum tubes in question.

Getting American and British cooperation for a renewed—but brief—inspection program was no small task. When the Security Council agreed to send UN inspection teams back into Iraq in November 2002, ElBaradei; Hans Blix, the chief UN weapons inspector; and Jacques Baute, a French physicist at the IAEA in charge of hunting for Iraq's nuclear program, expressed concern that the American and British intelligence services were balking at turning over meaningful leads for the inspectors. In January 2003, Blix complained that the two countries had briefed inspectors about what banned weapons they believed Iraq was hiding but not where they were hidden. Senator Carl Levin, a Democrat from Michigan, agreed. He charged that Tenet, the director of central intelligence, had withheld information from the inspectors. Tenet denied that and told Levin that the CIA had "provided [to the inspectors] detailed information on all of the high value and moderate value sites" in Iraq. But the CIA revised that statement a year later, finally admitting publicly that it had not shared the location of 21 of 105 sites it believed to be of high or medium priority.

The Bush administration maintained a stony silence for more than a week after ElBaradei's authoritative refutation of the very foundation for the impending US action against Iraq. When a response came, it was brazen. On March 16, four days before the invasion, Vice President Cheney appeared on MSNBC's *Meet the Press* and said, "I think Mr. ElBaradei frankly is wrong."

Cheney had no credible evidence to back his claim that ElBaradei was wrong, and a number of US analysts had also reached many of the UN official's conclusions months earlier. Unable to rebut the charges, Cheney turned his ire on ElBaradei himself and began serious efforts to have the veteran Egyptian diplomat fired by the United Nations.

The reaction was no surprise, but singling out ElBaradei was an outrage to many in the United States and internationally. "They totally misjudged the fact that outside of this group of neocons, ElBaradei was a hugely respected guy," said a retired senior CIA officer.

The Bush administration not only scoffed at the UN agency's inspection program in Iraq, but also ordered American intelligence operatives to eavesdrop on ElBaradei, Blix, and their offices. The spying operation took place both at UN headquarters in New York and at the headquarters of the International Atomic Energy Agency in Vienna.

The IAEA had been based since 1957 in Vienna, the capital of neutral Austria. Vienna was attractive to new international organizations, especially those involved in nuclear proliferation issues, because Geneva, home to many UN agencies, had become too expensive. US and many other intelligence services had long been attracted to Vienna, where they could monitor Eastern Europe during the Cold War and beyond; but with the arrival of the nuclear agencies, espionage activities also targeted agencies that dealt with proliferation. The United States based about 250 intelligence personnel in Vienna, making it one of the CIA's largest stations. The intelligence collectors ranged from specialists at the Air Force Technical Application Center, which monitored compliance with nuclear test ban treaties, to CIA officials posted at the US Mission to International Organizations in Vienna (UNVIE), which represents American interests before the IAEA, the Comprehensive Test Ban Treaty Organization, and other UN-related bodies. CIA officers and analysts also were attached to the other two US missions in Vienna—the US embassy and the US Mission to the Organization for Security and Cooperation in Europe (OSCE), a fifty-six-country alliance that deals with all regional issues, including border security and terrorism. Ten of the thirty-five members of the US mission to UNVIE were CIA personnel from WINPAC, the Center for Weapons Intelligence, Nonproliferation, and Arms Control.

It is not clear what the intelligence personnel reported back home from the IAEA listening post in the months preceding the Iraq invasion, but they would have heard officials at the UN-affiliated agency saying they were deeply skeptical about the US claim that Iraq was reconstituting its nuclear weapons program. Such reports would have clashed with WINPAC's own assessment on Iraqi armaments, influenced by groupthink and pressure from Cheney and other top administration officials.

Besides organizations that should have been regarded as friends, the United States was also spying on other targets: Delegations and missions in Vienna also included Iran and North Korea, which in turn loaded their staffs with spies. Iraq also conducted spy operations in Vienna, even though it did not have a nuclear program. US and allied intelligence services persistently sought to penetrate those delegations, sometimes with great success.

The United States continued to listen in on ElBaradei and his agency even after the Iraq invasion, because Cheney and other administration hawks considered him too soft in dealing with Iran and wanted to gather evidence for their effort to replace him with someone more malleable. The US eavesdropping was not limited to the UN's Vienna offices. Some was conducted at UN Plaza in New York, where US agencies monitored Blix, ElBaradei's predecessor at the IAEA. Blix had become head of the nonnuclear weapons inspection team in Iraq, the United Nations Monitoring, Verification and Inspection Commission. Several weeks before the war started, Blix met with

John Wolf, the assistant secretary of state for nonproliferation. Wolf showed him two photographs of Iraqi weapons, one of a cluster bomb and the second of a drone. Blix realized that the pictures could have originated from only one place—his own UN weapons office. Blix had no doubt that the Iraqis bugged him, but he was miffed to discover that the United States spied on him as well. "You are cooperating with the people who sit across the desk one day, and if the next they are listening to you, it is an unpleasant feeling."

Blix's predecessor as chief weapons inspector in Iraq, Richard Butler, learned from his sources that he also had been bugged by US, British, French, and Russian intelligence. Butler discovered, he said, that the same countries that spied on him "would come to me and show me the recordings that they had made on others to help me do my job disarming Iraq."

The most sweeping monitoring activity was discovered in early 2003, when an employee at Britain's counterpart of the National Security Agency, the Government Communications Headquarters (GCHQ), leaked a top-secret NSA cable. It revealed that the United States had monitored the secret conversations of delegations from six Security Council states that wanted to give UN inspectors more time before voting on a war resolution.

The United States was preeminent in espionage against some of the country missions assigned to the IAEA. The volume of espionage activity worried John Ritch, who had been ambassador to the US UNVIE mission during the Clinton administration. He was concerned that mission creep would set in and that spying activities would expand to target the IAEA and the United Nations itself.

Ritch, who received degrees from the US Military Academy at West Point and from Oxford University in England, supported the United Nations and admired ElBaradei. But neoconservative critics of the United Nations, including John Bolton, who was appointed US ambassador to the United Nations in 2005, thought ElBaradei was too soft on what the United States considered to be rogue states, particularly Iraq and Iran. But Ritch "believed that ElBaradei was really trying to do the right thing, but to do it he had to be friends with everyone," according to a former senior administration official who knew him well. Over drinks, the official told Ritch that the CIA would limit its activities to penetrating foreign delegations assigned to the IAEA, and Ritch "went along with that."

The restriction was lifted under Ritch's successor, Ambassador Kenneth C. Brill, a conservative Foreign Service officer more in tune with the worldview of Cheney, Bolton, and Bush. US spy agencies bugged ElBaradei during Brill's tenure, seeking evidence that might convince the thirty-five member countries of the IAEA ruling Board of Governors to dismiss ElBaradei. The spies found nothing they could use. Brill, meanwhile, was promoted to become the first director of the National Counterproliferation Center, under the director of national intelligence, John Negroponte.

IAEA officials were not surprised to learn that the most powerful member of its governing board, the United States, had spied on their director. "We've always assumed that this kind of thing goes on. We wish it were otherwise, but we know the reality," said the agency's spokesman at the time, Mark Gwozdecky.

The IAEA had rules to inoculate itself from charges that it favored certain foreign governments and their intelligence services. The organization's 2,200 employees, citizens of ninety nuclear and nonnuclear states, were instructed to keep sensitive information confidential and not pass it to diplomats and technocrats from various missions, including some who were assigned by their nations' intelligence services. There was concern that IAEA staffers were more likely to transfer sensitive data to representatives of their own countries. The result was often an awkward working environment. "You're actually watched in a funny way by colleagues," said David Albright, who had been an IAEA consultant.

Meanwhile, it was obvious that intelligence services could not be isolated from political pressure at home. Baute, as the agency's chief nuclear weapons hunter in Iraq since 1994, had regular dealings with the US mission to UNVIE. "The fact that the Agency has 137 Member States forces it to put great distance from any single political agenda and its associated pressure," he wrote in the June 2004 *IAEA Bulletin*. On the other hand, he added, analysts from individual countries "may feel under the pressure, explicit or implicit, from a single political line." He did not identify which national analysts he was thinking of, but he easily could have been referring to the CIA.

The IAEA's effectiveness was weakened by failings in intelligence sharing. Member nations, in theory, were required to provide the IAEA with all actionable intelligence that had to do with nuclear treaty violations. But national intelligence services, no matter what the country, are by training and culture unwilling to share anything, even with partner agencies in their own countries. The terrorist attacks on September 11, 2001, succeeded in part because critical dots of intelligence were not connected, but also in part because the CIA and FBI did not fully communicate with one another. Their job was to spy, not to share and give away the results of their spying. The case of Iraq was somewhat different, because the CIA had little information available to show the IAEA that would prove the existence of Iraq's nuclear program. Even if they had had such information, CIA officials were constrained by rules that inhibited dissemination of third-country intelligence, and the original information on Niger had come from Italy's intelligence service.

Italian intelligence officials, for their part, traveled to Vienna in 2002 to secretly brief the agency, according to a former senior CIA officer intimately familiar with what transpired at the IAEA in the months before the invasion. A key component of Italy's SISMI intelligence, of course, was the uranium allegations based on the forged documents.

Italy's defense minister, Antonio Martino, also confided to a small group of Italian parliamentarians in November 2005 that SISMI briefed the IAEA to help prepare inspectors for their return to Iraq in November 2002.

While ElBaradei's disclosure of the Niger uranium fraud on March 7 was a last-minute attempt to stop the march to war, his agency only weeks earlier had obtained copies of the Italian letter. The IAEA's attempt to get to the bottom of the US charge about Iraqi uranium purchases in Niger was an exercise in cross-purposes and obstacles presented by intelligence agencies from the United States, Britain, and Italy.

IAEA officials had heard since at least the fall of 2002 that the uranium charges were based on suspect documents in the possession of Britain and the United States. Blix recalled being told before the dossier was turned over that the Niger claim was based on documents that included a copy of a contract. The package of forgeries never included a contract. He said the revelation came from the United States, not Italy. Asked by the Italian newspaper *La Repubblica* in 2005 when he had first learned of the intelligence pinpointing Niger as the would-be supplier of uranium, he said:

> I was informed by the offices of the IAEA in Vienna in the autumn of 2002, even if I don't recall the exact date. However, I can remember perfectly well my reaction. I thought it was absolute rubbish. We knew precisely that Iraq had large reserves of yellowcake accumulated over the years, and above all we knew that [Iraq] was not able to enrich it. So this Niger story made no sense logically. . . . I was told that the IAEA had heard from the Americans about the existence of a contract for a supply of yellowcake to Iraq by Niger. And it was added that Jacques Baute [director of the IAEA Iraq Action Team] was trying without success to obtain those documents in order to evaluate them.

David Albright, the nuclear specialist who had helped the IAEA teams in Iraq in the 1990s and knew Baute well, also remembered that the Iraq action team leader "knew what was in them [the documents], which is why Jacques wanted to get them. He wanted to check it out."

The IAEA had asked the British mission in Vienna for details after the British government on September 24, 2002, published its dossier claiming that Iraq had been seeking uranium in Africa. British officials said they could not help because their information was provided by a third country's intelligence service. That did not keep Baute from looking elsewhere, including checking with the US UNVIE mission. "I cannot be 100 percent definitive as of today because I usually didn't take notes," Baute said. "But I would say that when we had a question mark in mind, the United States was one of the natural nations we would ask."

Baute's Iraq Nuclear Verification Office, the IAEA's Iraq action team, became even more curious when the State Department on December 19, 2002, repeated the British dossier's claim, with the additional information that Niger was the suspect African country. Officials from the IAEA were on the phone with the Americans soon after they saw the declaration, which had been posted on the State Department's Web site.

The United States had the same Italian intelligence that had provided Britain's MI6 with the excuse for not sharing the Nigerien uranium story with the IAEA. But, courtesy of Elisabetta Burba, it also had the forged documents, which underpinned—and undermined—that intelligence.

The United States delayed giving the evidence to the IAEA for weeks. Baute pressed hard for the information, telling investigative journalist Seymour Hersh that at one point he even "started to harass the United States" to get his hands on the intelligence. Hersh said that Baute often pushed the US government for information and quoted the IAEA spokesman, Gwozdecky, as confirming that Baute routinely asked for "actionable evidence" but "was getting almost nothing."

Three years after his initial assessment, Baute told us that his comments to Hersh might have been exaggerated under the pressure of the moment. "When you're in the eye of the tornado, you want to have the things now. That's why I'm probably approaching things in a cooler way today."

Baute said that, even though the forged documents certainly were not obtained through a clandestine US operation, he believed they still had to be cleared through "a dozen [US] offices" before they were turned over to him. On February 4, 2003, he managed to get a briefing on the information from the US UNVIE mission in Vienna about the content of the documents, but still did not receive the documents themselves. The United States finally gave Baute the Italian letter and the accompanying dossier later that day; the next day, Powell delivered his factually wrong but very effective critique before the Security Council of Iraq's growing threat. Baute said it took him a few hours of searching on the Internet to see that the documents belonged in the garbage. In a matter of days, the IAEA concluded categorically that the US and British evidence was based on fraudulent documents. It was news to many at the CIA, especially at WINPAC. A simple Internet search—what Baute did—would have exposed the hoax more than a year earlier, long before the CIA received the documents themselves. The "verbatim text" of the so-called "accord" provided by SISMI to the CIA on February 5, 2002, contained so many factual errors that it should have been evident that the document could not have been drafted by officials from either Niger or Iraq.

Less than two weeks after ElBaradei was unable to win an extension, UN weapons inspectors were withdrawn and the US invasion was launched. In 2005, as the US failure in Iraq became apparent, the shrewd Egyptian lawyer and diplomat was awarded the Nobel Peace Prize.

Chapter 11

Mr. and Mrs. Wilson

In the early days after the US invasion, President Bush and his administration basked in victory: The war had gone well. Baghdad fell on April 9, 2003, just three weeks after the US attack. On May 1, Bush was triumphant as he donned a flight suit and boarded a navy S-3B Viking jet at the naval air station in San Diego. The jet made a tail-hook landing on the USS *Abraham Lincoln* stationed just offshore. On board the carrier, Bush declared before cheering sailors and a banner reading "Mission Accomplished": "Major combat operations in Iraq have ended."

By late spring, the early euphoria at the White House began to wane. Military and CIA investigators on the ground in Iraq had not found any weapons of mass destruction. The news media began to grumble that the administration had exaggerated intelligence to garner support for the war.

The 16 words of the State of the Union address, in particular, were coming back to haunt Bush. Those Americans who had been aware of it at all had been forgiving after ElBaradei declared on March 7 that the Nigerien uranium claim was based on forgeries. People assumed that the president was the victim of bad intelligence from the British, the CIA, and its partner spy agencies.

But Ambassador Joseph Wilson was angry. He believed that the White House, especially Cheney, must have read the March 8, 2002, CIA debriefing report of his visit to Niger. Therefore, he figured, Cheney would have known the 16 words were false. After all, his fact-finding trip was the CIA's response to Cheney's order to find out more about the Iraq–Niger uranium agreement, and Wilson had concluded that there was no deal.

In fact, the CIA had not bothered to send the report directly to Cheney, since officials there concluded Wilson's information did not add a great deal to what was already known. Instead, the CIA disseminated the report through routine channels—a wide distribution, but addressed to no one in particular. There was no evidence that Cheney or other senior officials in the Bush administration had read the report of his conclusions, despite Wilson's assumption that they must have seen it.

Wilson decided to set the record straight, at first testing the media waters in May by anonymously providing information about his CIA-sponsored trip. Wilson's first leak was to columnist Nicholas Kristof at the *New York Times*. On May 6, Kristof wrote that a "former US ambassador to Africa" had been sent to Niger the previous year and had reported to the CIA and the State Department that the Niger intelligence had been "unequivocally wrong" and that the documents "had been forged." Kristof said that the former ambassador's "debunking of the forgery was passed around the administration and seemed to be accepted—except that President Bush and the State Department kept citing it anyway." Wilson had no way of knowing in

2002 that there had been underlying documents or that they were bogus. He called Kristof on the same day to correct the impression in the article that he had been aware of the forgeries when he undertook the trip.

Nevertheless, the same impression was carried through in subsequent anonymous interviews with the *Washington Post* and the *New Republic*. Wilson later admitted to the Senate Intelligence Committee that he had "misspoken" in interviews and had inadvertently jumbled together what he personally had learned in Niger with what he had later read about the IAEA's report to the Security Council. The Kristof column and the *Washington Post* and *New Republic* articles were distributed at the White House, where Bush, Cheney, and others read them with great concern because these were attacks on their credibility. The *Post* article also did not identify Wilson by name but mentioned that the retired ambassador had told the CIA that the uranium story was false. The *New Republic* article was even more damaging. It quoted the unnamed ambassador as claiming that administration officials "knew the [Niger] story was a flat-out lie."

Before the last two articles appeared, Cheney's top aide, I. Lewis "Scooter" Libby, on or about May 29, asked the number three official at the State Department, Undersecretary Marc Grossman, to look for anything the department had on the Niger trip and who the unnamed former ambassador cited by Kristof was. The seemingly innocuous request marked the first in a series of missteps by Libby that would result in his indictment two and a half years later on charges of lying to a grand jury and to investigators. Grossman, who on that day was the acting secretary of state because the department's top two officers were away, assigned the task to INR director Carl Ford. Ford, a straight-talker, had been a marine and followed orders. "He didn't tell me why he wanted to know," Ford recalled. "I didn't ask questions. The undersecretary asks you to do something, you go do it."

Within days, Grossman had had a number of conversations on

the matter with Libby. At first, Grossman only told Libby that Wilson was the former ambassador who had been dispatched to Niger.

Then, on either June 11 or 12, Grossman told Libby that Wilson's wife had been involved in planning the trip. He did not identify her by name. On June 11, a senior CIA officer also told Libby that Wilson's wife "was believed to be responsible for sending Wilson on the trip." The officer did not name her. Libby said that Cheney, on June 12, for the first time identified Wilson's wife by her maiden name and the one she used at the CIA—Valerie Plame. Cheney also told him that Plame worked at the Counterproliferation Division of the CIA—a section of the clandestine service. This suggested but did not confirm that she was an undercover CIA operative whose identity should remain confidential under federal law.

Libby was now equipped with enough information to go after Wilson. On June 23, he met with reporter Judith Miller of the *New York Times* at the Old Executive Office Building adjacent to the White House. He told her that Wilson had been dispatched to Niger by the CIA and, according to Miller's notes, "that Mr. Wilson's wife might work for the CIA."

Miller said that Libby had been "angry about reports suggesting that senior administration officials, including Mr. Cheney, had embraced skimpy intelligence about Iraq's alleged efforts to buy uranium in Africa while ignoring evidence to the contrary. . . . Mr. Libby said the vice president's office had indeed pressed the Pentagon and the State Department for more information about reports that Iraq had renewed efforts to buy uranium."

Contrary to Miller's version, there was no evidence that Libby or anyone in Cheney's office asked the State Department's Bureau of Intelligence and Research to look into the Niger uranium claim. Miller did not write a story based on the meeting with Libby.

In late June, Bush and Cheney took steps to counter growing criticism that they might have been misleading in their statements about Iraq's weapons program. Court papers said that Bush told Cheney that he had on his own authority declassified portions of the October 2002 National Intelligence Estimate and that this action gave Cheney the authority to leak some conclusions in the estimate. Cheney notified Libby on that basis.

The resulting leaks, of course, were selective. The first recipient was Bob Woodward, assistant managing editor of the *Washington Post*. In sworn testimony to Special Counsel Patrick Fitzgerald, who later obtained the indictment against Libby, Woodward said that on June 27 Libby had cited to him the NIE passage about Iraq's alleged attempts to obtain uranium yellowcake in Africa. Libby described Iraq's efforts to obtain the material as "vigorous," Woodward said.

Libby was accurate in describing the National Intelligence Estimate to Woodward. The October 2002 document said that Iraq "also began vigorously trying to procure uranium ore and yellowcake." It was a passage lifted right out of the assertive DIA report of February 12, 2002, that had captivated Cheney's attention and prompted him to ask the CIA to investigate further.

But Libby didn't provide the full context. He did not tell Woodward that the uranium claim was buried deep in the report and was not included in the ninety-six-page document's "key judgments," an intelligence term that indicates consensus among the intelligence agencies that the information is of central importance. The key judgments, printed in bold type, made up the first five pages of the report. He also did not mention that the NIE said the intelligence was unconfirmed and that Iraq already had a large supply of uranium in storage.

Woodward, in fact, was the first journalist to learn of Plame's role at the CIA. Two weeks before his meeting with Libby, Richard Armitage, then the deputy secretary of state, told Woodward in a "casual and offhand conversation" that Plame worked at the CIA "as a WMD analyst." He never wrote a story based on what he had learned.

Then, on July 6, Wilson stepped up his media offensive with an essay on the opinion page of the *New York Times* headlined "What I Didn't Find in Africa." This was his first public declaration identifying himself as the former ambassador dispatched by the CIA to Niger the previous year. He set the tone in the first sentence in the form of a question: "Did the Bush administration manipulate intelligence about Saddam Hussein's weapons programs to justify an invasion of Iraq?" Wilson then detailed why he had concluded that there had been no agreement to sell uranium to Iraq and repeated his wrong assumption that the CIA had reported directly to Cheney the results of his trip. Wilson wrote that his visit had been prompted by Cheney's questions about the alleged uranium deal. That part was accurate. But therefore, he said, the CIA must have provided the vice president "with a specific answer" based on his trip. That apparently was not true.

"I have every confidence that the answer I provided was circulated to the appropriate officials within our government," Wilson wrote. But it had been distributed only through routine channels and not to any specific policymaker. Then-CIA director George Tenet later said that his agency did not brief Bush, Cheney, or any other senior administration official on the results of Wilson's trip.

Wilson continued: "The question now is how that answer was or was not used by our political leadership. If my information was deemed inaccurate, I understand (though I would be very interested to know why). If, however, the information was ignored because it did not fit certain preconceptions about Iraq, then a legitimate argument can be made that we went to war under false pretenses."

Cheney and others at the White House were deeply angered by

the charge that he had disregarded Wilson's report about Iraq's uranium purchase. Cheney's integrity had been challenged, and he did not like it. "The . . . op-ed by Mr. Wilson was viewed in the Office of Vice President as a direct attack on the credibility of the Vice President (and the President) on a matter of signal importance: the rationale for the war in Iraq," Special Counsel Fitzgerald noted in one of his briefs. A clipping of Wilson's piece in the *Times* ended up in Cheney's office, and the vice president scribbled notes on the margin: "Have they [the CIA] done this sort of thing before? Send an amb[assador] to answer a question? Do we ordinarily send people out pro bono to do work for us? Or did his wife send him on a junket?" Cheney apparently had never traveled to Niger, an impoverished desert nation that was not a draw for tourists. Bush supporters bandied about the term "junket," but Wilson and others ridiculed the thought. "To go to Niger is not exactly a benefit," a top CIA official said. "Most people you'd have to pay big bucks to go there." Wilson received only reimbursement for travel expenses and was not paid for his services.

White House officials, nevertheless, reacted with a strong attack. What followed, in the words of Fitzgerald, was a decision by multiple people in the White House "to discredit, punish, or seek revenge against Mr. Wilson." Fitzgerald, in one of his court filings, wrote that President Bush played no role in the decision to leak Plame's identity, but the prosecutor did not make a similar assertion about Cheney. After Bush's secret declassification of portions of the October National Intelligence Estimate, top White House officials, including Libby and Karl Rove, Bush's top political adviser, embarked on a leak campaign designed to savage Wilson. The NIE material was used to show that the White House had every reason to believe that the Niger story was true.

On July 8, 2003, Bush administration figures continued a new round of leaks to the news media. Armitage was the first government official to tip off conservative columnist Robert Novak that Plame worked at the CIA. Novak later confirmed her employment via Karl Rove who then wrote a column on July 14 exposing her to the world, saying, "Valerie Plame is an Agency operative on weapons of mass destruction. Two senior administration officials told me Wilson's wife suggested sending him to Niger to investigate the Italian report." Novak's column was referred by the CIA to the Justice Department for investigation into possible unauthorized disclosure of classified information. Fitzgerald eventually took over the probe, and Libby was subsequently indicted for allegedly lying to prosecutors and to a grand jury investigating his role in the leaks.

After eventually being exposed as Novak's initial source, Armitage insisted his reference to Plame had been a casual aside. "I said, 'I don't know, but I think his wife worked out there [the CIA].'" But Novak later wrote, "Armitage did not slip me this information as idle chitchat. . . . He made clear that he considered it especially suited for my column."

Also on July 8, Libby again met with Judith Miller, this time over breakfast at the St. Regis Hotel, two blocks from the White House. Libby reminded Miller that Wilson's wife worked at the CIA, but wrongly described her office as WINPAC, an analytical, not operational, department. At the same time, Libby muddled the substance of Wilson's debriefing report and tried to use it against him. Libby told Miller that Wilson had in fact helped support the conclusion that Iraq had been uranium shopping. Libby discussed Wilson's report of meeting briefly with Ibrahim Mayaki, the former Nigerien foreign minister who recalled having spoken with a member of an Iraqi delegation in 1999. The Iraqi had wanted to discuss trade, and this was "interpreted [by Mayaki] as an effort by Iraq to obtain uranium."

On July 12, Cheney and Libby plotted a new attack during a short return flight from Norfolk, Virginia, to Washington on *Air Force Two*. There was no evidence that Cheney directed Libby to discuss Plame, but he urged the selective leaking of Wilson's classified debriefing to show that Wilson, rather than closing the book on the uranium story, had actually bolstered it by referring to Mayaki's speculation.

Libby and perhaps other officials spoke with at least three reporters that day, including Matthew Cooper at *Time* magazine. A day earlier, Rove had told Cooper, "Don't get too far out on Wilson," suggesting that the White House had the goods on the former ambassador. He wouldn't say what it was, although he told Cooper that neither Tenet nor Cheney had dispatched Wilson to Niger. He only hinted at who it might be. Wilson's wife, Rove said, worked at the "agency on WMD," according to Cooper's notes of the conversation.

So on the following day, Cooper asked Libby if he had heard that it was Wilson's wife who had sent the diplomat to Niger. "Yeah, I've heard that, too," Libby replied, according to Cooper's recollection.

Libby also chatted on the phone with Judith Miller, who was at her home in Sag Harbor, New York. He again discussed Wilson's wife and the fact that she worked at the CIA and criticized Wilson's Niger investigation, saying it was unclear whether Wilson had talked to any of the Nigerien officials who had dealt with the 1999 Iraqi delegation.

Also on July 12, a White House official talked to Walter Pincus, the *Washington Post*'s distinguished intelligence reporter. The source, who spoke to Pincus on grounds of anonymity, told him that the White House "had not paid attention to the former ambassador's CIA-sponsored trip to Niger because it was set up as a boondoggle by his wife."

Wilson's op-ed prompted a steady flow of articles questioning not only Cheney's but also Bush's veracity. Tenet had already apologized for not having reviewed the speech and for failing to direct that the 16 words be removed. As the controversy about Wilson's Niger trip grew, the White House decided to go public in explaining how the 16 words had gotten into Bush's State of the Union speech. At a news conference on July 22, Hadley used the same argument Libby had used with Judith Miller of the *New York Times* about Mayaki, the former Nigerien foreign minister. Hadley admitted that he had coordinated the content of the speech and also apologized. He said he had forgotten that Tenet had previously raised this issue, arguing that a reference about uranium purchases had to be removed from a Bush speech delivered in Cincinnati three months earlier. But Hadley also contended that the CIA debriefing of Wilson showed that the 16 words had been "factually . . . accurate" because of Mayaki's sheer speculation. US intelligence had wrongly assumed that Mayaki had been referring to Ambassador Wissam al-Zahawie's 1999 visit to Africa. In fact, Mayaki had been talking about Foreign Minister al-Sahhaf's visit later that year during an Organization of African Unity meeting in Algiers. Sahhaf—Baghdad Bob—did not bring up the subject of uranium at their inconsequential encounter in June 1999.

On July 30, the CIA filed a report with the Justice Department alerting the prosecutors that a crime might have been committed in the disclosure of Plame's identity. On September 29, the Justice Department asked the FBI to investigate. On December 30, then-attorney general John Ashcroft recused himself, and his deputy, James Comey, appointed Fitzgerald as special counsel. The investigation continued into 2007.

Fitzgerald's preliminary findings showed that the revelation of Plame's name was crass politics tinged with malice and that officials sought to get even with Wilson, undermine his credibility, and at the same time attack his wife. When her name was revealed, she was still classified by the spy agency designation "non-official-cover officer," or NOC. NOCs, unlike most CIA case officers, do not work out of embassies. They do not have diplomatic cover, and if they are detained or arrested in a foreign country, they have no diplomatic immunity. One of Plame's unofficial covers had been as an "energy analyst" for Brewster Jennings and Associates—a private, Boston-based CIA front company. Plame may have been phasing out of her NOC assignment when the White House blew her cover, because she had been talking about spending more time at home with her two children. But the revelation of her identity immediately ruined her career.

The White House campaign of innuendo against Wilson also suggested that he had been selected for the plum assignment not for his investigative acumen but because of nepotism, further impugning Plame. A Senate Intelligence Committee report on Iraq intelligence failures said that Plame did recommend Wilson for the trip; Wilson said that was not so. Wilson said that Plame's boss at the CIA had asked her if her husband might be interested in undertaking the trip and to write up a brief memo about why he might be a good choice. A senior CIA official at the time confirmed that Plame had not volunteered her husband's name.

Wilson said one of the White House's motives for leaking his wife's identity was "pure vengeance," but he thought that Bush administration officials also used the case to divert attention from the real issue. They avoided focusing on the fact that Bush had misled the public about Iraqi nuclear plans and were able "to change the subject from the 16 words to Wilson and his wife." Wilson wrote a memoir that included details about his trip to Niger and conducted a survey when he traveled around the country for speaking engagements to discuss the Iraq invasion. He asked audience members: Raise your hand if you know who wrote the 16 words in Bush's State of the Union address. "Nobody raises their hand," Wilson said. But he asked the follow-up question in the opposite way: How many of you don't know my wife's name? "Again, nobody raises their hand." No one had heard of Michael Gerson, Bush's chief speechwriter, nor of Robert Joseph, who got approval from Alan Foley of the CIA to insert the

16 words in the 2003 State of the Union message. But everyone knew Valerie Plame. Wilson also viewed the aggressive White House attacks against him as a warning to others who might have contemplated publicly criticising the administration's prewar claims about Iraq's weapons. "Should you do to us what Wilson did to us, we will give you grief," Wilson said in describing what he believed was the implicit admonition from the White House. "Be afraid. Be very afraid."

While White House public relations operatives worked overtime to combat the damage done by Wilson's revelations, fallout from the fake Italian letter was causing problems for the British government, which was closely aligned with the Bush administration throughout the run-up to the Iraq war, and for the Italian intelligence service, SISMI, whose operatives had first made up the fraud about Niger.

Beyond supporting the Iraq invasion, Britain allowed the Bush administration to engage in circular reporting by pretending that the British MI6 reporting on Iraq's nuclear program was somehow different or separate from what the US Intelligence Community had. In fact, the half-baked evidence presented by Britain came from the same sources, most if not all of it from Rocco Martino and the Italian letter.

Chapter 12

Tony Blair, a Friend in Deed

President Bush's 16 words, lifted almost exactly from the British white paper on Iraq's alleged weapons of mass destruction, also haunted British prime minister Tony Blair.

The fifty-page dossier, released on September 24, 2002, was written by the Joint Intelligence Committee, a cabinet office that oversees British intelligence collection and produces for the government assessments based on the intelligence. The dossier was presented as a factually based summary of Saddam Hussein's illicit weapons and of his intentions to use them. But the public document, drafted with significant guidance from Blair, his chief of staff, and numerous Whitehall public relations advisors, would later be described by critics inside and outside of government as shoddy propaganda, blending bad intelligence with crass political overtones.

One of its key statements, "There is intelligence that Iraq has sought the supply of significant quantities of uranium from Africa," was a precursor to President Bush's 16 words, written some four months later.

The White House speechwriting team improved on the British report, personalizing it by inserting Saddam Hussein's name in place of Iraq and adding urgency by saying that the shopping had been conducted "recently."

Blair wrote the foreword to the white paper, which was presented to Parliament and the British public to encourage a vote to support Britain's impending participation in the US-led invasion of Iraq.

"What I believe," he wrote, is that "the assessed intelligence has established *beyond doubt* that Saddam has continued to produce chemical and biological weapons, that he continues in his efforts to develop nuclear weapons, and that he has been able to extend the range of his ballistic missile programme."

Blair had been less convinced several days earlier. In an unguarded comment while visiting Bush at Camp David on September 7, he admitted that virtually no intelligence had been developed about Iraq's weapons programs since UN inspectors had departed in 1998. "We haven't the faintest idea of what has been going on in the last four years other than what we know is an attempt to carry on rebuilding weapons," he said. "The details of it is something that the Iraqi regime should be forced to disclose."

While the uranium claim was the most resonant in the United States, in Britain, Blair's most controversial statement in the white paper was a frightening declaration that Saddam Hussein could launch WMDs on forty-five minutes' notice.

"His military planning allows for some of the WMD to be ready within forty-five minutes of an order to use them."

This alarming declaration was based on third-hand intelligence originating with an untested source in the Iraqi military. Two years later, it was withdrawn as not credible by MI6, Britain's foreign intelligence service. Military intelligence had warned that the intelligence was suspect even before it had gone into the dossier.

But that September 2002, before the ink on the white paper was dry, colorful London tabloids reacted with unabashed—if exaggerated—horror. "Brits 45 Mins from Doom," screamed Britain's mass circulation *Sun.* The competing *Daily Star,* meanwhile, proclaimed, "Mad Saddam Ready to Attack: 45 Minutes from a Chemical War."

Before MI6 killed the intelligence and before the white paper was published, British intelligence officials were aware that the hair-trigger claim referred only to battlefield arms, such as cannons and mortars, and not to strategic weapons, such as missiles. That distinction was not subtle, and the dossier cast an impression that cities in the Mideast and in Cyprus, where British troops were stationed, were at risk. Perhaps even London. Blair later told Parliament's Intelligence and Security Committee that he had been unaware that the warning applied only to battlefield weapons. The committee, which conducted one of several British investigations into the September white paper and the UK's underlying intelligence, strongly suggested that Blair had been eager to emphasize the forty-five-minute claim. Its report noted that in the dossier's first draft, dated September 10, the claim appeared twice—once in the executive summary and once in the main text. But by the time the document was published two weeks later and after careful vetting by Blair and his staff, it appeared four times, including in Blair's own foreword. The committee's report complains that because the manuscript was written "for the public and not for experienced readers of intelligence material," it should have "highlighted" that the intelligence referred only to battlefield, not strategic, weapons.

Blair could have avoided the doomsday impression he left with the forty-five-minute claim had he not deleted from the final report a passage he had penned in the first draft of his foreword. "The case I make," he had written, "is not that Saddam could launch a nuclear attack on London or another part of the UK (he could not)." The sentence was not included in the September 24 dossier.

The Bush administration, which had no independent evidence that the information was true, also found the dossier's forty-five-minute claim irresistible. On the same day the white paper was released, Ari Fleischer, Bush's press secretary at the time, alerted reporters to the "new information" contained in the British report—"particularly about the forty-five-minute threshold by which Saddam Hussein has got his biological and chemical weapons triggered to be launched."

Four days later, on September 28, Bush repeated Blair's statement in his weekly radio address. "The Iraqi regime possesses biological and chemical weapons. . . . And, according to the British government, could launch a biological or chemical attack in as little as forty-five minutes after the order is given." The United States had no intelligence whatsoever to corroborate that claim, according to a former CIA official.

Subsequent official investigations of prewar intelligence in both the United States and Great Britain concluded that the intelligence on each side of the Atlantic had been abysmal. But one of the British investigations, a judicial inquiry, took the matter where the American probes had not dared. It looked into how the government had used the intelligence. It found that the Blair government had exaggerated the intelligence, keying on the role of 10 Downing Street in the drafting of the white paper.

Officially, the author of the white paper—except for Blair's foreword—was John Scarlett, at the time chairman of the Joint Intelligence Committee (JIC) and now head of MI6. He was knighted on December 30, 2006. Blair and his top aides reviewed several drafts of the dossier and recommended a number of changes before publication. Among those reading the material were Blair's chief of staff, Jonathan Powell, and his top public relations adviser, Alastair Campbell. A number of midlevel Downing Street press officers and special advisers also reviewed the drafts, routinely urging Scarlett to emphasize claims in the report even if the underlying intelligence was thin.

Perhaps the most egregious example of 10 Downing Street manipulation came in a sentence that was to have preceded the forty-five-minute assertion. An early draft said that Saddam Hussein would use chemical or biological weapons "if he believes he is under threat." Scarlett dropped that line after he received a desperate e-mail from Powell, complaining that it presented "a bit of a problem" because it suggested that Iraq posed "no [chemical or biological] threat and we will only create one if we attack him."

In addition to the investigation by the Parliament's intelligence committee, other official inquiries were conducted by its Foreign Affairs Committee and by two panels appointed by the Blair government. The first, begun in August 2003, was a judicial inquiry chaired by Law Lord Hutton, a jurist who also went by the title of Baron Hutton. The Hutton inquiry, which documented much of the evidence of manipulation by Blair and his aides in the drafting of the dossier, was created after Britain's top defense WMD analyst, David Kelly, committed suicide. He had been a key source for the BBC's Andrew Gilligan, who charged that Blair's government, and notably Campbell, had intentionally "sexed up" the white paper.

Quoting an unnamed source, Gilligan had reported on March 29, 2003, that Blair's government probably knew ahead of time that claims in the September 24, 2002, dossier were exaggerated and that British officials had misrepresented the available intelligence about Iraqi weapons. The British government subsequently revealed that

Kelly, an internationally respected specialist on biological warfare and consultant in the development of the white paper, had been Gilligan's primary source. Kelly, who had also served as a UN weapons inspector in Iraq, committed suicide on July 18, 2003. Some attributed Kelly's death to personal problems and depression. Others said he was worried that he might be charged with perjury for lying to Parliament about his contacts with the BBC.

The Hutton inquiry exonerated the Blair government despite evidence and testimony elicited during the investigation disclosing that the wording of the dossier had been altered to present the strongest possible case for war, some of the changes had been instigated by Campbell, and Intelligence Community experts had expressed reservations about the wording of the dossier. The committee's report did say, however, that the JIC may have been "subconsciously influenced" by the pressure applied by the government.

E-mails introduced as evidence during the inquiry left little doubt that the pressure was enormous. Correspondence between Blair spokesman Campbell and JIC chairman Scarlett, which took place as the drafting process was concluding, showed that Campbell wanted to toughen the language about Iraq's illicit weaponry. He asked Scarlett whether the claim that Saddam Hussein had sought uranium in Africa could be changed to say that Iraq had "secured" the material. Scarlett in this instance refused. Campbell also told Scarlett that Blair wanted the dossier to include an item, deleted from an earlier draft, claiming that Iraq could produce a "radiological device," or dirty bomb, in the matter of months. Scarlett repeated what he had told Campbell the previous day: The UK had no intelligence that Saddam Hussein wanted a dirty bomb.

But Scarlett was more accommodating with other requests. On the forty-five-minute claim, for instance, an early draft had stated that Iraq "may be able to" or "could" deploy the chemical or biological weapons within forty-five minutes. After Campbell complained that "may" was too wimpy, Scarlett changed the final wording to assert that the weapons "are deployable" within forty-five minutes and that the Iraqi military "are able to deploy" the weapons inside the forty-five minutes.

Other Downing Street officials also chimed in with recommendations. Daniel Pruce, a Foreign Office press aide assigned to Blair's office, understood that attributing information to intelligence had a special cachet with reporters. "The more we advertise that unsupported assertions [e.g., Saddam attaches great importance to the possession of WMD] come from intelligence, the better." He also recommended greater demonization of Hussein—"a few quotes from Saddam to demonstrate his aggressive intent and hatred of his neighbors and the West"—and suggested "the need to personalize the dossier onto Saddam as much as possible, for example by replacing references to Iraq with references to Saddam."

The second probe, launched on February 3, 2004, headed by Lord Butler of Brockwell, limited its investigation to the quality of the intelligence and did not look into the government's use of the intelligence. Butler, née Robin Butler, a career civil servant who served five prime ministers, directed the July 2004 report, which was authoritative and also very British—understated and only mildly critical. It did not call for firings or punishments but did conclude that many of the claims contained in the Joint Intelligence Committee's dossier of September 24, 2002, were too assertive and did not reflect the ambiguity or thinness of the intelligence. Similar criticisms were made by the Senate Intelligence Committee about the summary of the CIA's National Intelligence Estimate on Iraq of October 2002 and the public white paper issued the same month.

Butler's panel reviewed hundreds of JIC reports on Iraq and found that the intelligence that formed the basis for war had been unreliable. It concluded that MI6 did not properly vet its sources and overrelied on Iraqi dissidents, whose interest was in toppling the Iraqi regime. The result, it said, was that "more weight was placed on the intelligence than it could bear" and as a consequence judgments stretched the intelligence "to the outer limits."

> In general, we found that the original intelligence material was correctly reported in JIC assessments. . . . We should record in particular that we have found no evidence of deliberate distortion or of culpable negligence.
>
> We examined JIC assessments to see whether there was evidence that the judgments inside them were systematically distorted by non-intelligence factors, in particular the influence of the policy positions of departments. We found no evidence of JIC assessments and the judgments inside them being pulled in any particular direction to meet the policy concerns of senior officials on the JIC.

However, Butler made clear that there had been a "strain" between Downing Street and the JIC in producing the white paper and recommended that the government, not the Intelligence Community, take responsibility for future documents. A member of his team, Field Marshal Lord Inge, agreed that the line between intelligence and propaganda had been blurred too much. "Intelligence and public relations should be kept apart," he said.

The Butler report shed some light on how MI6 concluded there was merit to the claim that Iraq had shopped for uranium in Africa. It disclosed that MI6's conclusions were based in part on Iraqi ambassador Wissam al-Zahawie's uneventful journey to Niger. The British government acknowledged that one of its reports came from SISMI and was based on the phony Italian documents. Pinning its intelligence on al-Zahawie's trip showed that MI6 fell into the same deductive trap that blinded other intelligence services, including many at the CIA: The Iraqi diplomat's visit could only have been to negotiate a uranium sale because Niger had little else to offer and Hussein was a bad guy.

The Butler report also said there was intelligence that in 1999 Iraq had inquired about buying uranium from the Democratic Republic of the Congo. The CIA, too, had that intelligence, but it was not considered reliable by most analysts at the time. It was later judged not credible and recalled.

The British government and intelligence services insisted that they had some other secret bit of information, but since it came from a foreign intelligence service, they could not divulge any of the details, even to the CIA. The mysterious unshareable intelligence also pointed to al-Zahawie's trip to Niger, suggesting that it may have been based on the same Italian intelligence, perhaps provided by another country. In intelligence, this is known as circular reporting. Most intelligence services seek to protect themselves from inadvertent duplicative reporting, which they can mistake as corroboration; the third-country rule always made it difficult to learn the pedigree of shared intelligence.

Sir Richard Dearlove, who retired as head of Britain's foreign espionage agency, MI6, in 2004, told Parliament's intelligence committee that his agency had obtained the Niger intelligence from two separate sources—the first time in June 2002 and the second that September.

Foreign Secretary Jack Straw echoed that claim. "The information on which we relied, which was completely separate from the now notorious forged documents, came from foreign intelligence sources," Straw said, even after the White House acknowledged that Bush had erred in including the 16 words in his State of the Union speech.

Dearlove told the House of Commons intelligence panel that one of the pieces of evidence was based on documentary sources. Officials on both sides of the Atlantic confirmed that the provenance of the documentary evidence was SISMI, and it was the same faux intelligence shared earlier with the United States. Dearlove's second source has never been identified, even to MI6's most trusted ally, the CIA.

In correspondence with us, Dearlove declined to discuss with us the uranium intelligence. He cryptically cautioned us to "not fall into the trap of thinking that the fake Italian documents had anything to do with the original intelligence."

But the dominant view of the Intelligence Community in the United States is that Britain was faking it. A senior CIA officer who retired after the US invasion of Iraq and who oversaw much of the agency's collection of intelligence at the time faulted the British government for having given prominent yet undeserved credibility to the Niger claim. "What you're dealing with is sort of a bureaucratic screwup . . . in the way they handled the third-country rule and handling of intelligence," the CIA source said, adding that all the British really had was the phony SISMI intelligence. "There was only one body of intelligence. They actually had it right after it was sent to us."

He dismissed Britain's claim that its hands were tied because of the rules governing intelligence sharing. "They actually shared with us far more sensitive intelligence" than whatever information might have been provided by the so-called "second" source, he said.

The former senior CIA officer said that MI6 was more responsive to the political winds coming from the prime minister's office than the CIA was to pressure from the White House. The CIA also came under criticism for caving in to administration pressure by casting Iraq as a more serious threat than the available evidence supported. MI6 "is much more a part of policy than we are, and that's why they can't back off" the claim of having independent intelligence on Niger, the former CIA officer said. Admitting they had nothing, he said, would be embarrassing to Blair and his government.

Whatever it was, Britain's "other" intelligence did not impress

Brian Jones, a senior Defense Ministry intelligence analyst who reviewed the dossier before it was published. "There was other [than the SISMI] reporting," said Jones. "I can't remember the details of it, [but] from our perspective, that information didn't harden up any assessments." In other words, it was mostly fluff.

One dissenting comment came from Parliament's Foreign Affairs Committee, which declared it was totally puzzled by the government's explanations of why British officials stood by the Niger claim. The committee asked Blair to elaborate on what that intelligence was, and the prime minister answered that indeed "there was intelligence to that effect" that "at the time was judged by the Joint Intelligence Committee to be correct." Then he added, "Until we investigate properly, we are simply not in a position to say whether that is so."

The committee could make no sense of the story. "We conclude that it is very odd indeed that the Government asserts that it was not relying on evidence which has since been shown to be forged, but that eight months later it is still reviewing the other evidence." It said the dossier's assertion that Iraq had been uranium shopping should at the very least have been qualified to "reflect the uncertainty."

In 2002, intelligence on Iraq was at the top of the list for American and British collection and analysis. Some British intelligence analysts dissented in much the same way that their counterparts in America did, complaining that there was little evidence that Iraq was seeking nuclear weapons. Brian Jones, head of the Ministry of Defense's WMD intelligence branch at the time, told the Hutton inquiry that he had expressed concern about the information being made public by British officials, particularly in the September 24 dossier.

Jones and his staff objected to reliance on secondhand information from unknown sources to describe Iraq's weapons capability. One of Jones's internal documents, written a week before the release

of the dossier, criticized drafts submitted for review as drawing conclusions not sufficiently supported by evidence. Jones also had long-
standing complaints about the use of the term "weapons of mass
destruction," which he said didn't distinguish among chemical, biological, and nuclear weapons. Jones believed, as did many other members of the Intelligence Community and the military, that only nuclear
bombs constituted true weapons of mass destruction.

"There was a disjoint," Jones told us. "Mr. Blair was stating his
own view that there was no doubt about these things [Iraq's WMD
program] in a language [reflecting] that was the general view of British intelligence. Nobody at my lowly level was prepared to argue that
was the case."

Jones said his "argument with the whole process was that there
remained a big question mark over it. One couldn't make categorical
statements. My particular objection that indeed I wrote at the time in
September 2002 in official internal documents that came to
light . . . was 'you can't actually say that, we don't have the backup
from them. The assessments are not those that are being projected.'"

Jones compared the capitulation of Britain's intelligence leadership because of political pressure in London to former CIA director
George Tenet's assurance to Bush that America's intelligence on Iraq
was a "slam dunk." The British intelligence chiefs, represented at the
JIC, "were taking a similar line," Jones said. "They were acceding to
political pressure, to political requirements, trying to maintain credibility with the politicians for an organization that [was] under a lot of
pressure to justify [its] value, especially on the US side since 9/11."

Critics accused Blair of being Bush's lapdog for supporting the
war. Some speculated that Blair, among other things, had concluded
that he could pick up some favors from a grateful president, including
a pledge from Bush to follow through on his "road map" for Israeli
disengagement from the West Bank and Gaza Strip.

Blair also might have been considering Britain's historical role in

Iraq. The country's borders were drawn up in 1918 by the British colonial authorities, which had consolidated three separate provinces—the current Sunni, Shiite, and Kurdish regions—that had been part of the former Ottoman empire. They decided that Sunnis should run the country and selected a king as its titular head. Kurds were denied independence because Britain wanted to control the oil fields in their territory. The majority Shiites remained disenfranchised because British authorities said they were incapable of adapting to democracy.

Britain and the United States had an obvious, long-standing, and very close relationship on cultural, military, economic, and political affairs. The countries maintained superb cooperation on intelligence. Tenet, the head of the CIA, and his counterpart, Dearlove, met regularly, including an annual summit of the two intelligence services' top management and several other more private meetings.

A telling illustration of the closeness of the two agencies was the unpublicized visit by Dearlove and his top aides to CIA headquarters the day after the September 11 attacks. They had come to offer comfort and voice support during one of America's most traumatic moments.

One summit meeting, on July 20, 2002, attracted considerable attention, not for what was discussed, which was not revealed, but for what Dearlove told his government upon his return.

At the meeting with Tenet at CIA headquarters in Langley, Virginia, Dearlove learned that war with Iraq was inevitable, according to the so-called Downing Street Memos, leaked to the *Sunday Times* of London. Included were notes of Dearlove's meeting with Blair and his cabinet on July 23, 2002. Dearlove, or "C," the code name for MI6 directors, told Blair that the war would be justified in the United States through a "conjunction of terrorism and WMD. . . . The intelligence and facts were being fixed around the policy," according to the notes published in 2005.

In 2002, the Bush administration viewed British support for the looming war with Iraq as critical, and the CIA shared virtually everything it had on Iraq. Robin Cook, a former foreign secretary, told Parliament the following year that he would be "astonished" if British reliance on US intelligence to prepare the September dossier had not been "immense." Cook resigned from his post as leader of the House of Commons in the Blair government three days before the Iraq invasion, to protest British involvement.

"The United States and the United Kingdom have a unique intelligence relationship which has probably never existed in any period of history, in which on our side we have full transparency and we strive to secure full transparency on their side," he said.

Then Cook brought up a long-held British belief that has been a major sore point with CIA case officers. "As a rough rule of thumb, and it is very rough," Cook said, the British "tend to be rather better at gathering human intelligence. . . . The Americans are . . . more formidable in technological ways of gathering intelligence."

That was a salient point when a Foreign Affairs Committee report in Parliament concluded that Britain had relied too much on US technical intelligence.

CIA officers who worked closely with MI6 found that the relations were not always smooth. One described the service as beset by "British arrogance." "That's the way they are," said a retired CIA station chief in Europe who dealt regularly with MI6. "They still look at us as very much a junior partner when it comes to professionalism and competence. . . . If you give them 8,000 reports and they give you one, they handle that one like it was made of gold."

Another retired CIA officer said that the snobbery is a by-product of MI6's preference for recruiting officers from Britain's upper classes. "This is the third generation of sons and daughters who are now in the service, and they really think this is, like, born to royalty," he said. "They always know everything better."

The cultural tension between officers of the two intelligence services was of little consequence. The leaders of both countries realized the importance of shared intelligence, especially as they prepared for war and needed to convince their separate constituencies that a conflict was unavoidable.

Brian Jones, the former defense analyst, agreed that there were cultural differences in the intelligence services of both countries but emphasized that those differences were not as significant as their shared objectives. And they had one critical trait in common, Jones said: "Intelligence operatives in both countries were loath to stand up to their superiors when they saw something amiss." The consequence, in both countries, was disastrous. With no real challenge to the intelligence, the Niger uranium claim, the reconstituted nuclear program, and the forty-five-minute hair trigger for chemical and biological weapons made war inevitable.

But the lowly origins of the uranium claim were slow to emerge. Italian officials worked for more than a year to divert blame and responsibility from their own intelligence services, blaming France for propagating the ruse.

Chapter 13

Let's Blame France

Beginning in mid-2004, Italian officials tried to mute the growing public uproar that their own intelligence service, SISMI, had been behind Rocco Martino's forged documents by accusing the French of masterminding the scam. The Italian spin was that French intelligence, the General Directorate for External Security, had been engaged in a diabolical conspiracy to plant phony intelligence about Iraq's nuclear weapons program and then expose it as fraudulent.

The Italian argument was that France wanted to undermine America's claim that Hussein was pursuing banned weapons in the hope of slowing down, or even halting, the march to war. The French government, after all, opposed Bush's hard-line policy on Iraq and believed UN inspectors should be given more time to see if Iraq had complied with resolutions to disarm.

As evidence against France, SISMI leaked a surveillance photograph that showed Martino and the French DGSE station chief from Brussels huddled together at a meeting in Luxembourg, where Martino ran an intelligence consulting business. The DGSE acknowledged that the Luxembourg meeting had taken place in late June 2002 but said that was when Martino had passed the forged documents to the spy agency and asked for $100,000. The French had refused. But Italian officials said this contact was evidence not that Martino tried to peddle the documents, but that the French were using Martino to disseminate them. Italian intelligence had been tailing Martino—something he feared during his meetings with Burba on October 7 through 9, 2002, when he gave her the Italian letter and other documents he had peddled to the French.

The public scapegoating of France came shortly after London newspapers in August 2004 published stories that for the first time identified Rocco Martino as a key middleman in the forgery scam and quoted him as saying that SISMI was behind the plot. On August 1, the *Sunday Times* of London reported that a "small time tipster," whom it identified only as Giacomo, had admitted to disseminating the bogus documents. "SISMI wanted me to pass on the documents, but they didn't want anyone to know they had been involved," Giacomo told the *Times*. On the following day, the *Financial Times* disclosed that Giacomo was Rocco Martino.

SISMI, hoping to protect its image and derail criticism, launched a disinformation campaign on August 9, 2004, eight days after publication of the *Sunday Times* story, by planting a story in the newspaper *Libero,* a small, right-wing publication. Renato Farino, *Libero*'s deputy editor who was later discovered to have been on the SISMI payroll, penned a long story laying out for the first time the case against the French. In his thinly sourced essay, he wrote that Martino had passed the forgeries to Burba under the direction of his French intelligence handlers, who wanted to embarrass Bush. He said that after American intelligence analyzed Burba's documents, "they were induced to accept them as true by French confirmation," as well as by confirmation from the British, who had received them from the French as well. "Aren't they ashamed?" Farino indignantly asked about the French. Later, prosecutors in Milan discovered that SISMI had paid Farino at least 10,000 euros for his assistance in other operations.

SISMI had launched a major internal investigation and concluded the following year that at least some of its officers had conspired in creating and disseminating the forgeries. Not wanting that to be known, SISMI and the Berlusconi government had devised a cover story, saying that they had obtained the documents from a diplomat at the Nigerien embassy in Rome, but that the documents had been prepared at the behest of the French.

They presented that cover story when the Italian Parliament began an investigation. Italian senator Luigi Malabarba, a member of the legislature's intelligence oversight committee, COPACO, told us that SISMI officials had testified in closed session that they had "documentation" that "implicates the French secret service." He said that SISMI claimed to have "evidence of a transmission of [the phony] documents [from the Nigerien embassy in Rome] to France, and back to Rome." But Malabarba told us he was not totally convinced of SISMI's story. "There may be a desire to make it look like France guided the whole thing right from the beginning," he said. "It would be in SISMI's interest to say that they [the French] did it."

Indeed, some SISMI officials, including its then-director, Nicolo Pollari, might have believed for a while that France had some culpability, if not in the creation of the documents, then perhaps in their dissemination. While they knew that some of their own people were involved in the scam, they decided to pursue the French angle in any case. Thus, they staged a bizarre unannounced visit by a SISMI delegation to DGSE headquarters in Paris in early 2004. Locals refer to the compound, in the working-class twentieth arrondissement of the

French capital, as *La Piscine*, the swimming pool, because of its proximity to the French Swimming Federation. Built in the nineteenth century, the nondescript cluster of barrackslike buildings, hidden from view by a high wall, was formerly a women's prison.

The purpose of the visit by the Italian delegation was a puzzle, and the DGSE learned through official channels that SISMI was blaming them for the hoax. DGSE officials refused to talk with the SISMI delegation.

"They [DGSE] literally threw them out," chortled a former senior CIA officer who had been posted in Paris at the time. "I'm not sure they even got to [Pierre] Brochand [DGSE's director]. I think he made them see the deputy director. It was the deputy director who threw them out. . . . The French were really angry about [being blamed for the forgeries]. They told the Italians to get the hell out of there, get out of the office, and get out of town." The CIA officer said he did not remember the name of the official who had headed the SISMI delegation, but said it was the agency's director at the time. That would have been Pollari. Pollari and other SISMI officials declined our requests for interviews.

The confrontation between the two intelligence services was so unusual that word of it leaked as soon as it happened. "I knew about the Italians coming to Paris and formally charging the French," said the former CIA officer. "I knew it the day it happened. I knew all about it before they [the DGSE] raised it with me."

CIA officers close to the case said that the French government had nothing to do with the hoax. DGSE, in fact, shared intelligence with the United States and routinely debunked reports flowing to the CIA that Iraq was seeking uranium from Niger or elsewhere in Africa. But the Italian attempt to blame the French government played well in Washington as the Berlusconi government had hoped, because the Bush administration had been angered by French opposition to the US invasion of Iraq. Top officials such as Douglas Feith, the undersecretary of defense who founded the Office of Special Plans, and other administration supporters of military action routinely leaked questionable intelligence suggesting financial, political, and military links between France and Saddam Hussein. Many of the stories were tall tales attributed to US "intelligence sources" that France had sold Iraq nuclear and missile technology equipment. One of the most spectacular claims appeared in the *Washington Times,* a favorite of Bush administration neoconservatives. The newspaper reported that the French government had issued French passports to Hussein's most hated cronies so they could escape to Europe in the early weeks of the invasion.

Wilkerson, Powell's chief of staff, scoffed at those stories. "Contrary to what you were hearing in the papers and other places, one of the best relationships we had in fighting terrorists and in intelligence in general was with guess who? The French. In fact, it was probably the best. And they were right in there with us."

French intelligence was key to tracking down and debunking reports of illicit uranium sales because French companies dominate the global uranium business, and its former colonies are the most active producers. "Our interest in Niger, or any of those places in Africa that produce uranium, is long-standing," a former CIA case officer said. "And the question of where they're selling the uranium is a long-standing issue that we covered [with DGSE] over and over and over again: . . . what Iraq, Syria, Libya, and Egypt were doing looking for uranium in various places. I had fairly regular contact with the French checking out various rumors related to the export from those mines. And the reason we went to the French, of course, was because the French owned those mines."

The CIA asked the DGSE to check into SISMI's Niger intelligence at least twice in 2002. The most urgent request came after Vice President Cheney took an active interest after reading the February 12

DIA report that prompted Ambassador Joseph Wilson's trip to Niger.

DGSE's point man on proliferation issues was the chief of the agency's security intelligence service, Alain Chouet, described by Americans who knew him as an intelligent, hard-drinking, and occasionally foul-mouthed professional spy with a well-trimmed beard and a Gallic contempt for US policy. Chouet left DGSE's Security Intelligence Service in October 2002 because of a political shakeup. An expert on the Middle East and Islamic fundamentalism, Chouet was a tough man for the CIA to deal with.

"Chouet is very anti-American," said a former senior CIA officer who had some run-ins with him. "He had this ingrained belief that every time we went to him, we were holding something important back from him, stuff that he really needed to know. He always saw a skunk out on the woodpile somewhere. He could never get down to the business and answer the goddamn question. We asked him that question [about Niger's uranium] because we kept having people coming in and saying the Iraqis have a deal with the Nigeriens for uranium, and we're duty bound to check with the French. Chouet was always reading something into that shit."

Most of the CIA's dealings with the DGSE over African uranium issues were with Chouet's deputies and with liaison officers. These officials, according to the former CIA officer, provided solid, credible answers. Chouet was also cooperative when pressed—especially after Cheney triggered the new urgency. At one point in the late spring of 2002, Chouet dispatched a small team of clandestine operatives to Niger to double- and triple-check whether anything may have been missed in earlier assessments. Again, the French agents concluded that yellowcake had not been diverted from the two operating uranium mines and no back-channel deal was in the works.

Chouet said he considered the CIA request for information about

Niger a "high priority urgency." "I arranged a deep undercover mission. . . . Five of our best men were part of the team, with deep knowledge of Niger and all of the issues connected to yellowcake. My men stayed in Africa for a couple of weeks, and once back they told me a very simple thing: 'The American information on uranium is all bullshit.'"

Chouet declined to be interviewed by us, citing an order by the French government to make no public statements pending completion of fraud investigations into the hoax that are being conducted in Italy and the United States. "I have to comply with that order," he wrote us in an e-mail.

Chouet gave at least two interviews before the gag order in late 2005 about France's role, and those accounts differed in significant ways. One was published in the Italian newspaper *La Repubblica,* which reported that he said that the CIA in late June 2002 had provided his agency with "samples" of the forgeries. "I can remember they were no more than a dozen pages," the Italian daily quoted him as saying. "There was a short introduction where the CIA explained the meaning of the documents and no more than three complete documents, I would say. After a quick scrutiny, we decided it was all rubbish, gross fakes."

He told the *Los Angeles Times,* however, that the CIA asked questions about the content of Rocco Martino's documents, which the DGSE had recently obtained and dismissed as bogus. "We thought they [the Americans] were in possession of the documents," he told the *Times.* "The words were very similar."

The former Paris-based CIA officer said that the US government did not have the documents at the time. "There never was a time when we had a formal discussion with the French about the Iraq–Niger documents," he said. "I asked about specific questions [based on the SISMI reports] and would submit the stuff on that basis. We talked about Niger, Iraq, but never about the documents."

And, according to *La Repubblica*, Chouet maintained that the DGSE met with Martino only twice. Once was at the end of June, when Martino passed the documents in Luxembourg to Jacques Nadal, who had been appointed DGSE station chief several weeks earlier, and asked for $100,000 for the entire lot. Their encounter was photographed by SISMI. The second time, Chouet told the Italian newspaper, was at the end of July, "when we told him his stuff was a trashy forgery."

"The French didn't say that so clearly," said Martino's attorney, Giuseppe Placidi. "But he [Martino] understood [from the French] that the documents were false." Nevertheless, he said, the French paid him a small amount, "maybe 2,000 or 3,000 euros."

It was unclear why Chouet told *La Repubblica* that his agency had only two meetings with Martino. A few weeks later, he admitted to the *Times* that Martino "came to us and others on his own during this period, frequently trying to sell bits of intelligence he could get from former colleagues in the Italian service about the former Yugoslavia." In fact, Chouet told an acquaintance, Martino was someone the DGSE had used over the years. "He was well known and had been useful in getting information about Bosnia. He generally had been reliable," according to Chouet's acquaintance. Nevertheless, Chouet described Martino as "a little fish" in the world of informants.

A likely explanation for Chouet's claim to *La Repubblica* that his agency met Martino only twice was that he did not want to lend support to the Italian spin that Martino was a longtime DGSE asset working with his French spymasters to spread the phony intelligence.

DGSE's cooperation with the CIA in 2001 and 2002 and its detailed accounts that Iraq had not been seeking uranium from Niger were not included in the 2004 Senate Intelligence Committee's report on US intelligence failures in assessing Iraq's weapons programs. The Senate report made no mention of DGSE's important, if underappreciated, contribution to the CIA. "I talked to them [committee staff members] about that," said a former CIA officer. He said the committee staffers told him "they didn't feel [the French input] closed the issue" of whether or not Iraq had sought Niger's uranium.

Yet the report, directed by the committee's Republican majority, devoted several pages to Joseph Wilson's fact-finding trip to Niger, criticizing him for alleged minor inconsistencies in what he told the staff and what he had told the media. It concluded that Wilson's trip, too, did not close the issue, even though Wilson had reported back that no sale or agreement had occurred and that there had not even been any discussion of a possible sale.

The committee report did include, however, a claim made on November 22, 2002, by France's Ministry of Foreign Affairs director for nonproliferation that his country "had information on an Iraqi attempt to buy uranium from Niger." This assertion was made during a meeting with State Department officials. The French official told the Americans that Paris had determined, however, that no uranium had been shipped.

The CIA station in Paris was directed to check with the DGSE and reported back that the French service did not believe that Iraq had tried to buy uranium in Niger.

The Senate report subsequently noted that the United States had discovered on March 4, 2003, that the French official's conclusion had been based "on the same documents" that the United States had finally turned over to the IAEA on February 4, 2003. In other words, the Foreign Ministry had based its information on the bogus dossier—documents that the DGSE months earlier had determined to be forgeries.

If the French Foreign Ministry had been misled by Martino's documents, it suggested that relations between France's intelligence service and its diplomatic corps were, at best, dysfunctional. Or, in the words of a longtime CIA case officer, "It could be that Foreign Ministry was not interested in the opinion of the DGSE spooks. That was the case with us and the US government. At the State Department, they turn up their noses at us. We're just a bunch of lowlifes. Their general view is that we're sort of a waste of space in an embassy."

Chouet said that the Foreign Ministry was never told of his secret dispatch of five undercover operatives to Niger to check on the uranium story. "Our foreign office does not know what the DGSE does," he said. "That's a rule. It's standard procedure not only in the French [intelligence] services." It is not standard procedure in the United States, where US ambassadors must be fully briefed of all activities by CIA stations. CIA officers grumble that some ambassadors even try to micromanage their operations.

The comment by the Foreign Ministry's nonproliferation director about alleged attempts by Iraq to obtain uranium was not the only one that came to the attention of the State Department. The ministry's director for Africa and the Indian Ocean, Bruno Joubert, triggered a wildfire at State after he told his hosts at a diplomatic dinner in West Africa that France had intelligence that Iraq had been stockpiling chemical and biological weapons. Some US officials considered Joubert's comments credible because he had been a DGSE official in the late 1990s.

The problem was that French intelligence never believed Joubert's claim. Instead, the DGSE had concluded that Iraq did have ongoing research programs, because it hoped that one day it could reconstitute its weapons of mass destruction program, but it had no significant stockpiles. The US Intelligence Community, in its October 2002 National Intelligence Estimate, also reported that Iraq was continuing research into WMDs, but it concluded that Iraq had not destroyed all of its banned weapons; had begun production of mustard gas, sarin, and VX chemicals; and was in the process of reconstituting its nuclear weapons program.

The Bush administration seized upon Joubert's unfounded claim, and once again the Paris CIA station was ordered to find out more. "They were basically grabbing at any straw they could find to justify what they already knew they were going to do," said the former Paris-based CIA officer. "And I had to go back to French intelligence and say, 'Listen, what's this all about?'" Since Joubert "had been for a while in DGSE as director of strategy," he said, US officials figured his statement "must reflect the thinking of French intelligence. And it never did. French intelligence never said that. Ever. [But] Joubert made that statement. I don't know why he did it. Maybe he had too much wine, because he's a fairly cautious man."

While there were internal political issues in France between intelligence agencies and politicians, there was near unanimous criticism of US policy. None of that had anything to do with the spurious claim by SISMI that France had in any way helped develop or disseminate the Italian letter. By mid-2004, it was highly unlikely that top SISMI officials believed that French intelligence had masterminded the Niger hoax; if they ever had believed it. The Italian intelligence service could not avoid the clamor that blamed Italy for the deception.

Chapter 14

Italian Intelligence

Ever since the IAEA had disclosed just before the invasion that the Niger uranium story had been based on forged documents, there had been considerable public conjecture about who was behind the hoax. Seymour Hersh, writing in the *New Yorker* on March 31, 2003, speculated that the documents may have been concocted by Britain's MI6 as part of an anti-Iraq disinformation campaign the agency waged in the late 1990s. Later in 2003, Italy's *La Repubblica* became the first to publish images of some of the forged documents. In its July 16 edition, the newspaper also was the first to report that SISMI had purchased the forgeries from the Nigerien embassy in late 2001. It gave no hint that some SISMI officials may have been coconspirators in the hoax or that SISMI had relayed the bogus intelligence culled from those documents to some other intelligence services, including the CIA.

La Repubblica had obtained some of the Italian letter documents and published its July 16, 2003, exposé linking SISMI to the affair. But that story still downplayed Italian responsibility, saying that a corrupt diplomat at the Niger embassy in Rome had hoodwinked the Italian service into buying the documents. It even suggested that SISMI may have "brokered their purchase on behalf of the British from MI6." The story quoted a SISMI official as saying that it was "highly likely" that it was the British who had initially provided the Niger intelligence to the CIA. "We do not know if it was the British who passed the stuff on to the CIA. It is highly likely. . . . The British are under no obligation to tell us to whom they give the intelligence they share with us."

The more Elisabetta Burba read the numerous articles speculating about the forgeries, the angrier she became, unable to publish her own version as other newspapers wrote about the Niger documents. She knew, of course, that Martino, who had given her the bogus documents, had been a paid SISMI agent. It was her story, but every time she asked her editors at *Panorama,* they refused to let her write it. She had become quite a pest with her editors, who always rejected her entreaties. Burba kept up her lobbying and acknowledged, "I was really becoming a ballbuster."

Finally, on Friday night, July 18, 2003—two days after the *La Repubblica* exposé—the Rome daily, *Corriere della Sera,* figured out that Burba was somehow enmeshed in the document saga and called her for an interview. Burba left a voice mail message with her editor, Carlo Rossella, with whom she had maintained a frosty relationship since her trip to Niger: *Corriere* wanted to interview her, she said; the reporters there had figured it all out and planned to name her in their story whether or not she spoke to them. What should she do?

Rossella called her right back. They hadn't spoken for months and hadn't seen each other because Burba had been out on sick leave for a few weeks, but the tone and tenor of the conversation did not betray the strain between them. "We have decided you should do the interview," Rossella told her. "And when you come back, you can write your own version." She would be permitted to tell her own account of her encounter with Martino and include a detailed description of his phony documents.

The *Corriere della Sera* story came out on Saturday, July 19, the following day, under the headline, "That Is How I Gave Those Uranium Documents to the Americans."

"I realized it could be an extraordinary scoop, which is why I was especially worried," she told *Corriere*. "Were it to prove a hoax, and were I to publish it, my career would be over. I discussed the matter with my editorial staff and began to run all possible checks. There were several details that failed to convince me, and that is why I decided to go to Niger."

Burba went to the office and wrote her own version, which appeared in the July 24, 2003, edition of *Panorama*. The title was "The Scoop That Wasn't."

"The story of alleged uranium trafficking between Niger and Iraq has become an embarrassment to the White House," she wrote in Italian. "After careful investigative work, I can tell you that the intelligence on uranium trafficking is a howling mistake." Without identifying Martino by name—she referred to him instead as Mr. *Patacca*, or Garbage Intelligence—Burba said she had investigated the story in Niger and found it was a fake. As a result, she wrote, *Panorama* had broken relations with the source and decided not to publish the story.

Together with Burba's firsthand account, *Panorama* reproduced some of the forgeries Martino had given her the previous year. *La Repubblica*, which also had reproduced some of the documents, provided copies to NBC News. Soon the Internet was filled with examples of the phony documents, some more legible than others. They were incomplete, but the whole world now could play detective. Blogs bristled with analysis, and some produced astute commentary. If there was consensus, it was that the forgeries were amateurish. The CIA was ridiculed for having bought into the intelligence.

We obtained most of the documents Martino provided Burba, including some she never turned over to the US embassy and that the IAEA never received. Viewed in their entirety, they lead to a telling conclusion. They are so full of serious errors about Nigerien government officials and institutions that Nigeriens could not have fabricated them.

The fake documents had been a work in process, some dated from 1999 through the fall of 2000. These were the ones SISMI used in reporting to the CIA in October 2001 and February 2002 that it had intelligence that Iraq had been seeking uranium from Niger. Others, purportedly drafted in 2001 and 2002, were obtained by Burba but not by *La Repubblica*. Indeed, it appeared that the forgers had an ongoing press run of phony documents, many of which have not surfaced. At one point, when Martino was trying to convince Burba to buy his Niger uranium package, she recalled he had boasted, "I've got a case load of these documents."

One of the early documents was legitimate—a February 1, 1999, telex from Niger's Rome embassy notifying Niamey that Wissam al-Zahawie would be arriving in four days. The eight pages obtained by *La Repubblica*—five documents plus a title page entitled "Accord," or agreement—were the ones SISMI relied on when it passed the intelligence to the CIA and that helped Bush sell the Iraq invasion. *La Repubblica*'s documents had come from SISMI's own files.

The five early documents were initially offered in the spring of

2003 to Dina Nascetti, a reporter for the newsweekly *L'Espresso*. She would not identify her source other than to describe that person as someone she had known for a long time and who had been "always reliable." She put the source in touch with two investigative reporters at *La Repubblica*, *L'Espresso*'s partner newspaper in Rome. *La Repubblica* purchased the documents in June 2003 and became the first news outlet to report that SISMI had acquired the forgeries from a "diplomat" at the Niger embassy in the fall of 2001. When *La Repubblica* received the documents, the IAEA had already declared the Niger story to be a hoax, and the newspaper knew it was purchasing them as forgeries.

That had not been the case several months earlier, when Burba received a much larger package from Martino. In October 2002, Martino had tried to sell the eight pages that eventually ended up with *La Repubblica* together with at least another nine pages of documents—including one dated as recently as June 2002—as legitimate diplomatic reports.

Both *La Repubblica* and Burba's *Panorama* had copies of the Italian letter. It, like virtually all of the faux documents, contained glaring errors. The Italian letter, dated July 27, 2000, was purportedly signed by Niger's president, Mamadou Tandja, and directed to "Mr. President," i.e., Saddam Hussein. The fictional Tandja confirmed the uranium deal under presidential powers granted by Niger's 1966 constitution. The real Tandja would have known better, because the 1966 constitution was only in effect until 1991, when it was replaced by three subsequent constitutions ratified in the 1990s.

It is unclear whether SISMI ever cited to the CIA the constitutional basis for Tandja's approval. The Senate Intelligence Committee report summarizing the CIA's intelligence failures in Iraq says only that the agency's report on SISMI's initial information, dated October 15, 2001, included a claim that Tandja had given Saddam Hussein "his stamp of approval."

But at least one of the phony documents indicated that someone at SISMI was cleaning up glaring errors before passing on the intelligence to the CIA. The document, in the hands of both *La Repubblica* and *Panorama*, was an October 2000 cover letter from Niger's foreign minister to the Rome embassy purporting to accompany a copy of the agreement on the uranium sale. *Panorama*'s and *La Repubblica*'s version of the letter was signed by Allele Elhadj Habibou—who had last served as foreign minister in 1989.

Yet according to the CIA report of October 15, 2001, SISMI alleged that the letter had been signed by Foreign Minister Nassirou Sabo, who actually occupied that position in October 2000. How, where, and when the correction was made remains a mystery. One possibility is that the SISMI official assigned to write the report for the CIA station in Rome did not see the documents but was working from someone else's report. When he saw Habibou's name, he might have concluded that it was an honest mistake and replaced it with the name of the current foreign minister. Another possibility was that he was working from a report that had been prepared by a member of the forgery team inside SISMI's counterproliferation department. The conspirator, aware that the report would be passed on to the CIA, could simply have decided to clean up one of the most glaring errors.

The documents obtained by the two Italian publications provide strong clues that the SISMI conspirators relied heavily on dated material already in their files when they created the documents. Martino, for example, gave Burba two pages from a Nigerien codebook. A Nigerien embassy aide later admitted to a Rome prosecutor that she had provided SISMI with Niger's codebook in 1996. Three key documents that make up the bulk of the intelligence SISMI provided to the CIA were forged on old correspondence from Niger government agencies in Niamey to the embassy in Rome or relied on dated information. The October 2000 cover letter that SISMI told the CIA had been sent by Foreign Minister Nassirou Sabo to Niger's Rome embassy, for example, was written on a document with a Supreme Military Council letterhead. The military council did not exist after 1989.

Other documents were more contemporary and appeared to have been altered by the conspirators after a real or staged break-in of Niger's Rome embassy over the 2000–2001 New Year's holiday. None of the newer documents were used by SISMI in the intelligence it shared with the CIA, nor were any of them turned over to *La Repubblica*, and only Burba received them.

Little of value was stolen during the reported break-in—a cheap watch and three small vials of perfume, according to police reports. A Nigerien embassy official told us that no official documents had been stolen during the break-in. "What is bizarre is that they didn't break into where the authentic documents are filed," the official said. Yet within months, some authentic documents were lifted out of the embassy, and the Nigerien diplomat said that the break-in may have served as a cover for the subsequent purloining of official documents by an insider.

The original content of those documents was erased and replaced with the tall tales of the uranium deal. One, for example, was the August 2001 letter from Maiga Djibrilla Aminata, at the time secretary general of Niger's foreign ministry and now Niger's ambassador to Washington. She had written the letter to approve a vacation request for a diplomat at the Rome embassy and to wish him a good holiday. That letter was altered by the forgers, who substituted the original text with a message saying that the uranium had been delivered to a shipping company for overland transport to the port of Cotonou. Another, in code, had her signature on it and was also dated August 2001. Aminata, who later began using the last name Toure, said she had never sent correspondence in code. At the same time, US intelligence sources said it made little sense—and was highly risky— for a government conducting covert or illicit activities to bring into its confidence an embassy that was not part of the operation.

Two of Burba's documents were drafted on letterhead from Niger's Rome embassy and one appeared to be legitimate: a letter to the foreign ministry in Niamey that is a formal reproduction of the 1999 telex announcing al-Zahawie's visit to Niger. The other one was an obvious forgery, a May 3, 2002, letter from Niger's ambassador to four Islamic countries, along with "Korea," proposing secret meetings during a conference of the UN Food and Agriculture Organization scheduled for the following month. It was allegedly sent to representatives of the Sudan, Iraq, Pakistan, Libya, and Korea (presumably North Korea, which, formally known as the Democratic People's Republic of Korea, is unlikely to be referred to in a diplomatic document as Korea). Minutes of the alleged meeting, held at the Iraqi ambassador's residence on June 14, 2002, detailed plans for a jihad to be waged by "specialists" from their respective militaries against Western interests. Korea, either North or South, is not an Islamic country and was not listed as an attendee, but was replaced by Iran, an equally improbable coconspirator. Iran would be unlikely to share a military venture with its blood enemy, Iraq.

Both *La Repubblica* and *Panorama* had copies of "Annex 1," which SISMI, in February 2002, had told the CIA was the actual accord when it had provided a "verbatim text" of the agreement. A Google search based on that verbatim text alone would have unraveled the hoax, but CIA analysts apparently didn't bother to do so. The positions of the officials listed in the document and the name of the authorizing court, the State Court, were either wrong, archaic, or both. The State Court, for instance, changed its name to the Supreme Court in 1990. The named officials appeared together only at a court ruling in April 1989. The document described Bandiaire Ali as Iraq's attorney general, apparently reversing the name of Ali Bandiaire, who had served as Niger's attorney general.

Another of the five documents that formed the basis of the intelligence passed to the CIA was a letter signed by Foreign Minister

Sabo and dated July 30, 1999. But Sabo didn't assume that post until the following year. The letter mentioned uranium accords reached *a year later*, on June 29, 2000, when Sabo was indeed foreign minister. *Panorama*'s version of the document had a correction that did not appear in the *La Repubblica* copy. The year 1999 was crossed off in pen and 2000 was handwritten and boxed above 1999. But that still didn't fix a conspicuous problem. The letterhead was from Niger's National Reconciliation Council, which had gone out of existence in 1999.

Most of Burba's set of the forgeries ended up with the US government and the IAEA. SISMI tried, without success, to obtain it from the IAEA in February 2003, an indication that the agency itself may not have had Burba's more complete package—only the forgeries that formed the basis for its reports to the CIA and ended up with *La Repubblica*.

Burba did not give the US embassy five of her documents—a page from Niger's codebook, two letters describing shipping arrangements for the uranium, and two pages in code. Martino had faxed them to her on October 10, the day after her visit to the US mission.

Had SISMI perpetrated the fraud? Retired CIA officers who worked with the Italian service were convinced the forgeries were not hatched by SISMI as an institution. They described the agency as bloated (there are more than 33,000 employees) and mismanaged. "It is a huge organization with an awful lot of lack of central direction and organization," said a former CIA officer who had extensive dealings with the Italian service. "It's not well managed. It's never been well managed."

Another former senior CIA officer who knew many top SISMI officers agreed, recalling his experience in coordinating CIA operations with the Italian service. SISMI is so inept "they couldn't mount this type of operation," he said. "Believe me. I know that it is absolutely not true. . . . It was not an Italian government thing."

Meanwhile, he said, neither the SISMI leadership nor the government of Silvio Berlusconi wanted war with Iraq. "The Italians were trying to stop us from doing this." Indeed, Berlusconi did not believe that Iraq possessed banned weapons. On a visit to Moscow on October 16, 2002, he drew criticism from conservative newspapers that normally fawned over him when he declared that he believed Iraq had been disarmed.

But the fraud did involve several SISMI officials. The former senior CIA officer who coordinated operations with the intelligence service said that SISMI launched a major internal investigation as soon as the *La Repubblica* and *Panorama* stories were published. "The senior guys were reacting," he said. He said that the spy agency's chief of WMD counterproliferation, Alberto Manenti, "was called to the carpet when the shit hit the fan in 2003." Manenti "almost went to jail. I mean, he was going to be prosecuted. And he panicked. I've known Manenti for years. He wouldn't fake it." He said that Manenti's deputy, Col. Antonio Nucera, "and a couple of other SISMI folks" were targeted in the probe. Nucera had been Martino's "handler," or control officer. He retired in 2002 but stayed on during the investigation as a paid consultant. The former CIA officer said he did not believe that Manenti had been involved in the hoax but didn't know what finally happened to Manenti and the others. Martino told an acquaintance in 2004 that the SISMI officers behind the hoax were Nucera, an Italian army major who served as one of SISMI's branch chiefs, and an officer who had been brought in from Italy's fiscal police (Guardia di Finanzia), by SISMI director Nicolo Pollari. SISMI and the Italian government never disclosed that there was an internal investigation, much less what the outcome was.

SISMI's role in the fraud became unmistakable, however, when in early August 2004, Rocco Martino revealed in an interview with the *Sunday Times* of London that SISMI had hatched the Niger deception, and the disclosure shook the government of Prime Minister Silvio Berlusconi.

"Like most European [secret] services, they [SISMI] don't like to face problems until it hits them on the head," said a former senior CIA official. "Unless they're faced with an issue where they have to make a decision, the default thing is just to ignore it until they absolutely have to do something. And nine times out of ten they're okay, because it just goes away."

Once he broke his silence, Martino was out of control. SISMI, concerned about his activities, shadowed a production crew of CBS's *60 Minutes,* which had been working on the Niger story for several months; and SISMI operatives photographed some of the CBS meetings with Martino. By that point, too, SISMI officials also knew about Martino's contacts with Burba in 2002 and the documents she had turned over to the US embassy. SISMI also found out that Martino had sold the documents to French intelligence in 2002 and that, in the spring of 2003, Martino had tried to sell the bogus documents to the British as well—even after the IAEA had exposed them as fraudulent.

With the disclosure that Martino had been a key player in the dissemination of the documents, a Rome prosecutor launched an investigation, and Martino started changing his story. In late September, the pro-Berlusconi newspaper *Il Giornale* asked him if he had "played France's game" in peddling the documents. Martino responded that he now was unsure who was behind the fraud but declared, "SISMI had nothing to do with it."

While SISMI's investigation remained a deep secret, another one drew broad attention. Shortly after London newspapers publicly identified Rocco Martino and reported his claim that SISMI had been behind the hoax, Franco Ionta, chief of the Rome prosecutor's office, launched a criminal investigation. Nearly a year after the sensational disclosures published by *La Repubblica* and *Panorama*, he began taking sworn testimony from the principal players.

Edited portions of the testimony published in 2006 in *Il Giornale* weaved an incomplete story of two-bit hustlers unencumbered by questions of morality. The testimony hinted at a possible SISMI role, but Ionta had no authority to compel the spy agency to reveal its secrets or the Nigerien diplomats to testify under oath.

The cast of characters included Martino; Nucera, who had been Martino's former handler at SISMI; and Laura Montini—code-named La Signora—the secretary at the Nigerien embassy who acted as a facilitator in the scheme. Montini had been a longtime SISMI spy who in the 1990s reported directly to Nucera. In 1996, she had even provided Nucera with Niger's codebook. For many countries, the pilfering of such intelligence jewels, the key to coded messages, would be a capital offense. But ten years later, she was still employed at the Rome embassy by a very forgiving Niger government.

Ionta, the prosecutor, interrogated the three in late 2004 and early 2005 and was able to piece together a version of what had taken place. Nucera introduced Martino to La Signora in 2000, and she then became a paid informant for Martino. She admitted passing him embassy documents about unspecified agreements between Niger and Iraq, as well as rough drafts of agreements by Niger to supply uranium to China and Korea. She did not elaborate on which Korea. Martino, meanwhile, testified that La Signora also provided him with the phony documents on the uranium deal between Iraq and Niger.

The Nigerien government itself did not investigate the embassy's role, a Nigerien diplomat told us. "They didn't do anything," the diplomat said. "It's not good. To have your name in the papers three or four times a year, and there is no reply, no complaint, no investigation." The source said that Niger had become an embarrassment to the tight-knit African diplomatic community in Rome because it put up no defense to the now very public scandal and gave no indication that it took the matter seriously.

In testimony before Ionta's prosecuting team, Nucera portrayed himself as a disinterested go-between, doing a favor for Martino and La Signora, both of whom wanted to make some money. "I don't remember if I arranged the encounter at the behest of the woman or Rocco Martino, each for his own personal reasons interested in undertaking a collaboration between themselves," he said.

In an interview with *Il Giornale* after he testified before Ionta, Nucera said that he arranged the initial meeting at La Signora's behest. He said La Signora needed money and complained that SISMI was not using her as much as in previous years. "I thought that she might be interested in cooperating with Rocco. . . . It's like when you introduce a bricklayer to a friend who needs him to refurbish his house. I cannot take the blame if, at the end of it, the bricklayer screws everything up."

La Signora, meanwhile, confessed to Ionta that she had been a SISMI spy for years and had pilfered documents out of the Nigerien embassy, where she worked as a secretary. She said that Nucera had initiated the contact with Martino in 2000, when he showed up at the Nigerien embassy one day to tell her that SISMI was undergoing "internal restructuring" and her espionage services would not be needed for a while. Luckily, however, he offered a new plan, and La Signora agreed: Nucera said she could make up for the lost wages by working for a new sponsor, whom he described as a "friend and acquaintance" who worked for "an intelligence agency in Brussels."

Martino said Nucera had also approached him about taking on Montini as a paid informant. "Nucera asked me in 2000 if I was interested in meeting someone who worked for an African embassy and was in a position to supply intelligence and classified papers."

Nucera and La Signora said the first meeting with Martino was at a bar in Rome's Largo Gancia district, not far from the Nigerien embassy. Montini recalled that their first meeting was on her birthday, February 16, and Martino brought her a small box of chocolates. Martino had kept his receipts to prove the date was accurate. He also secretly tape-recorded that meeting and his future encounters and phone conversations with both La Signora and Nucera. He turned the tapes over to Ionta, hoping they would prove that he had been set up.

In his testimony to Ionta, Nucera tried to put as much distance as possible between himself, SISMI, Martino, and La Signora. With no prodding, he volunteered at several points that he had no knowledge of what the two were up to after the initial introduction. "I want to specify that the relations between the two were of no interest to my service [SISMI] branch. . . . I was never interested in knowing if a relation between [La Signora] and Rocco had developed, nor was I interested in their affairs. . . . I want to emphasize that I had no interest whatsoever, professional or personal, in the relations that developed between the two. . . . I never received information on the nature of their collaboration."

Nucera also belittled their value as spies. While admitting that he had been La Signora's handler for several years in the 1990s, he complained that the "said relation was never productive." This opinion, of course, clashed with SISMI's claim to the CIA that she had been a "very reliable source." Nucera described Martino as something of a mixed bag, providing poor intelligence on arms deals but decent information on Islamic fundamentalism.

Martino has changed his version of events several times. He told the Rome prosecutor that Nucera introduced him to La Signora, but had previously told Elisabetta Burba that he approached La Signora directly as a possible new informant. This account, no doubt, was a cover story. He told Burba that he had devised a subterfuge to meet her at an exhibition of wooden sculptures he knew she would be attending. "I looked for information about wooden sculptures on the

Internet in order to be able to say something. . . . We started talking, and one thing led to the other."

La Signora told the Rome prosecutor that she stopped dealing with Martino in 2003 on orders from her unnamed SISMI handler at the time. By 2003, SISMI was fully aware that Martino was peddling the phony Niger documents to anyone naïve enough to buy them. Any link back to SISMI had to be erased.

Martino also finally realized in that year that he had been played for a fool. It finally sank in that not only had the documents been fraudulent (Burba had told him that, and so had the French), but that people whom he trusted had used him. He told the Rome prosecutors that on May 3, 2003, he called La Signora to complain that the documents were bogus. "I'm sure you're in good faith, but it's clear there's a problem to sort out," he told her. There were two possibilities: Either someone at the embassy forged them, or someone brought them to her from the outside. La Signora was indignant and denied knowing that the documents were rubbish.

Martino tried in his own mind to reconstruct events. The chain of events he had put together by early 2004 finally convinced him that he had been deceived. He was bitter. For a brief period, he even described to journalists and acquaintances how he had been conned. In the early summer, he confided to an acquaintance that three SISMI officers, including Nucera, had provided La Signora with the phony documents, and he named the SISMI officials. This was followed by the interview he gave the *London Times,* under the cover name of Giacomo, when he charged that SISMI had been behind the fraud. At about the same time, he was interviewed by CBS's *60 Minutes,* which did not broadcast his comments until last year as part of a broader exposé on Bush administration exaggerations of Iraqi intelligence. Martino told the network that he had been duped. "I thought I had my hands on some important papers. And this same woman [La Signora] was telling me they were very important," he said. The period of candor was fleeting. When Ionta opened his investigation, Martino apparently decided that there was no benefit in taking on Italy's powerful intelligence service.

Ionta's investigation got that far but then languished. The sworn testimony left him with contradictory and confusing answers. In March 2006, when we visited his office after two years of off-and-on probing, Ionta was still preoccupied with the question of which of Martino's documents were phony and which were real. The forensic analysis was made more difficult because he had only copies, not the originals, one of his top aides said. If any of the originals were still on file at the Nigerien embassy, they were protected by diplomatic immunity. If the original bogus documents were not on file, it could mean they had not originated at the embassy. The aide said that one of the suspects was a diplomat at the Nigerien embassy who was protected by diplomatic immunity. Nevertheless, the aide said, it remained a "fluid investigation" made a bit more difficult by the apparent mendacity of the suspects whom the office had interviewed.

Ionta and other well-informed Italians knew full well that a rogue operation inside SISMI was nothing new. The service was plagued by a history of scandals, many of which involved the illicit sales of arms. In other instances, SISMI officers were implicated in—and occasionally convicted of—involvement in massive fraud, assassinations, and politically motivated terrorist explosions.

There was a catchphrase in Italy for questionable, and often unauthorized, operations. It was said they were the product of a "deviated service" within SISMI, one involving officers either freelancing for money or working off the books for powerful politicians. Retired admiral Falco Accame, a former socialist senator who once chaired a military oversight committee, told us that the strange conspiracy surrounding the Italian letter and the accompanying forgeries fit well in the long history of intrigue and side deals within SISMI. Accame, who had personally known several SISMI directors, said he was not surprised by the CIA officers' conclusions that the bogus documents had been the product of corrupt SISMI officers.

He also agreed that SISMI, whose creation after World War II was enormously influenced by the CIA's primary mission of thwarting Soviet-sponsored communism in Europe, was an agency riddled with problems. "Yes, I agree. They are nothing. . . . They are not very credible or competent."

"When something happens that shouldn't happen, then the secret services say, 'The problem is the deviated service.' That's the key," said Accame. "This thing of Niger, with Rocco Martino, it was the deviated service. It's a way of saying, 'We don't know anything about it.' Officially, it didn't happen. Unofficially, it happened, but we don't have control over what happens in the deviated service. It's Machiavelli."

In late 2005, SISMI director Pollari testified before Parliament's COPACO that Martino had been the sole source behind the phony dossier. Virtually to the man, COPACO members were willing to accept that version and praised the intelligence service for its "exhaustive" reconstruction of what had happened. But Martino refused to shoulder the blame by himself. He surfaced again briefly, telling reporters that he had been duped by a "parallel structure, an internal SISMI faction." He did not elaborate.

Italy's official line remained that Martino was the main villain in the uranium hoax, probably with the assistance of the French. There was no indication that the new left-of-center government of Prime Minister Romano Prodi, who succeeded Berlusconi in May 2006, would push for a more aggressive (or honest) investigation.

In the United States, a less-than-aggressive FBI counterintelligence investigation was opened in mid-2003 at the behest of Senator Jay Rockefeller of West Virginia, at the time the ranking Democrat on the

Senate Intelligence Committee. The FBI was asked to determine what foreign powers or individuals had created the fake documents to lure America into war. It was, at best, a lukewarm probe. FBI agents in Italy were unable to interview key sources because the State Department and the Justice Department refused to open doors in Italy by appealing directly to the Italian government and its relevant departments, such as the Justice Ministry or prosecutor Ionta.

The Bush administration had reasons to avoid embarrassing SISMI. It depended on SISMI's cooperation in the war on terrorism. SISMI had assisted in the kidnapping by CIA officers in 2003 of terrorism suspect Hassan Mustafa Osama Nasr, who was flown to Cairo under the CIA's controversial extraordinary rendition program. The operation was in violation of Italian law, a Milan magistrate concluded. Nasr claimed he was tortured while under interrogation in Egypt. The magistrate issued warrants for the arrest of twenty-five CIA operatives, and six top SISMI officers, including Pollari, were charged. Pollari was dismissed as head of SISMI in November 2006.

Another issue of considerable political controversy in Italy was the fatal shooting by US troops in Baghdad in March 2005 of a widely respected SISMI officer, Maj. Gen. Nicola Calipari. The highly decorated officer had just completed the successful rescue of an Italian journalist kidnapped by terrorists. The United States said that Calipari, who became an Italian national hero, was killed when National Guardsmen manning a roadblock near the Baghdad airport opened fire because they believed his car failed to obey signals to halt. Italian prosecutors sought unsuccessfully to interview one of the guardsmen as they contemplated homicide charges against him. The US government refused to turn the guardsman over to Italian authorities.

Without the active cooperation of the Bush administration, FBI agents had to rely almost exclusively on what SISMI, their liaison partner in Italy, told them. They did talk to Burba and her boss, Rossella, at the American consulate in Milan, sovereign US territory.

They would have needed permission from the Italian government to interview the two at their homes or office. Rossella had very little to contribute, and Burba, while friendly and cooperative, refused to identify Martino because she was protecting him as an unnamed source.

Some months later, in early August 2004, London newspapers "outed" Martino, and the FBI knew who he was. But the investigation went nowhere. "They [FBI agents] were interested in doing more, but everything, every logical path, required some political clout behind them to go to the Italians and required cooperation. . . . That political clout had been withheld," said a source who had been briefed by agents.

The FBI had not spoken to Martino, his attorney told us. By July 2005, the FBI shut down its investigation. Director Robert S. Muller III sent Pollari a private letter, thanking him for his agency's cooperation and declaring that the FBI had concluded that the forgeries were the creation of one or more persons for personal profit—not to influence US policy.

Not everyone was happy, least of all Senator Rockefeller. In late 2005, the FBI, claiming it had obtained some new information, reopened the investigation. Like the first one, the second investigation was a washout. The FBI knew that politically the case was a tinderbox and was in no rush to pursue it. Investigators believed that trying to unravel the strings could ensnare them in political disputes with the White House and the still-powerful neoconservatives or in diplomatic disputes with the French or the Italians. In the view of a top FBI official, the investigation was "so politically charged that whatever slant you take, you hit somebody you don't want to hit. . . . From a national security or political standpoint, for the bureau, this is as bad as it gets." Since the forgeries probably did not occur on US soil and the most likely suspects lived abroad, there was little chance the FBI could ever bring charges. But it could have embarrassed powerful constituencies, like the White House, if it became too aggressive in gathering evidence. The FBI had already conducted investigations that were politically sensitive for the administration, including those of I. Lewis "Scooter" Libby and others allegedly linked to the leaking of Valerie Plame's CIA identity, several Republican lawmakers who reportedly obtained favors from lobbyist Jack Abramoff and Pentagon officials and employees of the powerful American Israel Public Affairs Committee for alleged national security violations. Politics also were to play a role in official probes in the United States.

Chapter 15

The Aftermath: Majority Report

"If you ever injected truth into politics you have no politics."
WILL ROGERS

In the months after the Iraq invasion, as it became clear that no weapons of mass destruction were to be found, the then-Republican-controlled Congress launched official investigations into the failures of the American Intelligence Community. The first of these, by the Senate Select Committee on Intelligence, began in the spring of 2003. The committee and its House counterpart historically have been the least political of Congress's authorization panels. But the Senate committee, under Chairman Pat Roberts, a Kansas Republican, became a protective shield for Bush and his administration, the most secretive in US history.

Intelligence committees had a reputation for relative nonpartisanship.

Most lawmakers don't fight for an assignment to intelligence committees since they deal with classified matters and rarely offer opportunities for public posturing or allocating pork for their constituents. But
things changed when Roberts, the son of C. Wesley Roberts, chairman of the Republican National Committee under Dwight Eisen-
hower, took over as chairman of the Senate committee in 2003.

The committee became so politicized that Byron York, White
House correspondent for the conservative *National Review,* sounded
an unusual alarm that a Republican on the committee had the temer-
ity to hire an aide with a questionable pedigree. The committee member, Chuck Hagel of Nebraska, had hired Eric Rosenbach, a former
army military intelligence company commander and Fulbright scholar
who had advised John Kerry on Iraq reconstruction policy during the
2004 presidential campaign. York quoted a Senate Republican as saying, "This is an intensely political committee. The whole track record
of the committee is political." Rosenbach's hiring, York reported,
"raises plenty of Republican eyebrows."

The committee released its 511-page report on July 2004, after a
year of taking secret testimony from 200 intelligence officials and
experts and reviewing 45,000 pages of classified documents. It
received generally solid reviews for its critique of the Intelligence
Community. The community's fatal flaw, the report said, was a col-
lective assumption that Iraq possessed banned weapons, prompting
analysts to discount conflicting intelligence. It said US intelligence,
especially the CIA, suffered from a "broken corporate culture and
poor management" and charged that Tenet, who had resigned the
previous month, had blocked dissenting views from the CIA's partner
agencies. Conclusions reached in the October 2002 National Intelligence Estimate, it said, were "either overstated or were not supported
by the underlying intelligence." Roberts summed up the report's conclusions by saying that American intelligence had been guilty of
"groupthink," leading analysts to interpret "ambiguous evidence,

such as the procurement of dual-use technology, as conclusive evidence of the existence of WMD programs."

The report found no fault with the Bush administration. But it heaped criticism on former ambassador Joseph Wilson, another sign that the committee suffered from more than a tinge of partisanship. The report devoted seven pages to Wilson's fact-finding mission to Niger, an event that the CIA itself had concluded was of little intelligence value. But Wilson had rankled the Bush White House a year earlier when he went public to assert that the administration must have known that he had found no Niger uranium deal with Iraq when Bush delivered his 16 words. The committee report went into great detail over minor inconsistencies, comparing what Wilson told the CIA in his debriefing with what he told the committee and what he had told the press.

"I think that what the report was trying to do was to embarrass Joe Wilson," said Vicki Divoll, who had been the committee's general counsel until 2003. "I think it was politically far less concerned with [intelligence] documents and more concerned with making Wilson look bad."

Meanwhile, the larger questions of manipulating information and coercing intelligence analysts were sidetracked. The committee report asserted that it "did not find any evidence that administration officials attempted to coerce, influence, or pressure analysts to change their judgments related to Iraq's weapons of mass destruction capabilities." That provided welcome cover for Bush and his aides, who were under the gun after warnings about mushroom clouds and uranium purchases in Niger were revealed to be empty rhetoric.

The Democratic minority on the Senate committee challenged the committee's conclusion that there was no pressure on analysts from the White House. Vice Chairman Jay Rockefeller of West Virginia, Carl Levin of Michigan, and Richard Durbin of Illinois insisted in a dissenting statement that the administration's aggressive campaign to sell the war in itself had created "significant pressure on the Intelligence Community to conform to the certainty contained in the [administration] pronouncements." They also cited the internal investigation led by one of the CIA's former deputy directors, Richard Kerr, which concluded that repetitive orders from senior policymakers to find a link between al Qaeda and Iraq had "created significant pressure on the Intelligence Community to find evidence that supported a connection."

Paul Pillar, the CIA's top Middle East analyst from 2000 to 2005, who had witnessed the pressure tactics at the White House, ridiculed the idea that an analyst would confess to having cooked the books because of outside pressure. "The method of investigation used by the [committee]—essentially asking analysts whether their arms had been twisted—would have caught only the crudest attempts at politicization," he said. "It is unlikely that analysts would ever acknowledge that their own judgments have been politicized, since that would be far more damning than admitting more mundane types of analytical error."

The Senate report did not address the contentious issue of whether the administration cherry-picked, distorted, or manipulated the intelligence to deceive Congress and the American public in its campaign to sell the war. Roberts answered critics by saying that this would be studied in a separate investigation. He and Rockefeller had announced in February 2004 that the committee would expand its probe to include an investigation into whether there was a disconnect between what senior administration officials had claimed publicly and the intelligence behind those claims. They had agreed to release the report after the November 2004 election. By early 2007, with Democrats now in the Senate leadership, there was still no sign of the report.

Even as the Senate intelligence panel was conducting its probe, many Democratic lawmakers, joined by moderate Republicans who were increasingly questioning the administration, campaigned for a truly independent investigation into the intelligence failures. Bush resisted the creation of such a probe, saying that it was unnecessary, but was forced to relent after encountering increased pressure from within his own party and because of concern over an upcoming election.

A catalyst in this effort was David Kay, a strong supporter of the Iraq war, who headed the postinvasion Iraq Survey Group, the 1,400-member CIA–Pentagon team dedicated to finding Saddam's banned weapons. Kay quit unexpectedly on January 23, 2004, and immediately went public with his conclusion that Iraq had no weapons of mass destruction. He joined Republican senator John McCain of Arizona in urging the creation of an independent commission to investigate why the intelligence had been so bad.

In February 2004, Bush empanelled the nine-member committee. It was called the Commission on the Intelligence Capabilities of the United States Regarding Weapons of Mass Destruction.

But Bush, focusing on his reelection bid in November, maneuvered to control the results. First, he diluted the commission's mandate, directing the probe to include not only the Iraqi case, but also the Intelligence Community's performance on all WMD threats, including those from Libya, Pakistan, North Korea, Iran, and al Qaeda. Second, he placed a central issue out of bounds: the question of how the administration had used the intelligence it received.

Third, Bush withheld giving the commission authority to issue subpoenas; and finally, he directed that it report back to him by March 31, 2005—five months after the presidential election.

The commission's makeup had the veneer of bipartisanship. One of the two cochairs was Laurence H. Silberman, a retired federal judge who was an activist conservative Republican; and the other was former Virginia senator Charles S. Robb, a conservative Democrat. Most of the other commissioners were respected establishment figures, including former government bureaucrats, lawyers, and academicians.

Many had served on other blue-chip panels, and they were unlikely to rock the boat.

An exception was McCain, who had presidential aspirations of his own and had pushed for the creation of the commission in the first place and was appointed as one of its nine members. He lobbied the Bush administration to give the commission some teeth by insisting that it be granted subpoena power, even calling Vice President Cheney to ask for his help. Cheney refused.

As expected, the final product, a 692-page report delivered to Bush on the appointed date of March 31, 2005, contained nothing to upset the administration. Much of the report remained classified, including its assessments of US intelligence performance in analyzing Iran and North Korea. As with the Senate Intelligence Committee report, it effectively exonerated the administration in its decision to go to war by focusing the blame on the Intelligence Community. The community, the report concluded, had been responsible for one of the "most damaging intelligence failures in recent American history." US intelligence had been "dead wrong" in its assessments of Iraq's banned weapons, and its data had been "riddled with errors" and "either worthless or misleading." Like the Senate report, it concluded that in "no instance did political pressure cause [analysts] to skew or alter any of their analytical judgments."

On the contrary, the commission suggested that the Intelligence Community might have misled the administration in its zeal to please policymakers. The panel's report disclosed that analysts occasionally withheld information from top officials, notably Bush, if such material might cast doubt on reports of Hussein's illicit weapons. The omissions were from the highly classified President's Daily Briefs and Senior Executive Intelligence Briefs. "In other instances," the report said, "intelligence suggesting the existence of weapons programs was conveyed to policymakers, but later information casting doubt upon the validity of that intelligence was not. In ways both subtle and not so subtle, the daily reports seemed to be 'selling' intelligence—in order to keep its customers . . . interested."

The postwar inquiries had something in common with official probes in Italy and Britain: The leaders of the investigations paid attention to the political winds and protected their respective governments. Even where parliamentarians or members of the US Senate criticized their intelligence agencies, they avoided broader criticism of top leaders.

British lawmakers and government-appointed panels offered only mild rebukes in response to Prime Minister Blair's warnings of Iraq's capability of launching a WMD attack within forty-five minutes. They concluded that MI6's, Blair's, and Bush's claims that Iraq had been seeking uranium in Niger were "well founded." Italy's Parliament exonerated the Berlusconi government and the head agency for Italian military intelligence, SISMI.

Chapter 16

Postmortem at the CIA

In May 2003, within two months of the invasion, it became clear that something had gone wrong with prewar intelligence, and George Tenet commissioned a panel to analyze the failure. Without waiting for the congressional- or White House–appointed panels that were certain to come, he called on Richard Kerr, a former deputy director for intelligence, and a small team of retired analysts to conduct the internal investigation. Kerr's work would help organize the Intelligence Community's massive reports and assist the CIA in providing answers.

Tenet's decision also fulfilled a pledge he had made to Secretary of Defense Donald Rumsfeld, a frequent luncheon companion, the previous October that the Intelligence Community would compare its prewar intelligence with the facts on the ground after the invasion.

Rumsfeld had been highly critical of the CIA in the run-up to the war, especially about Iraq's alleged connection to al Qaeda. There was also constant pressure from Vice President Cheney, who routinely invoked the alleged link between Iraq and al Qaeda as an illustration of the threat Iraq posed to the United States. Ruffled but uncompromised by Rumsfeld or Cheney, the CIA had produced a document in June 2002 entitled "Iraq and al-Qa'ida: Interpreting a Murky Relationship."

The report's introduction said the agency had used a "purposely aggressive" approach in trying to connect al Qaeda with Iraq. This worst-case scenario is typically used by the military for war planning but seldom by the CIA in preparing assessments. The "purposely aggressive" approach this time was in response to the administration's badgering of analysts to find links. CIA analysts and managers involved in the report concluded that the "hammering" they received from the administration was the worst he had seen in his thirty-two-year career. Nevertheless, the report did not support a link between Iraq and the 9/11 attacks and concluded (along with the FBI's reports) that Mohammed Atta had never met with an Iraqi intelligence officer.

The Kerr team found poor performance both at the White House and at the CIA. It said that Bush administration officials tended to rely on oral briefings rather than documentation, that the agency depended on reports with unknown sourcing, and that analysis was not as specifically targeted as it should have been.

For example, the Kerr committee said, even as the White House was preparing for war with Iraq, it had not directed the CIA to shift priority on WMD intelligence gathering from North Korea and Iran to Iraq "until late 2002." It noted that some of the flawed intelligence on Iraq's weapons used by the administration to sell the war had come from allied intelligence services that refused to produce their sources. That, of course, is what had happened with the fraudulent Niger uranium claim, an invention of rogue SISMI intelligence officers. The CIA had asked SISMI about its source, but the Italian service only responded that the information had come from "a very credible source." Secretary of State Powell's dramatic revelation that Iraq had clandestine mobile labs producing germ warfare agents came from a German intelligence asset, code-named "Curveball," who even before the invasion was found to be a fabricator.

Kerr's investigators also complained that the CIA, in establishing single-issue centers, such as WINPAC and the Counterterrorism Center, and crisis-response task forces, diminished the importance of regional offices. SISMI's Nigerien uranium reports, including the so-called "verbatim text" of the Nigerien court approval, were forwarded by the CIA's Near East and South Asia Office to Africa analysts in February 2002. But the Africa analysts did not catch the glaring factual errors contained in the text. "Part of the problem is you don't always have the right people looking at the right document at the right time," said an intelligence official. "For instance, if you had the right people looking at these documents, they would have said, gee, these terms are hosed up, they're out of date." Kerr's report said that the stripping of experts from regional offices diminished their ability to provide "complete perspectives on country and regional issues." A reconstruction of how the Nigerien uranium intelligence flowed through various departments revealed that few people with special expertise on Africa saw it. The only mention of a CIA Africa specialist commenting on the intelligence is a notation that a "senior Africa analyst," on February 11, 2003, wrote an assessment concluding that the "documentary evidence contains several questionable details and could be fraudulent." His assessment, apparently based on his review of some of the forged documents, was never published and disseminated. Similarly, Africa analysts at the Pentagon were unaware of the alleged uranium deal with Iraq until hearing Bush's 16 words in the January 28 State of the Union address.

One of the Kerr team's most significant criticisms involved the overreliance by top Bush administration officials, including the president himself, on oral briefings by CIA officials. "Too close association with policy deliberations can be troublesome," it concluded. "In the case of Iraq, daily briefings and other contacts at the highest levels undoubtedly influenced policy in ways that went beyond the coordinated analysis contained in the written product. Close and continuing personal contact, unfettered by the formal caveats that usually accompany written production, probably imparted a greater sense of certainty to analytic conclusions than the facts would bear." A telling illustration occurred on December 21, 2002, when Tenet, accompanied by his chief deputy, John McLaughlin, visited the White House to give the president the Intelligence Community's most authoritative assessment of Iraq's WMDs. Bush, after listening to McLaughlin's summary of the intelligence, replete with satellite photographs, transcripts of intercepts, and other top-secret intelligence, turned to Tenet and asked, "This is the best we've got?" He told Tenet the intelligence would not convince "Joe Public." Bush's chief of staff, Andrew Card, also concluded that there was "no there there." Bush then turned to Tenet and asked how confident he was. Tenet responded, "Don't worry. It's a slam dunk."

Two major external investigations followed soon after the Kerr commission: The Senate Intelligence Committee investigation and the Robb-Silberman Commission, both of which provided detailed—and disturbing—insight into the Intelligence Committee's production of the October 2002 National Intelligence Estimate, the most authoritative document assessing Iraq's weapons and intentions. The report helped convince a number of lawmakers to support Bush's decision to wage war, although virtually all of its major conclusions were wrong. And virtually none of the lawmakers read the report in its entirety.

Analysts who prepared the NIE knew their product would not help shape the decision to go to war or give UN inspectors more time. A CIA analyst told the Senate Intelligence Committee that the document "was written [with a] going-in assumption [that] we were going to war, so this NIE was written with that in mind. We were going to war, which meant that American men and women had to be properly given the benefit of the doubt of what they would face. That was what was said to us. We're going to war."

As a consequence, the bogus Niger uranium intelligence became part of the report. The NIE was prepared in three weeks, coordinated by the National Intelligence Council, a collegial organization of intelligence veterans and academic experts. The staff represented ten of the fifteen agencies that composed the Intelligence Community at the time. The key writers and editors, national intelligence officers, each had regional or subject matter expertise. The final product was the result of give-and-take among the National Intelligence Officers and senior analysts from different intelligence agencies, who had struggled to represent the consensus (more or less) of the Intelligence Community.

The senior analysts had to cast a vote on whether there was enough evidence to claim that Iraq was reconstituting its nuclear weapons program. Most of them voted yes, based largely on their conclusion that Iraq had been buying aluminum tubes intended for centrifuges to process uranium into bomb-grade material. They were wrong; the tubes were being purchased for exactly what Iraq had been insisting they were for—artillery rockets.

The Department of Energy analyst on the NIE team, relying on the technical evaluation of scientists and engineers at the department's nuclear weapons labs, argued that the tubes were not suited for centrifuges. He accepted that some of the other dual-use material US intelligence believed Iraq was trying to buy, such as high-power magnets and a variety of machine tools, could be used for an enrichment program, but there was no supporting evidence that that was their intended use. The flimsy intelligence was not enough to bring him to the conclusion that Iraq had embarked on a nuclear program.

Then he looked at the Niger story, which the other analysts viewed with considerable skepticism. Based on the Niger intelligence, the analyst voted that, yes, Iraq was reconstituting, according to the Robb-Silberman Commission report. His logic surprised the other senior analysts. One later told the commission that the Energy Department representative's reasoning had "made sense politically, but not substantively." Though insisting that there was no political pressure on his department, the DOE analyst conceded that his agency "didn't want to come out before the war and say [Iraq] wasn't reconstituting" a nuclear weapons program.

The NIE team left the Niger story in the report but not in its "key judgments" section, which highlighted what the group believed to be the most significant intelligence.

Stu Cohen, as acting chairman of the National Intelligence Council, the powerful coordinating body for the fifteen agencies that at the time comprised the Intelligence Community, oversaw the drafting of the NIE. Cohen wrote an unusual apologia on the CIA's Web site in November 2003 that shed some light on the dangers of bad intelligence once embedded in the system. He said that the claim that Iraq had been seeking uranium from Iraq was included in the document but not emphasized, merely "for the sake of completeness."

Cohen might have assumed that the consumers of the intelligence, in this instance Bush administration officials and members of Congress, would read the intelligence with trained eyes and open minds.

"Mentioning with appropriate caveats even unconfirmed reporting is standard practice in NIEs and other intelligence assessments; it helps the consumers of the assessments understand the full range of possibly relevant intelligence."

The problem was that administration officials were not interested in the "full range" of intelligence, but only in whatever information might help make their case for war. Many analysts understood that, although feeding policymakers information they wanted to hear had the very natural consequence of generating bad intelligence. Even after the invasion, on June 12, 2003—three months after IAEA's declaration that the Niger intelligence was bogus—the DIA wrote Wolfowitz a classified memorandum claiming that Iraq's African shopping spree for uranium still held up. At the time, special units of the Pentagon were scouring Iraq in a futile search for weapons, and the news media were beginning to question the underpinnings of Bush's case for war. In addition, the Pentagon had received a memorandum in April from the national intelligence officer for Africa, Ambassador Robert Houdek, who concluded that the Niger intelligence "looks like crap," according to an official who had read it. But the June memo focused on the good news, saying that there still was separate intelligence suggesting that Iraq had been shopping for uranium. It said that the DIA had "unconfirmed reporting that suggested that Iraq attempted to obtain uranium and yellowcake from African nations after 1998." The only evidence the agency offered was the navy's report on the uranium once stored in Cotonou warehouses that an informant, never subsequently contacted, had claimed was destined for Iraq. The problem was that DIA officers had inspected the warehouses and found no uranium, and the French had told the CIA that what uranium had been stored there had been destined for France.

The Intelligence Community's most puzzling error of tradecraft was the failure of most of the agencies to review copies of Martino's forged documents for a critical four months after they were delivered in October by Burba to the US embassy in Rome. When analysts finally looked at the documents, they were slow in accepting the fact that virtually all of the documents were crude forgeries, something that embassy personnel, who are not trained intelligence specialists, spotted immediately.

In the intervening four months, the administration aggressively used the phony intelligence as one of the two key props—the other was the aluminum tubes—to convince America and Congress that Iraq was on the verge of becoming a dangerous nuclear power. Greg Thielmann, a senior INR analyst, said the president "was creating dual pillars" to support the nuclear threat—the uranium and aluminum tube stories.

Shortly after the IAEA presented its conclusion in March 2003, a top CIA official was unable to explain why the CIA had failed to obtain copies of the forged documents when they became available. "I guess we figured we had the accounts of what was in them, and that was close enough," he said. "And the whole thing [the Niger claim], we didn't take it that seriously to start with. It wasn't central to any of our assessments and our reportings [about Iraq's nuclear weapons program]. Since we didn't put a whole lot of stock in these reports from Niger for a variety of reasons, we didn't rush around to get the actual documents."

Asked, then, why those doubts were not reflected in the public assertions from Bush administration officials during the run-up to war, he said, "We probably didn't convey it well enough for them to understand it. We probably should have smacked them between the eyes."

Another intelligence official familiar with the CIA's assessment of what went wrong conceded that the agency should have been more aggressive in determining the sourcing of the Niger claim. Ironically, he said, had the CIA put more stock in the original intelligence, it would have devoted more energy to learning its provenance.

It is possible that some CIA analysts were reluctant to look at the newly available forgeries or to raise a flag about the Niger intelligence because it would have exposed them to ridicule for having approved its inclusion in the NIE on Iraq's illicit weapons, published just eleven days earlier. The NIE claimed that Iraq, already sitting on 550 tons of yellowcake at Tuwaitha, "also began vigorously trying to procure uranium ore and yellowcake." The key evidence: "A foreign government service reported that, as of early 2001, Niger planned to send several tons of 'pure uranium' [probably yellowcake] to Iraq."

Not all the postinvasion assessments came from formal investigations. Many retired CIA officials, including Paul Pillar, the national intelligence officer for the Near East and South Asia until 2005, went public with scathing critiques of what they had seen go wrong. Others kept quiet until asked. One of those was John Gannon, a respected former CIA director for intelligence.

"It was policy and politics that prevailed over tradecraft," Gannon told us. "I can give examples that go back twenty-five or thirty years, but I don't think there has been an issue where a bias for the presence of weapons of mass destruction has been so strong—apart from the Soviet Union . . . where it was always assumed the Soviets were behind every potted plant," he said. An important distinction, however, was that the Soviet threat was real, if sometimes exaggerated; the Iraq threat was not real and was routinely exaggerated.

Gannon said that the intelligence system collapsed, in part, because traditional checks and balances were abandoned and possible biases were overlooked. Division chiefs at CIA headquarters failed to challenge the case officers on the intelligence coming in from the field, and the officers did not in turn challenge their chiefs. Analysts did not press the officers to detect biases. Reporting officers did not challenge analytical conclusions. Increasingly, Gannon said, the blame went right to the top. Tenet, he said, had been too disengaged from the intelligence flow to make the hard calls when they were needed.

"How this stuff [the Niger story] got through the system and how it got into the State of the Union could only have happened because leadership failed and failed badly. I think it failed at the director of central intelligence [Tenet] level. You certainly didn't have a director there who was encouraging people to tell it like they saw it and bring all the information to the top so that it could fairly be evaluated. And you certainly didn't have a White House saying, 'Are you sure you're right here? I want you guys to be respecting dissent and make sure we understand where people agree or disagree.'"

He explained why policymakers, including Cheney, had the upper hand in confronting analysts to produce assessments more to their liking. "If they [administration officials] have very strong views that are embedded in the policy they are responsible for—like I think it's very clear the vice president and others in this administration had— you don't go back a second time and tell them what you told them the first time and they didn't like it," Gannon said. He said that when intelligence is weak, as was the case with the reporting on Iraq's alleged banned weapons, analysts are more likely to cave to the bias of policymakers. So when the briefer returns with a revised analysis, it often reflects the policymaker's bias. "The bias of power tends to trump the bias of analytical objectivity," Gannon said.

Chapter 17

Double Negatives

"The level of activity that we see today [in Iraq] from a military standpoint, I think, will clearly decline. I think they're in their last throes, if you will, of the insurgency."
VICE PRESIDENT CHENEY, MAY 30, 2005

"[The] bottom line is that we've had enormous successes [in Iraq] and we will continue to have enormous successes."
CHENEY, INTERVIEWED BY WOLF BLITZER, CNN, JANUARY 24, 2007

In early 2007, as the fourth anniversary of the Iraq invasion approached, the Bush administration appeared unable and unwilling to change course. The rationale for going into Iraq—preventing an eventual nuclear attack engineered by Saddam Hussein—was given less debate than how to extricate US forces safely, without further casualties, and without further damaging the overall stability of the Middle East.

First Bush announced a so-called "surge" of 21,000 additional troops into Iraq in an effort to stabilize Baghdad. The plan was criticized across the political spectrum as a weak idea—as hardly a plan at all. But soon afterward, Vice President Cheney told a national audience that the critics had it wrong, describing instead the United States' "enormous successes" in Iraq, past, present, and future. His declaration prompted strong derision, even from Republican lawmakers once in lockstep who challenged the administration's decisions on the conduct of the war. Even Bush himself a week earlier had admitted on PBS's *NewsHour with Jim Lehrer* that the war was headed to a "slow failure" if more troops weren't dispatched to Baghdad and Anbar province.

Senate majority whip Richard Durbin, an Illinois Democrat, issued an unusually strong critique of Cheney's declaration, describing the vice president's remark as "delusional." Patrick Lang, a retired DIA intelligence officer who was the top Middle East adviser to then-defense secretary Cheney during Operation Desert Storm in 1991, agreed with the characterization. "Delusional is a good word. I don't think it's an act at all. He's deluded. He's living inside some little psychodrama that has constructed an artificial idea system, and he won't listen to anyone who in any way contradicts what [he] says." Lang said that he had noted a change in the behavior of his former boss, whom he described as a rational and well-focused man when he served as defense secretary.

Within the Bush administration, Cheney was described as the leading architect of and cheerleader for war with Iraq. Behind the scenes, former administration officials told us, Cheney and his secretive team of loyalists had maneuvered to make war inevitable.

Cheney at times had faced challenges inside the White House. Before the 2004 election, Karl Rove, the president's powerful political adviser, privately sounded out social and fiscal conservative activists, who were unhappy with America's foreign adventurism, about the possibility of dumping Cheney as Bush's running mate. It is unclear whether Rove had the clout with Bush to arrange such a makeover of the ticket or whether he was simply "playing to the conservative base," according to a source who is a personal friend and consultant to many of these conservative stalwarts. Nevertheless, Cheney soon found out about Rove's secret conversations with the influential conservative backers. He was not happy. Yet Rove had reason to be concerned. His own internal polling six months before the election showed that Bush would gain 3.5 percent more votes if Iraq, strongly identified with Cheney, ceased to be an issue—a critical margin in what would certainly be a close election.

The antagonism between Rove and Cheney played out in dramatic fashion in January 2007 during the first day of the trial of I. Lewis "Scooter" Libby, Cheney's former chief of staff, on charges of perjury and making false statements. Defense attorney Theodore Wells Jr. told the jury in his opening statement that the White House had "sacrificed" Libby to protect Rove, who also had leaked Valerie Plame's identity to journalists. Wells produced a handwritten note from Cheney indicating that the vice president agreed with that tactic. "Not going to protect one staffer [apparently referring to Rove] + sacrifice the guy who was asked to stick his neck in the meat grinder because of the incompetence of others," the note said. Whether Cheney tried to do anything to help pull his chief of staff from the meat grinder is unclear. If he did try, he didn't succeed.

Nevertheless, according to the source familiar with Rove's 2004 overture to conservatives, "All of this goes to the point that there is no love lost between the two men."

If Cheney became delusional as vice president, that could explain why he saw evidence that no one else could see in the intelligence. And when he talked about Iraq being a nuclear threat, he wasn't lying. Cheney, according to Lang, had "constructed a kind of world in which what he believed was correct and everything else was bullshit."

"You can't be lying if you believe it," said Lang.

The administration's hyping of the Iraq threat, then, was not lying at all. "Any suggestion that prewar information was distorted, hyped, fabricated by the leader of the nation is utterly false," Cheney told a friendly audience of neoconservatives at the American Enterprise Institute on November 21, 2005. He was, of course, referring to himself as well.

Carl Ford, who served under Cheney both as a principal deputy at the Pentagon during Desert Storm and then as head of the State Department's Bureau of Intelligence and Research during the run-up to the invasion, also is puzzled by Cheney's performance. He said that Cheney has always been an avid consumer of intelligence, with a sharp mind and practiced eyes well capable of sifting wheat from chaff. He recalled a meeting of top civilian Pentagon officials in Cheney's office during the administration of George W. Bush's father. It involved North Korea, a potential nuclear threat.

As he left his own office for the meeting, Ford noticed an intelligence report on North Korea sitting atop his inbox. He had had no chance to read it. As the meeting progressed, it became awkwardly clear that none of the other officials had read it either—except for Cheney. "Cheney was the only one in that room who had actually read the report," Ford recalled. That moment stayed with Ford for years afterward.

Yet something changed when Cheney became vice president. Ford, who had access to virtually every snippet of intelligence on Iraq's alleged nuclear program before the 2003 invasion, described it as "so piss-poor that everybody was simply guessing based on very fragmentary information . . . I had never seen such limited data making such important calls. In my career I'd never seen anything like it.

"The fact is that [Cheney] read the same things I did," Ford continued. "And if he thought there were a lot of good things there [proving that Iraq was rebuilding its nuclear program], then he's not as smart as I thought he was during the four years I worked for him" at the Pentagon.

Nonetheless, Ford remains a devoted Cheney supporter. When he testified at Senate hearings on the nomination of John Bolton to be UN ambassador [Ford opposed the nomination] on April 12, 2005, Ford told the panel that he remained "a huge fan" of Cheney.

But not everyone was a fan of the vice president or his Iraq policy.

The invasion was controversial as the first application of George Bush's new national security strategy, adopted on September 20, 2002, that broadened the meaning of preventive force, which is accepted under international law, to include preventive war. This policy sea change allowed for the use of force even without evidence of imminent attack. The administration argued that the spread of WMD technology to states with a history of aggression was an unacceptable risk, thus presenting a compelling "case for taking anticipatory action to defend ourselves, even if uncertainty remains as to the time and place of the enemy's attack."

Nevertheless, only a few officials—none of them senior staff— resigned in protest, including three State Department diplomats; others quietly took early retirement. Many more went public with their dissent after leaving government service. The clamor against war was far more pronounced overseas than in America. In Britain, for instance, two of Blair's cabinet officers, Robin Cook and Clare Short, stepped down in protest of that country's Iraq policy.

Lt. Col. Karen Kwiatkowski, the Pentagon analyst at the Near East desk, protested anonymously while in her position and then accelerated her planned retirement in 2003, just after the invasion. Before leaving the Pentagon, Kwiatkowski had started anonymously posting analytical pieces about the neoconservatives' agenda on Web sites. She had been worried that, as an insider, she would get in trouble for her complaints about the radical politics and war planning at the newly formed Office of Special Plans (OSP), led by Douglas Feith. Once she left the Pentagon, she wrote a three-part series in the magazine *American Conservative* in which she described the operations of Bush administration neoconservatives in the Defense Department and beyond. She also described her concerns on television and in online forums.

"I witnessed neoconservative agenda bearers within OSP usurp measured and carefully considered assessments, and through suppression and distortion of intelligence analysis promulgate what were in fact falsehoods to both Congress and the executive office of the president. . . . I was morally and intellectually frustrated by my powerlessness against what increasingly appeared to be a philosophical hijacking of the Pentagon."

Another who spoke out after retirement is Tyler Drumheller, who had been chief of the CIA's Europe Division and in charge of covert operations there until 2005. The position gave him access to reports about the Niger uranium forgeries. Drumheller said in a televised interview that he had warned George Tenet and others about the weakness of the intelligence on Iraqi weapons. Drumheller said on CBS's *60 Minutes* in early 2006 that intelligence analysts had warned policymakers that the intelligence was thin. "It just sticks in my craw every time I hear them say it's an intelligence failure, it's an intelligence failure. This was a policy failure," Drumheller said.

Drumheller said that intelligence agencies had voiced their skepticism about the Niger uranium claim to the intelligence consumers in the administration and in Congress. He described it as "such a low-level, unimportant thing. But once it was in that State of the Union address, it became huge."

He said that policymakers were looking for information that would provide an excuse for going to war. "The idea of going after

Iraq was US policy. It was going to happen one way or the other," Drumheller said.

Wayne White, a State Department intelligence official, spoke out against the shoddy intelligence after he retired following a twenty-six-year career. He took an interest in the Niger uranium intelligence because he, like Joseph Wilson, had served in Niger as a junior Foreign Service officer in the 1970s. A staff member brought him the documents at the State Department and he perused them. He and the staff member joked about typographical errors. The State Department had already determined the mistakes about dates and names of officials in Niger.

White and other analysts were summoned to testify before the House Intelligence Committee. One by one, the lawmakers asked White and other WMD intelligence specialists whether they had been pressured to support conclusions favored by policymakers. "Some of the other analysts should have said yes when they said no, but they were probably cowed by their supervisors or by the corporate culture," White said.

One of the critics who was most vocal after retiring was Lawrence Wilkerson, who had had the unique role of standing next to Colin Powell, the secretary of state who never wavered in public even as he privately doubted the wisdom of invasion. Wilkerson knew that many people hoped that Powell would stand up at the last moment, apologize for mistakenly supporting the march to war, and resign because it was the right thing to do.

But anyone who thought Powell might do that "didn't know him very well. He had achieved a rationalization at that time; he had actually sat down and weighed the reasons."

Wilkerson left the State Department when Powell did and started teaching national security policy at the College of William and Mary and the George Washington University. But unlike Powell, he began to lash out at those whose lies had provided justification for the invasion.

He said that Cheney and Defense Secretary Rumsfeld were leaders of a "cabal" that had railroaded US policy. "I believe that the decisions of this cabal were sometimes made with the full and witting support of the president and sometimes with something less," Wilkerson said. More often than not, he said, then-national security advisor Condoleezza Rice was shunted aside. Critics complained that Rice was weak and ineffective, unable or unwilling to arbitrate disputes between strong-willed cabinet and national security officials. The cabal's "insular and secret workings were efficient and swift—not unlike the decision-making one would associate more with a dictatorship than a democracy. This furtive process was camouflaged neatly by the dysfunction and inefficiency of the formal decision-making process, where decisions, if they were reached at all, had to wend their way through the bureaucracy, with its dissenters, obstructionists, and 'guardians of the turf.'" Wilkerson was the highest-ranking government official in the United States to break ranks over the Iraq war. Long after he delivered the speech that effectively clinched the invasion, Powell publicly acknowledged that his United Nations speech had been based on erroneous information. He was slow to reach that conclusion. As late as June 8, 2003, when it was becoming clear that significant stashes of banned weapons were unlikely to be discovered, he told Fox News that he stood by each of the claims he had made to the United Nations.

Based on the information he had seen before the war, Wilkerson also thought the United States was certain to find chemical or biological weapons in Iraq within months of the March invasion, but it didn't happen. "I was in disbelief all summer long. Did I think we were going to find incredible stores? No, but I did think we'd find something, it was just so convincing what the analysts presented to us."

Eventually, in the fall of 2003, Tenet began informing Powell, item by item, that the material in his speech was mostly wrong. Wilkerson's conclusion was that a closed circle of neoconservative operatives was cooking the books. "If you could fool George Tenet, you could certainly fool Cheney, because Cheney's information comes through a straw," Wilkerson said. Wilkerson's experience was that Cheney was predisposed to believing the people working for him and that counterarguments were futile. "You can't penetrate that with a bulldozer."

Chapter 18

Repeated History

A letter cannot start a war: Elisabetta Burba should not have blamed herself for handing over the Niger dossier to the Bush administration. Understandably, she thought that if she had kept the intelligence dossier to herself, she might have exposed Rocco Martino's fake documents and deflated US invasion plans. But if the Italian letter and the other false pages hadn't existed, George Walker Bush probably would have ordered the invasion anyway.

Nevertheless, the administration's retrieval of the uranium documents from the intelligence garbage heap made war more acceptable to Congress and to Americans in general. Without the overarching fear of the mushroom cloud, it would have been a harder sell.

At the same time, the impact of the phony dossier did not end with the invasion. The documents helped open a Pandora's box of consequences. The war itself threatened to destabilize the Middle East; its drain on the US military in blood, money, and available troops severely hindered America's ability to use force in other potential flashpoints, such as Iran and North Korea; its unpopularity at home dramatically weakened Bush's authority and resulted in the overthrow of twelve years of Republican control of Congress; abroad, the war shattered the goodwill and moral authority that the United States had cultivated since the end of World War II.

One week after Cheney declared that America had had "tremendous successes" in Iraq the Intelligence Community published a new National Intelligence Estimate about the ravaged country—the first since the flawed October 2002 report—concluding that conditions on the ground were disastrous and getting worse.

"Iraqi society's growing polarization, the persistent weakness of the security forces and the state in general, and all sides' ready recourse to violence are collectively driving an increase in communal and insurgent violence and political extremism," the report's unclassified Key Judgments section declared. This section, released on February 2, predicted that unless "measurable progress" was achieved over the next eighteen months, "the overall security situation will continue to deteriorate at rates comparable to the latter part of 2006," the most violent period since the invasion. And even if violence were reduced over the next year and a half, "given the current winner-take-all attitude and sectarian animosities infecting the political scene, Iraqi leaders will be hard pressed to achieve sustained political reconciliation."

While the NIE projected events through mid-2008, respected analysts said the fallout from Bush's preemptive attack on Iraq will likely last for years, even decades.

"The strategic blunder that this administration has made in invading Iraq has caused the United States to face its most precipitous loss of power and prestige in history," said Joseph Cirincione, a former congressional defense staffer and now vice president for national security and international affairs at the Center for American Progress. "The last six years have been devastating for the United States. Never have we been so isolated, so hated, so weakened before. . . . How much power we've lost in these last six years. Military power, economic [power] because of deficits, and diplomatically because of the way we treated our allies. This is historic turning-point stuff. This isn't just partisan rhetoric; this is people genuinely worried about what has happened to us."

Cirincione had foreseen an emerging disaster within three days of the invasion, even as Bush, Cheney, and colleagues gave each other high fives for their success.

Bush had shrugged off warnings from the CIA that Iraq, a tribal nation with deep sectarian divides, could well break apart in the aftermath of an invasion. He did not heed the pleas for caution from doubters at home, from European allies, from the United Nations, even from the likes of Brent Scowcroft, his father's national security adviser. Scowcroft had warned in the summer of 2002 that attacking Iraq "is certain to divert us for some indefinite period from our war on terrorism. Worse, there is a virtual consensus in the world against an attack on Iraq at this time. . . . Ignoring that clear sentiment would result in a serious degradation in international cooperation with us against terrorism. And make no mistake, we simply cannot win that war without enthusiastic international cooperation, especially on intelligence."

When Bush disregarded warnings and ordered the invasion, many critics predicted that the result would be a heavier landing than his arrival on an aircraft carrier in the Pacific on May 1, 2003, when he declared, "Major combat operations in Iraq have ended."

Four years after the US invasion, some true believers thought they still would find weapons caches in the Iraqi desert if they searched hard enough and that the discovery would exonerate the administration for invading Iraq. Others were convinced the WMDs were smuggled across the border to Syria or Iran just before the war started. At least one freelance operation to search for underground laboratories and caches of WMDs was planned in 2006.

For some administration officials, the acceptance of reality was difficult. Lawrence Wilkerson, Colin Powell's former chief of staff, said reality and belief were twisted together in the drive toward war in Iraq. "Once you get to the point where you're reinforcing your own beliefs with cherry-picked stuff, it's hard to start drawing a line between where you knew a particular fact was really false but accepted it anyway, because it conformed and buttressed your case."

Wilkerson said he thought Cheney still believed the story that Iraq tried to buy uranium from Niger. "I think Cheney still thinks that Iraq, however ineffectually, . . . attempted to explore the possibility of getting uranium from Niger as late as possibly the early 2000s. I think he still believes that."

The faulty WMD intelligence served as a crutch that Cheney employed repeatedly.

"While he did not have stockpiles—clearly the intelligence that said he did was wrong," he told Tim Russert on September 10, 2006, on *Meet the Press*.

"That was the intelligence we saw, that was the intelligence all of us believed, it was—when, when George Tenet sat in the Oval Office and the president of the United States asked him directly, he said, 'George, how good is the case against Saddam on weapons of mass destruction?' the director of the CIA said, 'It's a slam dunk, Mr. President, it's a slam dunk.' That was the intelligence that was provided to us at the time, and based on which we made a choice."

At the same time, he said, the intelligence didn't matter. Even without the WMD intelligence, he told Russert, America would have invaded Iraq anyway because "it was the right thing to do and if we had to do it all over again, we'd do exactly the same thing."

Four years into the war, Bush administration officials had not detailed exactly why they felt it was necessary to invade, especially if the specter of mushroom clouds was illusory.

Richard Clarke, chief counterterrorism adviser at the National Security Council, described the Bush administration's preoccupation with Iraq hours after the 9/11 attacks and months before the CIA ratcheted up its assessments on Iraq's alleged WMD programs. Before 9/11 the CIA said it thought Saddam Hussein aspired to having a nuclear program but did not. In 2002, the revised estimate was that Iraq was planning to build a nuclear bomb.

In his book, *Against All Enemies*, Clarke described a meeting with Bush and other top officials on September 12, 2001:

> I left the video conferencing center and there, wandering alone around the situation room, was the president. He looked like he wanted something to do. He grabbed a few of us and closed the door to the conference room. "Look," he told us, "I know you have a lot to do and all, but I want you, as soon as you can, to go back over everything, everything. See if Saddam did this. See if he's linked in any way."
>
> I was once again taken aback, incredulous, and it showed. "But, Mr. President, Al Qaeda did this."
>
> "I know, I know, but—see if Saddam was involved. Just look. I want to know any shred—"
>
> "Absolutely, we will look—again." I was trying to be more respectful, more responsive. "But you know, we have looked several times for state sponsorship of Al Qaeda and not found any real linkages to Iraq. Iran plays a little, as does Pakistan, and Saudi Arabia, Yemen."
>
> "Look into Iraq, Saddam," the president said testily and left us.

By December 2001, Bush's speechwriter, David Frum, was asked to come up with a justification for the Iraq war. "Can you sum up in a sentence or two our best case for going after Iraq?" Frum then helped coin the term "axis of evil"—Iraq, Iran, and North Korea—a trio of states with little in common other than their threat to join the once-exclusive group of nations that have nuclear weapons. Frum said that Saddam Hussein was inherently bad, whether or not he had anything to do with al Qaeda or 9/11. In an early draft he penned for Bush's 2002 State of the Union speech, he wrote, "Indeed, Saddam Hussein's Baathist ideology was cobbled together in the 1940s by Arab admirers of Hitler and Mussolini. So there was our link—and our explanation of why we must act: Together, the terror states and the terrorist organizations formed an axis of hatred against the United States. The United States could not wait for these dangerous regimes to get deadly weapons and attack us; the United States must strike first and protect the world from them." The final draft dropped the last sentence, replacing it with the more elegant "Time is not on our side. I will not wait on events, while dangers gather. I will not stand by as peril draws closer and closer." The warning was the same and the die was cast. Several months later the White House declared that its new national security strategy embraced the principle of preventive war—military action even if there was no evidence of an imminent attack by the enemy.

The Intelligence Community's failure to connect the dots to prevent the September 11 al Qaeda attacks, followed by its woeful performance in assessing Iraq's banned weapons, prompted the administration and Congress to order the largest reorganization of the American Intelligence Community since the creation of the CIA in 1947.

Under the 2004 reorganization act, the CIA remained the primary foreign intelligence–gathering agency, but its director, who also had held the title of director of central intelligence, lost his coordinating authority over the rest of the Intelligence Community. That function was taken over by a new layer of bureaucracy overseen by the director of national intelligence.

As the new Democratic-controlled Congress took over, there were pledges by key committee chairmen that they would conduct aggressive oversight investigations. One of the promises was to conclude the Senate Intelligence Committee's long-delayed investigation of the administration's use—or manipulation—of the Iraq WMD intelligence. Another issue left hanging was a 2005 pledge by the committee's then-ranking member and now chairman, Senator Jay Rockefeller of West Virginia, to investigate the Pentagon Office of Special Plans. In 2006 the committee tried to obtain copies of reports produced by Special Plans and to interview members of its staff, but deferred to an ongoing Pentagon Inspector General investigation. The inspector general issued a classified report in February 2007 saying that Feith's shop had conducted "inappropriate" activities.

Many questions still surround the Italian letter. At publication time, the trial of I. Lewis "Scooter" Libby on charges of perjury, obstruction of justice, and making false statements to the FBI was underway. Special Prosecutor Patrick Fitzgerald had not yet closed his investigation. Plame and her husband, Joseph Wilson, were suing government officials, alleging that they blew her cover as a clandestine CIA officer in retaliation for Wilson's criticism of US policy following his 2002 fact-finding trip to Niger.

One confusing element in that story was the admission by Richard Armitage, deputy secretary of state under Colin Powell, that he had been the first to pass along Valerie Plame's identity to newspaper columnist Robert Novak and to Bob Woodward, assistant managing editor of the *Washington Post*.

Armitage's leaking of the information puzzled people who knew him. He was a retired navy officer who had served in Vietnam and been a deputy assistant secretary of defense and an aide to Ronald

Reagan, Bob Dole, and George W. Bush. Many of those who had worked with him said he was sometimes careless with gossip and that was the reason for his leaking Plame's name. They said he got along poorly with the neoconservatives and with Vice President Cheney's office; was intensely loyal to his boss, Powell; and was unlikely to have conspired with the White House in the attacks on Joe Wilson and the outing of Plame.

Others were not so sure. Powell's former staff director, Wilkerson, eventually wondered, admittedly without solid evidence, whether he might have been frozen out of one aspect of the Bush administration's operations in 2002 and 2003. "It could be that Rich [Armitage] and Powell were complicit together" with the White House, Wilkerson said.

The neoconservatives, meanwhile, were blaming others and pointing fingers over the disintegrating situation in the Middle East. Richard Perle, once the war's biggest booster, said the root problem was disarray within the administration. "At the end of the day, you have to hold the president responsible," he said in an interview in *Vanity Fair* late last year. "I don't think he realized the extent of the opposition within his own administration, and the disloyalty."

Frum, Bush's former speechwriter who helped coin the term "axis of evil," also put the onus on his former boss. "The insurgency has proven it can kill anyone who cooperates, and the United States and its friends have failed to prove that it can protect them." He called it a "failure at the center"—referring to Bush.

And Kenneth Adelman, a longtime Pentagon insider who famously had predicted that the invasion would be a "cakewalk," attributed the disaster in Iraq to Bush's national security team, which he described as one of "the most incompetent teams in the postwar [World War II] era. Not only did each of them, individually, have enormous flaws, but together they were deadly, dysfunctional."

Even as the Iraq morass was deepening, the administration and neoconservatives focused on another leg of the axis of evil—Iran. The administration railed against Iran's nuclear fuel enrichment program and its material and training support for Shiite factions inside Iraq.

But the White House and the Intelligence Community were far more circumspect in making intelligence claims about Iran. In early 2007, the administration promised to release an intelligence report on Iran's alleged role in supporting the insurgency in Iraq. A PowerPoint presentation, complete with photographs of the serial numbers of weapons seized inside Iraq that link them to manufacture in Iran, was delayed several times, in part because top officials wanted to make sure the intelligence would hold up. "This is one of many examples you can cite in terms of our heightened emphasis on tradecraft," an intelligence official told us. "You've got to make sure in what you put out there that the case stands up. . . . It's an awareness that when you go public with this stuff, it's got to be as good a presentation as it can be."

In some cases, US political statements about Iran mirrored the party line years earlier in the run-up to the Iraq invasion. In August 2006 the then-Republican majority on the House Intelligence Committee issued an alarming report that Iran was processing weapons-grade uranium. It was written by a neoconservative point man in the administration, Fred Fleitz, a former CIA official and ex-aide to UN ambassador John Bolton. He wrote that the processing was being conducted at Iran's nuclear facility in the town of Natanz.

As was the case with Iraq, UN weapons inspectors challenged the committee's assessment. The International Atomic Energy Agency, still led by Mohamed ElBaradei, sent a letter to US officials detailing at least five errors in the report issued by the subcommittee on intelligence policy.

The *Washington Post* obtained a copy of the IAEA letter. "Among the committee's assertions is that Iran is producing weapons-grade uranium at its facility in the town of Natanz. The IAEA called that 'incorrect,' noting that weapons-grade uranium is enriched to a level of 90 percent or more. Iran has enriched uranium to 3.5 percent under IAEA monitoring.

"Privately," the *Post* reported, "several intelligence officials said the committee report included at least a dozen claims that were either demonstrably wrong or impossible to substantiate."

The *Post* also quoted David Albright, president of the Institute for Science and International Security, who had criticized the US intelligence on Iraq's nuclear weapons program during the run-up to the invasion.

"'This is like prewar Iraq all over again,' he said. 'You have an Iranian nuclear threat that is spun up, using bad information that's cherry-picked and a report that trashes the inspectors.'"

The Iraq war was justified with distortions, if not outright lies; and the word "lie" was not easily and comfortably used in American public life or in journalism. Did Vice President Cheney lie when he cited links between Saddam Hussein and al Qaeda on September 8, 2002, three months after the CIA told him that was wrong, or, as a US senator declared, was he delusional?

Why did Bush recite those 16 words scrolling on his teleprompter at the 2003 State of the Union address that "The British government has learned that Saddam Hussein recently sought significant quantities of uranium from Africa"? Did he know that many in the Intelligence Community had serious doubts? His national security staff clearly did.

Why did Britain run interference for Bush, saying that they had independent sources of information about Iraqi uranium supplies and maintaining that position even years later? Britain never disclosed its evidence.

"Very, very rarely has an American president lied about such an important subject," said Cirincione. "It's one thing to lie about an affair," he said, referring to the righteous indignation expressed by Republican lawmakers spearheading the impeachment of Bill Clinton. "It's another thing to lie about a war."

A letter may not start or avert a war, but it can have a profound effect. The Italian letter was a fraud that helped promote the Iraq war; eighty-six years earlier, the Zimmermann Telegram brought the United States into the Great War. At the time of the Zimmermann Telegram, named for the German foreign minister in 1917, Arthur Zimmermann, the United States' role in world affairs was far different. President Woodrow Wilson advocated international cooperation to the extreme, eventually promoting the League of Nations, and sought to stay out of the European war. Britain saw US engagement as the path to victory, while Germany feigned neutrality with the United States.

The telegram was a secret transmission from Berlin to the German embassy in Mexico City, reporting that Germany was about to initiate U-boat attacks on US shipping vessels, an act of war. Germany proposed an alliance with Mexico and promised them the return of lost territory—Arizona, New Mexico, and Texas. Revelation of the telegram—intercepted by British code breakers—obviously provoked US public outrage, and Wilson had no choice but to declare war on Germany.

The final chance for the Germans and for opponents of war in the

United States to avert the conflict was for Zimmermann to disavow the telegram and claim it was a subterfuge by US and British warmongers. Zimmermann did not do so. "I cannot deny it," he said. "It is true."

Wilson declared war on April 6, 1917.

In 1917, the United States was immersed in political isolationism, and a wave of pacifism argued against war. In 2003, the Bush administration was engaged in another form of isolationism—disdaining the role of the United Nations, considering its hegemony a greater force, contemptuous of analysis and opinion originating beyond the small center of its own power. Even Bush's father, the forty-first president, and his father's closest advisers feared that the Iraq war would be a mistake. But he also feared telling his son that.

"I think it symbolizes . . . the general realm of unreality and untruth that marked US foreign policy in 2002–2003," said Walter LaFeber, a distinguished historian and professor at Cornell University. In 1917 and 2003, US political analysis was lacking but for different reasons.

"US officials never sufficiently understand the possible dimensions of their military interventions, sometimes out of cultural ignorance [as in 1917], sometimes out of cultural ignorance and the belief they don't have to pay attention to possible results anyway [as in 2003]."

Any pacifist argument in the United States against joining the European war against Germany collapsed with the revelation of the Zimmermann Telegram. Zimmermann might have deflected the US declaration of war and protected secret German planning a while longer by claiming the telegram was a fake. His choice in the lights of political discourse in 2006 was quaint. He was the enemy, but he was not willing to lie, even on a point that could affect the course of a war.

Endnotes

Chapter 1

Page 2   **It was his clearest statement**   Peter Baker, "2002 Doctrine of Preemptive War to Be Reaffirmed," *Washington Post,* March 16, 2006.

He said that Hussein   "With nuclear arms or a full arsenal of chemical and biological weapons, Saddam Hussein could resume his ambitions of conquest in the Middle East, and create deadly havoc in the region. And this Congress and the American people must recognize another threat. Evidence from intelligence sources, secret communications, and statements by people now in custody, reveal that Saddam Hussein aids and protects terrorists, including members of al-Qaeda. Secretly, and without fingerprints, he could provide one of his hidden weapons to terrorists or help them develop their own."

Page 3   **After the March 20, 2003**   The first prominent national mention of the "16 words" was on MSNBC's *Hardball* with Chris Matthews, June 13, 2003.

Mohammed ElBaradei   Colum Lynch, "UN Finds No Proof of Nuclear Program; IAEA Unable to Verify US Claims," *Washington Post,* January 29, 2003, 1.

He pleaded for more time   ElBaradei addressed the council on January 27, 2003: http://www.un.org/News/dh/iraq/elbaradei27jan03.htm.

the Italian Military Intelligence and Security Service, a government agency better known as SISMI   Servizio per le Informazioni e la Sicurezza Militar.

[Pag]e 4   **David Albright**   Interview, 2006.

[W]ithout turning over   Senate Select Committee on Intelligence report, [pa]ges 36 and 38.

[Page] 5   **Perhaps no single document**   The Zimmermann Telegram was an [int]ercepted message from the German foreign ministry. It was eventually [inte]nded for the Mexican president and offered the return of US border terri[tory] if Mexico joined the axis.

[Pres]ident Bush already had substantial support   Richard Morin and Clau[dia] Deane, "Support for a War with Iraq Grows After Bush's Speech; Half the [Nati]on Favors Military Action Without UN Backing," *Washington Post,* Feb[ruary] 2, 2003.

This time the draft   Interview with a former senior CIA official, [Octob]er 12, 2006, and SSCI report, page 64.

"When I see bin Laden issuing fatwahs . . . "   Interview of James [Woolse]y by Wolf Blitzer, CNN, September 12, 2001.

[S]eptember 2001   Elaine Sciolino and Alison Mitchell, "Calls for [Bu]sh into Iraq Gain Power in Washington," *New York Times,* December [200]9.

The Italian letter was the product of a different moment in history, of a mightily expanded US position in world affairs, of vastly
new dangers facing the planet. But the comparison can be made. I
the words of Barbara Tuchman, "The Zimmermann telegram w
only a pebble on the long road of history. But a pebble can kill a G
ath, and this one killed the American illusion that we could go a
our business happily separate from other nations. In world affa
was a German Minister's minor plot. In the lives of the An
people it was the end of innocence."

Page 9   **"I'm not here today . . . "**   Interview of Vice President Cheney on *Meet the Press,* September 8, 2002.

"The most reliable reporting . . . "   June 2002 partly declassified CIA report, "Iraq and al Qaeda: Interpreting a Murky Relationship."

Yet the administration's repeated suggestions   Dana Milbank and Claudia Deane, "Hussein Link to 9/11 Lingers in Many Minds," *Washington Post,* September 6, 2003, A1.

The chief al Qaeda–Iraq conspiracy theoretician   Peter Bergen, "Armchair Provocateur," *Washington Monthly,* December 2003.

Page 10   **Advocates of an invasion**   Interview with Patrick Lang, October 13, 2006.

The Intelligence Community   National Intelligence Estimate, October 2002.

In a scathing 2006 essay   Paul Pillar "Terrorism and US Foreign Policy," *Foreign Affairs,* February 2006.

Page 12   **"We know the Americans have concerns . . . "**   Rajiv Chandrasekaran and Colum Lynch, "UN Officials Say Intelligence to Prove US Claim Is Lacking; Best Information Still Being Withheld from Inspectors," *Washington Post,* January 27, 2003, A12.

Page 13   **The morning papers raised questions**   Dan Balz, "One Topic Rules Bush's Thinking," *Washington Post,* January 29, 2003, 1; and Ronald Brownstein, "War Now Drives the Presidency," *Los Angeles Times,* January 29, 2003.

CIA officials were immediately skeptical   Letter dated October 6, 1997, from Hans Blitz to the UN Security Council.

Page 14   **"Cheney's too smart."**   Interview with Carl Ford, April 17, 2006.

Page 15   **In sizing up President Bush's speech**   Interview with Elisabetta Burba, March 4, 2006.

Chapter 2

Page 16   **Pino Buongiorno, a fellow reporter**   Pino Buongiorno, "La Guerra? È cominciata (The War? It has begun)," *Panorama,* September 12, 2002.

Page 17   **The major export**   For details on uranium oxide, production and uses, see http://www.galleries.com/minerals/oxides/uraninit/uraninit.htm.

Page 18   **She did remember seeing**   British white paper, September 24, 2002, 6. The paper, issued by the British government, said that Iraq "sought significant quantities of uranium from Africa, despite having no active civil nuclear power programme that could require it."

Page 24   **Accompanying the Italian letter**   Interview with senior diplomat at Niger's embassy to the United States, September 27, 2006.

Page 25   **But there was no**   Interview with intelligence official, September 20, 2006.

It prompted the DIA a week later   Senate Select Committee on Intelligence, report on Niger, page 39; http://www.factcheck.org/UploadedFiles/US%20Report.pdf.

Page 27   **One person who refused**   Interviews with US government sources who knew C. C. refused requests for an interview.

Page 30   Rossella defended the story   Interview with Rossella, June 14, 2006.

Page 31   *Panorama* published a question-and-answer   Ledeen, *Panorama,* October 3, 2002.

Page 32   Because of his historical ties   Interview with Michael Ledeen, September 7, 2006.

Attending the three-day session   Knut Royce and Timothy M. Phelps, "Secret Talks with Iranian Sources: Meetings 'Unauthorized,'" *Newsday,* August 9, 2003, A4.

Page 33   There was no evidence   Laura Rozen, "Three Days in Rome," *Mother Jones,* July/August 2006.

Despite his murky past   Thomas B. Edsall and Dana Milbankm, "White House's Roving Eye for Politics; President's Most Powerful Adviser May Also Be the Most Connected," *Washington Post,* March 10, 2003, A1.

Kay cabled back   Bob Woodward, *State of Denial,* New York: Simon & Schuster, 259–60.

"Everyone tells me . . . "   Interview with Bill Murray, October 11, 2006.

Page 34   Burba had the impression   Colloquio Con Il Colonnello Antonio Nucera (Conversation with Col. Antonio Nucera), *Il Giornale,* November 6, 2005, quoted by www.warandpiece.com, Nucera on the Record, November 6, 2005.

Page 37   Associates said C.   Interview with CIA source, April 2006.

Page 39   The Western Europe Division   Interviews with State Department sources, March 2006.

Page 40   Carl Ford Jr., the blunt Vietnam War veteran   Interview with Carl Ford Jr., February 2006.

Page 41   Burba went to Niamey   Interviews with Burba, March 2006.

Page 45   "For me, she was not . . . "   Interview with Rosella, June 14, 2006.

Chapter 3

Page 47   . . . one of the estimated 62 million people who watched   "Bush Improves on State of Union TV Ratings (41.7MM viewers)," Reuter News Agency, February 2, 2006.

Page 48   "We saw the fireball . . . "   Interview on C-SPAN, April 2, 2006.

Page 53   Their report was delivered   Bob Woodward, *State of Denial,* 83–85.

Page 54   People knew the attitude   Interview with DIA official, April 10, 2006.

In a substantially declassified report   "The Use by the Intelligence Community of Information Provided by the Iraqi National Congress," a report of the Senate Select Committee on Intelligence, September 8, 2006.

Page 55   INC defectors   Ibid.

"At the time . . . "   Interview with a former senior CIA officer, December 10, 2006.

In late 2001   Ibid.

Page 56   The first two analysts   James Risen, "The Struggle for Iraq: Diplomacy," *New York Times,* November 6, 2003, 1.

Page 57   **The intelligence they**   Interview with Rand Beers, October 27, 2006.

Page 58   **NESA's Iraq desk grew from four to eighteen staffers**   Interview with senior OSP official, May 3, 2003.

It included a handful of professional analysts   Interview with Karen Kwiatkowski, February 23, 2006.

Page 58   **Special Plans was run by Abram Shulsky**   Interview with Vincent Cannistraro, September 28, 2006. Cannistraro had many dealings with Shulsky while serving on the National Security Council during the Reagan administration.

Page 59   **But the Office of Special Plans**   Interview with staff member, Senate Armed Services Committee, May 26, 2006. (The Intelligence Community scooped up and analyzed every possible source of intelligence, including from the supersecret National Security Agency, which vacuums the airwaves for virtually all forms of electronic transmissions—from cell and landline phones, radios, the Internet, missile tests, diplomatic and military correspondence, encrypted or in microbursts, at home and abroad. Special Plans also had access to the NSA intercepts. During confirmation hearings in May 2006, air force general Michael Hayden, the new CIA director, complained that when Feith headed the NSA in 2002, his office routinely sought transcripts of intercepted conversations it hoped would make the al-Qaeda link with Iraq. "I wasn't comfortable" with Feith's approach to intelligence, he told the Senate Intelligence Committee. Hayden said the NSA adopted a highly unusual practice of issuing disclaimers in the transcripts delivered to Feith's analysts, reminding them that the intercepted material, standing alone, "neither confirms nor denies" anything. That was largely true for much of what the NSA was vacuuming from the airwaves. The intelligence the NSA was collecting on Iraq "was mostly ambiguous," the Senate intelligence source said.)

Pages 59–60   **Officials ordered them never to confirm**   Karen Kwiatkowski, "Conscientious Objector," *American Conservative,* December 15, 2003.

Page 60   **Other than its access**   Interview with senior official at Office of Special Plans, May 3, 2003.

Ahmed Chalabi was a frequent visitor   James Bamford, "The Man Who Sold the War," *Rolling Stone,* November 15, 2005.

When asked to comment   Interview of Ahmed Chalabi by Chris Wallace, *Fox News Sunday,* April 25, 2004.

Page 61   **"There were a lot of the opposition forces . . . "**   Interview with Col. Patrick Lang, USA retired, May 2006.

According to Kwiatkowski,   Karen Kwiatkowski, "Conscientious Objector," *American Conservative,* December 15, 2003.

Critics have described   Seymour Hersh, "The Stovepipe; How Conflicts Between the Bush Administration and the Intelligence Community Marred the Reporting on Iraq's Weapons," *New Yorker,* October 27, 2003.

Page 62   **Some of the intelligence that flowed**   Mark Hosenball and Michael Isikoff, "Cheney and the 'Raw' Intelligence," *Newsweek,* December 15, 2003.

Kwiatkowski recalled   Interview with Kwiatkowski, February 23, 2006.

Page 64   **"The commitment of our forces . . . "**   Greg Newbold, "Why Iraq Was a Mistake," *Time,* April 9, 2006.

Chapter 4

Page 66   **"At the time . . . "**   Senate Select Committee on Intelligence, Report on the Intelligence Community's Prewar Intelligence Assessments on Iraq, July 7, 2004, 36.

One reason was   Interview with CIA source, 2006.

Page 68   **The errors were so**   Cannistraro said it should have been apparent that the original documents with appropriate letterheads were rifled from files and provided to the conspirators by an employee at the Rome embassy—La Signora eventually admitted to a Rome prosecutor that she did just that. Then Italian forgers with rudimentary knowledge of Niger deleted the original content of the letters, replacing them with phony official messages.

The DIA report   Patrick Conway, a doctoral candidate in Australia, analyzed the letters extensively.

Page 69   **Melvin Goodman**   Interview, October 11, 2006.

The DIA's ominous report   Karen DeYoung and Glenn Kessler, "Cheney Says Tax Cuts Eased Recession; Democrats Assail Speech to Foreign Relations Group as 'Revisionism,'" *Washington Post,* February 16, 2002.

Page 70   **It is a rare analyst**   Interview with John Gannon, April 14, 2006.

Page 71   **Cheney crossed**   Interview with Wayne White, February 23, 2006.

He said Cheney   Interview with Paul R. Pillar; and Paul Pillar, "Intelligence, Policy, and the War in Iraq," *Foreign Affairs,* March/April 2006.

Page 72   **A top-ranking former deputy director**   Richard Kerr, "The Path to War," *Vanity Fair,* May 2004.

Page 73   **"The sources were so bad."**   Interview with intelligence source, April 12, 2006.

Not everyone in the Intelligence Community   Senate Select Committee report.

Page 74   **At the same time**   Ibid, but Martinez is not mentioned by name.

Page 75   **The French officers found nothing**   Chouet first sent agents in the summer of 2001. Carlo Bonini and Giuseppe D'Avanzo, "Il Mercato della Paura [The market of Fear]," Rome: Giulio Einaudi Editore, 79–80.

Joseph Wilson was a logical choice   Interview with a senior CIA official at the time, July 2003.

Page 76   **Most important, he had conducted**   Edward Harris and Ellen Knickmeyer, "AP Investigation: Head of Pakistan's Nuclear Ring Made Repeated Visits to Uranium-Rich African," The Associated Press, April 18, 2004.

CIA case officers and analysts   Senate Select Committee report, 40.

A WINPAC analyst said   Ibid.

Page 77   **The agency called Wilson**   Joseph Wilson, *The Politics of Truth,* New York: Carroll and Graf, 18–19.

She was happy to receive her colleague   Ibid; and interview with Wilson, February 2006.

Page 78   **The Bush administration**   Report of Senate Intelligence Committee reviewing prewar intelligence, July 9, 2004, 46; http://www.gpoaccess.gov/serialset/creports/iraq.html.

Page 80   **"All these guys think they're spooks."**   Interview with retired CIA officer, March 2006.

"That organization is hopeless . . . "   Ibid.

The feeling was mutual   Interview with Lt. Col. Lawrence Wilkerson, April 25, 2006.

Page 81   **The CIA Directorate of Operations asked**   Senate Intelligence report, op.cit., 68.

Page 82   **"People knew what attitude the 'powers that be' . . . "**   Intelligence source interview, April 2006.

Chapter 5

Page 83   **The CIA's reporting had downplayed**   Senate Intelligence report on prewar intelligence, op. cit., 46. "The most important fact in the report was that the Nigerian officials admitted that the Iraqi delegation had traveled there in 1999 and that the Nigerian Prime Minister believed the Iraqis were interested in purchasing uranium, because this provided confirmation of the foreign government service reporting."

Page 85   **Each visited Africa**   Barton Gellman, "US Strikes at Iraqi Targets; Impeachment Vote Delayed," *Washington Post,* December 17, 1998.

Zahawie was suddenly ordered   Interview with Wissam al-Zahawie, April 27, 2006; and Raymond Whitaker, "The Diplomat: The Forgery and the Suspect Case for War," *The Independent,* August 10, 2003.

Page 86   **The urbane diplomat**   E-mail correspondence with Zahawie, April 27, 2006.

Page 90   **Was Zahawie aware**   Based on Zahawie's reconstruction of the conversation. E-mail from Zahawie, April 24, 2006.

Page 93   **"They are not near Baghdad."**   Sahaaf, April 5, 2003; http:// www.cfif.org/htdocs/freedomline/current/in_our_opinion/baghdad_bob.htm. Two days later, he may have been more prescient when he said: "This invasion will end in failure."

Hitchens wrote   Christopher Hitchens, "Wowie Zahawie: Sorry Everyone, but Iraq Did Go Uranium Shopping in Niger," *Slate,* April 10, 2006.

Page 95   **"We captured one . . . "**   Interview with Wayne White, February 22, 2006.

Before and after the invasion   David Albright, "Iraq's Aluminum Tubes: Separating Fact from Fiction," The Institute for Science and International Security, December 5, 2003, 33.

"By failing to acknowledge this point . . . "   An extensive analysis by Albright on March 10, 2003, is also available at http://www.isis-online.org/ publications/iraq/al_tubes.html.

Page 96   **There was no other**   The Butler Report (Review of Intelligence on Weapons of Mass Destruction), House of Commons, July 14, 2004.

The British claim   "The full transcript of evidence given to the Butler Inquiry," *The Independent,* London, December 15, 2006.

In retrospect, Wilson deeply regretted   Interview with Wilson, February 2006.

Chapter 6

Page 98   The WHIG team was assembled   Interview with former White House official, April 24, 2006.

Page 99   Wolfowitz, in an interview   Interview by Sam Tannenhaus, *Vanity Fair,* May 2003.

"The WMD that really . . . "   Interview with Greg Theilmann, March 23, 2006.

Page 101   The *New York Times*'s ominous story   Michael R. Gordon and Judith Miller, "Threats and Responses: The Iraqis; US Says Hussein Intensifies Quest for A-Bomb Parts," *New York Times,* September 8, 2002.

Page 102   But the administration was opening   Elizabeth Bumiller, "Traces of Terror: The Strategy; Bush Aides Set Strategy to Sell Policy on Iraq," *NewYork Times,* September 7, 2002, 1.

Page 103   "There is no doubt that . . . "   Michael R. Gordon and Judith Miller, "Threats and Responses: The Iraqis; US Says Hussein Intensifies Quest for A-Bomb Parts," *New York Times,* September 8, 2002, 1.

Cheney, for instance,   Interview with Dick Cheney on *Meet the Press,* September 8, 2002.

Four days after the *New York Times* exposé   Bush speech before the United Nations General Assembly, September 12, 2002.

Page 104   "Our guys weren't able to persuade the Brits . . . "   Interview with Paul Pillar, March 2006.

Page 105   Tenet told the intelligence committee   Walter Pincus, "CIA Did Not Share Doubt on Iraq Data; Bush Used Report of Uranium Bid," *Washington Post,* June 12, 2003, 1.

"In the case of prewar assessments . . . "   Commission on the Intelligence Capabilities of the United States Regarding Weapons of Mass Destruction, the Robb-Silberman Commission, named after cochairmen Charles Robb and Laurence Silberman.

Page 106   Bush had been warming up   A *Washington Post* staffer, "Not Seasick, Not Sleek, Just Ooching," *Washington Post,*October 5, 2002.

Over the weekend   Text of an early draft, Senate Select Committee on Intelligence Report, 55. One early draft said, "The regime has been caught attempting to purchase up to 500 metric tons of uranium oxide from Africa."

page 107   The intelligence, Tenet said   Senate Intelligence Committee report, 56.

Page 108   The White House public relations   Mike Allen, "Bush to Address US on Case against Iraq," *Washington Post,* October 7, 2002, A13.

In any case, the three major broadcast networks   Jim Rutenberg, "Threats and Response; The Networks; 3 Networks Skip Bush's Talk, Citing Absence of Request." The Associated Press,13.

Page 109   Bush went further   Zarqawi was killed by U.S. troops in Iraq in June 2006.

But the *Washington Post*   Dana Milbank, "For Bush, Facts Are Malleable; Presidential Tradition of Embroidering Key Assertions Continues," *Washington Post,* October 22, 2002, A1.

Three days later   Knut Royce, "CIA Reports Dispute Bush Pattern of Exaggeration on Iraq Seen by Sources," *Newsday,* October 10, 2002, A7.

Chapter 7

Page 113   **Under orders from John Robert Bolton**   Senate Select Committee on Intelligence.

The fact sheet specifically mentioned Niger   Chronology from the State Department's Inspector General.

The nonproliferation bureau   Senate Select Committee on Intelligence report.

Page 116   **When he returned to his office**   Interview with a former senior CIA official, October 12, 2006.

Several months after Bush's State of the Union   Senate Select Committee on Intelligence report, 65.

In an influential essay   Paul Pillar, "Intelligence, Policy and the War in Iraq," *Foreign Affairs,* March/April 2006.

Page 117   **"I doubt if . . . "**   Interview with Pat Roberts, *Meet the Press,* July 11, 2004.

Chapter 8

Page 119   **One day in December 2002**   There had been earlier indications that WINPAC had a keen antenna for sensing priority changes when the Clinton administration made way for the incoming Bush team and had the bureaucratic deftness to accommodate those shifting priorities. Under a 1997 congressional order, the CIA was responsible for a semiannual report on the global proliferation of weapons of mass destruction. During the Clinton administration, the unclassified documents paid scant notice to Iraq. In its first report, it devoted three paragraphs to Iraq, noting in passing that Baghdad possessed dual-use equipment that could be used for chemical and biological programs. There was no mention of a nuclear program. The last report during the Clinton years, the report made only a glancing reference to nuclear weapons, saying that Iraq had "probably continued low-level theoretical R&D [research and development]" and that its "most significant obstacle" to producing a bomb was that it had no fissile material. (Unclassified Report to Congress on the Acquisition of Technology Relating to Weapons of Mass Destruction and Advanced Convention Munitions, 1 January through 30 June 2000) The reports were drafted by the CIA's Nonproliferation Center. Beginning in 2001, the Bush administration's first year, the reports became more ominous. WINPAC, headed by Foley, reported in 2001 that the Intelligence Community was "concerned" about "a reconstituted nuclear weapons program" and warned that Iraq "may be attempting to acquire materials" to produce a bomb. (Unclassified Report to Congress on the Acquisition of Technology Relating to Weapons of Mass Destruction and Advanced Convention Munitions, 1 January through 30 June 2001)

Pages 121–22   **They were too narrow**   Barton Gellman and Walter Pincus, "Depiction of Threat Outgrew Supporting Evidence," *Washington Post,* August 10, 2003, A1.

Page 122   **Foley and WINPAC**   Report on the US Intelligence Community's Prewar Intelligence Assessments on Iraq, 57–58.

Chapter 9

Page 131   **While he avoided the substance of the Italian letter**   http://www. whitehouse.gov/news/releases/2003/02/20030205-1.html#6.

Page 133   **Mohamed ElBaradei, the director general of the International Atomic Energy Agency**   Colum Lynch, "UN Finds No Proof of Nuclear Program; IAEA Unable to Verify US Claims," *Washington Post,* January 29, 2003, 1.

Chapter 10

Page 135   **"Based on thorough analysis . . . "**   ElBaradei speech, March 7, 2003. http://www.un.org/News/dh/iraq/elbaradei-7mar03.pdf.

Page 137   **"They totally . . . "**   Interview with former CIA source, May 27, 2006.

Page 138   **Such reports**   Senator Pat Roberts, July 9, 2004, on the release of the SSCI report.

Besides organizations   Interview with former CIA source, May 27, 2006.

The United States continued   Dafna Linzer, "IAEA Leader's Phone Tapped; US Pores Over Transcripts to Try to Oust Nuclear Chief," **Washington Post,** December 12, 2004, A1.

Page 139   **Blix realized**   Ewen MacAskill, "Exclusive: Blix: I Was a Target Too: Chief UN Weapons Inspector Believes He Was Bugged," *The Guardian,* February 28, 2004, 1.

The most sweeping   Document reprinted by *The Observer,* London, March 2, 2003.

Page 140   **Over drinks**   Interview with former senior official, May 27, 2006.

US spy agencies   *Washington Post,* op.cit, December 12, 2004.

"We've always assumed . . . "   Ibid.

"You're actually watched . . . "   Interview with David Albright, May 15, 2006.

Page 141   **"The fact that . . . "**   IAEA Bulletin, June 2004.

A key component   Interview with former senior CIA officer, May 27, 2006.

Page 142   **Italy's defense minister**   Transcript of the Martino statement, November 3, 2005.

And it was added   "Nigergate, il dossier di Roma uno scandalo costato una guerra" (Nigergate, the Rome dossier, a scandal leads to a war), http://www. repubblica.it/2005/j/sezioni/esteri/nigergate/blix/blix.html.

Page 143   **"I cannot be 100 percent . . . "**Interview with Baute, May 25, 2006.

Hersh said that   Seymour Hersh, "The Stovepipe," *New Yorker,* October 27, 2003.

Page 144   **"When you're in the eye . . . "**   Interview with Jacques Baute, May 25, 2006.

Chapter 11

Page 146   **On May 6**   Nicholas Kristof, "Missing in Action: Truth," *New York Times,* May 6, 2003.

Page 147   **He called Kristof**   Joseph Wilson, *The Politics of Truth,* New York: Carroll & Graf, lvii.

Before the last two articles   Libby indictment, released on October 28, 2005.

"I didn't ask questions."   Interview with Carl Ford Jr., March 26, 2003.

Page 148   **He told her**   Judith Miller, "My Four Hours Testifying in the Federal Grand Jury Room," *New York Times,* October 16, 2005.

Miller said that   Ibid.

Contrary to Miller's version   Interview with Carl Ford Jr., March 26, 2003.

Page 149   **The resulting leaks**   Fitzgerald court filings.

Libby described   Barton Gellman and Dafna Linzer, "A Concerted Effort to Discredit Bush Critic," *Washington Post,* April 9, 2006, A1.

Two weeks before   Michael Isikoff, "The Man Who Said Too Much," *Newsweek,* August 28, 2006.

Page 150   **Then-CIA director, George Tenet**   Published statement, July 11, 2003.

Page 151   **"The . . . op-ed by Mr. Wilson . . . "**   *US v Libby,* Government's Response to Defendant's Third Motion to Compel Discovery, filed April 5, 2006.

"Do we ordinarily . . . "   Filings by special prosecutor, May 2006.

"To go to Niger is not exactly a benefit,"   Interview with CIA source, February 2006.

Page 152   **Novak later confirmed**   Libby indictment.

After eventually being exposed   R. Jeffrey Smith, "Novak Accuses Plame Source of Distortion," *Washington Post,* September 14, 2006.

But Novak later wrote   Novak column, *Washington Post,* September 14, 2006.

Libby discussed   Judith Miller, "A Personal Account: My Four Hours Testifying in the Federal Grand Jury Room," *New York Times,* October 16, 2005.

There was no evidence   Murray Waas, "Cheney Authorized Leak of CIA Report, Libby Says," *National Journal,* April 14, 2006.

Page 153   **Wilson's wife, Rove said**   Matthew Cooper, "What I Told the Grand Jury," *Time,* July 25, 2005.

So on the following day   Ibid.

Libby also chatted   Libby indictment; and Judith Miller, "A Personal Account: My Four Hours Testifying in the Federal Grand Jury Room," *New York Times,* October 16, 2005.

Also on July 12   Walter Pincus. "Side Issue in the Plame Case: Who Sent Her Spouse to Africa?" *Washington Post,* August 11, 2005, A8.

Page 154   **But Hadley also contended**   White House Press briefing, July 22, 2003.

Page 155   **Wilson said that**   Joseph Wilson, *The Politics of Truth,* New York: Carroll and Graf, liv–lv.

A senior CIA official   Interview with a senior CIA official, July 2003.

but he thought   *Interview with Wilson,* June 15, 2006.

Chapter 12

Page 158   **"There is intelligence . . . "**   British dossier, "Iraq's Weapons of Mass Destruction," 25.

"The details . . . , "   "I've No Idea What Saddam's Up To," *Mirror,* September 9, 2002.

Pages 158–59   **Two years later**   BBC News chronology, October 13, 2004.

Page 159   **Blair later told**   There were various versions of this statement. The Hutton inquiries analyzed drafts of Blair's dossier and noted changes and listed e-mail exchanges prior to the final version. One sentence from an early version of Blair's had been excised—"The case I make is not that Saddam could launch a nuclear attack on London or another part of the UK [he could not]."—was not included in the dossier published on 24 September. [The early inclusion of that sentence showed that drafters of the document were aware that a broad statement about the launch of weapons of mass destruction could be distressing. But the decision left open the most general possibility that any form of attack was possible.

But by the time   Intelligence and Security Committee. Iraqi Weapons of Mass Destruction—Intelligence and Assessments, September 2003.

Page 160   **The Bush administration**   Press briefing, Ari Fleischer, September 24, 2002.

Four days later   Radio address by President Bush, September 28, 2002.

Page 161   **Perhaps the most egregious**   Evidence submitted in the Hutton inquiry.

Page 162   **Campbell also told**   Campbell served Blair as his chief communications and policy adviser from 1994 to August 2003; he faced accusations, later dismissed, that he had helped in exaggerating the intelligence on Iraq.

The UK had no   The Hutton inquiry.

Page 165   **It was later**   Robb-Silberman Commission report.

Sir Richard Dearlove   Testimony before the Parliament Intelligence and Security Committee, investigating Britain's prewar intelligence on Iraq.

Foreign Secretary Jack Straw   BBC interview, July 2003.

Dearlove told   Intelligence and Security Committee, Iraqi Weapons of Mass Destruction—Intelligence and Assessments, September 2003, 28.

Page 166   **In correspondence with us**   Letter from Dearlove, April 24, 2006.

"There was only one . . . "   Interview with former CIA official, March 10, 2006.

Whatever it was   E-mail from Brian Jones, March 27, 2006.

Page 167   **Then he added**   Foreign Affairs Committee, Iraqi Weapons of Mass Destruction—Intelligence and Assessments, July 3, 2003, 52.

The committee could   Ibid.

Jones and his staff   Hutton report, 125.

Page 168   "There was a disjoint ... "   E-mail from Brian Jones.

Page 169   **Britain and the United States**   Interview with a former senior CIA official, May 17, 2006.

At the meeting with Tenet   Text of a secret British government document, "The Secret Downing Street Memo," *Sunday Times (London)*, May 1, 2005.

Page 170   **Robin Cook, a former**   Testimony before Parliament's Foreign Affairs Committee, Foreign Affairs Committee Report, July 3, 2003. Cook died in 2005.

CIA officers who worked   Interviews with former CIA officers, May 16, 2006.

Chapter 13

Page 173   **As evidence**   "Nigergate, lo 007 francese che smonta la tesi del Sismi" *La Repubblica*, December 1, 2005.

"SISMI wanted me ... "   Nicholas Rufford and Nick Fielding, "Tracked Down," *Sunday Times (London)*, August 1, 2004, 13.

On the following day   Mark Huband, "French Probe Led to 'Fake Niger Uranium Papers'," *Financial Times (London)*, August 2, 2004, 8.

Libero, **a small right-wing publication**   *Libero,* August 9, 2004.

Page 174   **They presented**   Interview with Luigi Malabarba, February 28, 2006.

Thus, they staged   Interview with former Paris-based CIA officer, February 10, 2006.

Page 175   **"They [DGSE] literally ... "**   Interview with former CIA officer, February 21, 2006.

Page 176   **One of the most spectacular claims appeared**   Bill Gertz, "France Gave Passports to Help Iraqis Escape," *Washington Times*, May 6, 2003, 1.

Wilkerson, Powell's chief of staff   Speech to New America Foundation, October 19, 2005.

"Our interest in Niger ... "   Interview with former CIA officer, February 21, 2006.

Page 177   **Chouet left**   Tom Hamburger, Peter Wallsten, and Bob Drogin, "French Told CIA of Bogus Intelligence," *Los Angeles Times*, December 11, 2005; and *La Repubblica*, December 1, 2005.

"Chouet is very ... "   Interview with former CIA officer, January 18, 2006.

Again, the French agents concluded   *Los Angeles Times*, op. cit.

Page 178   **My men stayed in Africa**   "Nigergate, lo 007 francese che smonta la tesi del Sismi," *La Repubblica*, December 1, 2005.

Page 179   **The second time Chouet told**   *La Repubblica*, December 1, 2005.

"The French didn't say that so clearly ... "   Interview with Giuseppe Placidi, March 1, 2006.

It was unclear why Chouet told   Bob Drogin and Tom Hamburger, "Niger Uranium Rumors Wouldn't Die," *Los Angeles Times*, February 17, 2006, 1.

"He generally had been reliable ... "   Interview with CIA source, May 12, 2006.

Chapter 14

Page 183   **It gave no hint**   Carlo Bonini and Giuseppe D'Avanzo, "Ecco il falso dossier sull 'uranio di Saddam (This is the false dossier about Saddam's uranium)" *La Reppublica,* July 16, 2003.

Page 184   **"I was really . . . "**   Interview with Elisabetta Burba, March 1, 2006.

Page 185   **"I realized it could be . . . "**   "Italian Correspondent Explains Role in Conveying Iraq–Niger Uranium Dossier," *BBC Monitoring Europe,* July 20, 2003.

    Burba went to the office   "Lo scoop che non c'era," *Panorama,* July 24, 2003.

Page 186   *La Repubblica***'s documents**   Conversation with one of the participants in the document transfer, January 13, 2007.

Page 189   **A Nigerien embassy official told us**   Interview with Nigerien diplomat, February 2006.

Page 191   **Most of Burba's set**   Transcript of portion of Martino interrogation by Franco Ionta, Rome chief magistrate, November 3, 2005.

    SISMI is so inept   Interview with CIA source, March 2006.

Page 192   **On a visit**   Law proposal, Deputies Folana, Violante, et al., February 10, 2002.

    "The senior guys . . . "   Interview with former senior CIA official, March 10, 2006, and on later occasions.

    Martino told an acquaintance   Source who spent several hours with Martino. The information tracks with an account provided in the *American Prospect,* March 10, 2006.

Page 193   **"Unless they're faced . . . "**   Former senior CIA official, May 27, 2006.

    Once he broke his silence   Interview with Italian journalist, March 3, 2006.

    Sismi also found   Defense Minister Antonio Martino briefing members of Italian Parliament, November 3, 2005.

    Martino responded   *Il Giornale,* September 21, 2004.

Page 194   **She did not elaborate**   "Niger-gate, ecco i verbali segreti di Martino," *Il Giornale,* February 17, 2006.

    "They didn't do anything"   Interview with Nigerien diplomat, February 7, 2006.

Page 195   **Nucera portrayed himself as a disinterested go-between**   Ionta interrogation on February 7, 2005.

    In an interview   "L'ex 007 del Sismi:«Io, Martino e la fonte segreta»," *Il Giornale,* November 6, 2005.

    She said that Nucera   Montino testimony, February 7, 2005.

Page 196   **He turned the tapes over**   *Il Giornale,* February 17, 2006. According to edited transcripts of the interrogations in Ionta's office.

    "I looked for information . . . "   Interview with Elisabetta Burba, March 1, 2006.

Page 197   **He told the Rome prosecutors**   *Il Giornale,* according to a tape recording he turned over to Prosecutor Ionta.

Page 198 **Nevertheless, the aide said, it remained a "fluid investigation"** Interview with Ionta aide, Rome, March 1, 2006.

Page 199 **He surfaced again** BBC *Worldwide Monitoring,* November 9, 2005.

Page 200 **Nasr claimed he was tortured** Dana Priest, "Italy Knew About Plan to Grab Suspect; CIA Officials Cite Briefing in 2003," *Washington Post,* June 30, 2005, A1.

Italian prosecutors sought Tracy Wilkinson, "Italy May Charge US Soldier; Rome's Inquiry into the Shooting Death of One of Its Agents in Iraq Focuses on a Guardsman Cleared of Wrongdoing by His Own Government," *Los Angeles Times,* December 23, 2005, 4.

Chapter 15

Page 204 **The committee became** Byron York, "The Kerry Campaigner on the Republican Staff of the Senate Intelligence Committee," *National Review,* June 21, 2006.

The committee released Report on the US Intelligence Community's Prewar Intelligence Assessments on Iraq, 29.

Roberts summed up "Panel Criticizes CIA For Incorrect Iraq Intelligence," *NewsHour with Jim Lehrer,* July 9, 2004.

Page 205 **"I think that . . . "** Interview with Vicki Divoll, January 23, 2006.

Page 206 **They also cited** Report on the US Intelligence Community's Prewar Intelligence Assessments on Iraq, 455.

Paul Pillar, the CIA's top Paul R. Pillar, "Policy,and the War in Iraq," *Foreign Affairs,* March/April 2006.

Page 208 **An exception was** "McCain and Bush Clash on Powers, Scope of Intel Probe," The Hill.com, March 4, 2004.

Chapter 16

Page 210 **Without waiting** Interview with a former senior CIA official, January 16, 2007.

Tenet's decision James Risen, "Prewar Views of Iraq Threat Are Under Review by CIA," *New York Times,* May 22, 2003, 1; and interview with Harlow, January 16, 2007.

Page 211 **For example, the Kerr committee** Intelligence and Analysis on Iraq: Issues for the Intelligence Community, July 29, 2004.

Page 212 **Kerr's investigators** Senate Intelligence Committee report, 68.

SISMI's Nigerien uranium Interview with CIA source, January 19, 2006.

"Part of the problem . . . " Interview with CIA source, October 11, 2006.

Similarly, Africa analysts Interview with Karen Kwiatkowski, February 23, 2006.

Page 213 **A telling illustration** Bob Woodward, *Plan of Attack,* London: Simon & Schuster, 248–49.

Page 214 **A CIA analyst** Report on the US Intelligence Community's Prewar Intelligence Assessments on Iraq, 505.

Page 215   Stu Cohen   "Iraq's WMD Programs: Culling Hard Facts from Soft Myths," http://www.gwu.edu/~nsarchiv/NSAEBB/NSAEBB80/NIC%20Speeches%20-%20Iraq's%20WMD%20Programs.htm.

Page 216   But the June memo   Report on the US Intelligence Community's Prewar Intelligence Assessments on Iraq, 65–71.

Page 217   Shortly after   Senior CIA source, June 11, 2003.

Page 218   "It was policy . . . "   Interview with John Gannon, April 14, 2006.

Chapter 17

Page 220   "The level of . . . "   Interview with Dick Cheney, Lynne Cheney, CNN, *Larry King Live,* May 30, 2005; http://transcripts.cnn.com/TRANSCRIPTS/0505/30/lkl.01.html.

"[The] bottom line . . . "   Interviewed with Dick Cheney by Wolf Blitzer, CNN, January 24, 2007.

Page 221   First Bush announced   Michael Abramowitz, "Bush Works to Rally Support for Iraq 'Surge'," *Washington Post,* January 9, 2007.

headed to a "slow failure"   "President Bush Defends Decision to Send Additional Troops to Iraq," Online NewsHour, January 16, 2007.

Senate Majority Whip   Interview with Illinois senator Richard Durbin, CNN, January 25, 2007.

"I don't think it's an act . . . "   Interview with Patrick Lang, January 30, 2007.

Within the Bush administration   Franklin Foer & Spencer Ackerman, "The Radical," *New Republic,* December 1, 2003.

Cheney at times   Interviews with retired CIA officer, well-informed about the Rove-Cheney case, January 30, 2007.

Page 222   "Not going to protect . . . "   Amy Goldstein and Carol D. Leonnig, "Defense Portrays Libby as Scapegoat; Jury Is Told About White House Rifts," *Washington Post,* January 24, 2007, A1.

Page 223   Carl Ford, who served   Interview with Carl Ford, April 17, 2006.

Page 224   Whether or not   Congressional Record, September 6, 2006, S8991.

The invasion was   Michael E. O'Hanlon, Susan E. Rice, and James B. Steinberg, The Brookings Institution, Policy Brief 113, December 2002.

Page 225   "I witnessed . . . "   The new Pentagon papers, Salon.com; http://dir.salon.com/story/opinion/feature/2004/03/10/osp_moveon/index.html.

Another who spoke out   "A Spy Speaks Out," CBS, *60 Minutes,* April 23, 2006.

Page 226   White and other analysts   Interview with Wayne White, February 23, 2006.

Page 227   Critics complained   Lawrence Wilkerson, "The White House Cabal," *Los Angeles Times,* October 24, 2005.

As late as   Interview of Colin Powell, *Fox News Sunday with Tony Snow,* June 8, 2003.

"I was in disbelief . . . "   Interview with Lawrence Wilkerson, August 3, 2006.

Chapter 18

Page 230   **One week after**   Unclassified key judgments of the NIE titled "Prospects for Iraq's Stability: A Challenging Road Ahead," released February 2, 2007.

Page 230   **"The strategic blunder . . . "**   Interview with Joseph Cirincione, October 18, 2006.

Page 231   **Cirincione had foreseen**   Joseph Cirincione, "Why We Are in Iraq," speech given at American Univerity, March 23, 2003.

Scowcroft had warned in the summer   Brent Scowcroft, "Don't Attack Saddam," *Wall Street Journal*, August 15, 2002.

Page 232   **At least one freelance**   Interview with former CIA officer, April 21, 2006.

Wilkerson said he thought   Interview with Lawrence Wilkerson, August 3, 2006.

"While he did not have . . . "   Transcript, *Meet the Press*, September 10, 2006.

Page 233   **"I left the video . . . "**   Richard Clarke, *Against All Enemies*, New York: Free Press, 2004.

By December 2001, Bush's speechwriter   David Frum, *The Right Man: The Surprise Presidency of George W. Bush*, New York: Random House, 2003, 224.

Page 235   **As the new Democratic-controlled**   Press conference, November 4, 2005.

One confusing element   R. Jeffrey Smith, "Novak Accuses Plame Source of Distortion; Armitage Minimizes Role in Leak," *Washington Post*, September 14, 2006, A14.

Page 236   **"It could be . . . "**   Interview with Lawrence Wilkerson, August 3, 2006.

Frum, Bush's former speechwriter   "Neo Culpa Please Don't Call Them 'Architects of the War'," *Vanity Fair*, January 2007.

Page 237   **A PowerPoint presentation**   David E. Sanger and Mark Mazzetti, "US Says Iran Meddles in Iraq but Is Delaying Release of Data," *New York Times*, February 2, 2007, 13.

"This is one of many . . . "   Interview with intelligence official, February 1, 2007.

In some cases   http://intelligence.house.gov/Media/PDFS/ IranReport082206v2.pdf.

Page 238   **As was the case with Iraq**   Dafna Linzer, "UN Inspectors Dispute Iran Report by House Panel," *Washington Post*, September 14, 2006, A17.

Page 240   **"I cannot deny it . . . "**   *New York Evening Post*, March 3, 1917, quoted in Barbara Tuchman, *The Zimmermann Telegram*, New York: Ballantine, 1985, 183.

Even Bush's father   Bob Woodward, *State of Denial*, New York: Simon & Schuster, 2006, 114.

"US officials never . . . "   E-mail exchange with Walter LaFeber, May 2, 2006.

Page 241   **The Italian letter**   Barbara Tuchman, *The Zimmermann Telegram*, New York: Ballantine, 1985, 200.

Index

Cheney, Richard Bruce ("Dick") *(cont.)*
ElBaradei and, 137
Ford (Carl) and, 223–24
Hussein's (Saddam) link to
    terrorism and, alleged, 8–9,
    71, 211, 238
Iraqi National Congress
    intelligence and, 62
Iraq invasion and, 100, 221
Iraq's purchase of uranium and,
    alleged, 65, 74, 232
Iraq's weapons of mass destruction
    and, alleged, 11, 13–14, 39,
    102–4, 112, 148–49, 220, 232
Jewish Institute for National
    Security Affairs and, 53
Lang and, 222–23
leaks by, authorized, 148–49
Ledeen and, 33
Libby and, 57, 148, 152–53
Pentagon and, 62–63
Plame and, 148
political experience of, 63, 70
power of, 63, 71, 219, 227
Rove and, 221–22
Senior Publish When Ready report
    and, 74
16 words of Bush and, 146
at State of Union address (2003), 2
Team B and, 59
US foreign policy and, 70
US Intelligence Community and,
    57, 70–72
Wilkerson and, 63, 227–28, 232
Wilson's report and, 146, 150–51
Chouet, Alain, 75, 177–81
CIA. *See also* US Intelligence
    Community
Benin warehouse report and, 81
British intelligence and, 169–70
Bush administration and, 51,
    71–72
Bush (George Herbert Walker) and,
    71
Cheney ("Dick") and, 14, 70–73,
    119–20
Cincinnati speech of Bush (George
    Walker) and, 107–8
Counterproliferation Division of,
    28, 75–76, 148
dissemination of information from
    other agencies and, 141

French intelligence and, 175–79
Harith's intelligence and, 55–56
Hussein's (Saddam) link to
    terrorism and, 18
International Atomic Energy
    Agency and, 141, 217
Iraq invasion and, inevitability of,
    130
Iraq's nuclear buildup and, alleged,
    6
Iraq's purchase of uranium and,
    alleged, 27–28, 66–68, 105–6,
    108, 123
Iraq's weapons of mass destruction
    and, alleged, 13, 50, 91
Italian letter and, 4, 25, 37, 40,
    107–8, 217–18
Kerr team's report and, 210–13
Marseille report and, 80
in post–Italian letter period, 210–19
rendition program of, 200
reorganization act (2004) and,
    234–35
review of White House speeches
    and, 107–8, 114, 118
ridicule of, for buying into Italian
    letter, 186
Robb-Silberman Commission and,
    213, 215
Rome station intelligence report
    and, 66–68
Rome station of, 27–28, 66–68
Rumsfeld and, 211
Senate Intelligence Committee
    investigation and, 213–14
Senior Publish When Ready report
    of, 74
September 11, 2001, terrorist
    attacks and, 141
SISMI and, 4, 25, 66, 187–89,
    191–92, 199
Wilson and, 76
Wilson's report and, 78–79, 83–84,
    150
Cincinnati speech of George Walker
    Bush (2002), 16, 38–39,
    106–10, 154
Circular reporting, intelligence, 165
Cirincione, Joseph, 230–31, 239
Clarke, Richard, 7, 233
Clinton, Bill, 239
Clinton administration, 85, 139

COGEMA (French government-run mining consortium), 78
Cohen, Stu, 215–16
Comey, James, 154
Commission on the Intelligence Capabilities of the United States Regarding Weapons of Mass Destruction, 207–8
Cook, Robin, 170, 224
Cooper, Matthew, 153
COPACO (Italian parliamentary committee), 174, 199
Corriere della Sera, 18, 184–85
Cotonou warehouses, 42–43, 80–81, 189, 216
Counterproliferation Division of CIA, 28, 75–76, 148
Cuban Missile Crisis (1962), 129, 131
Curveball (Iraqi fabricator code name), 55, 212

D

Dearlove, Sir Richard, 165–66, 169
Defense Intelligence Agency (DIA), 25, 28, 55, 61, 65, 68–70, 80–81. *See also* US Intelligence Community
DeMuth, Christopher, 53
DGSE, 75, 81, 172–77, 179–82. *See also* French intelligence
DIA, 25, 28, 55, 61, 65, 68–70, 80–81. *See also* US Intelligence Community
Divoll, Vicki, 205
Dodge, Simon, 40, 121–23
Downing Street Memos, 169
Drumheller, Tyler, 225
Durbin, Richard, 205–6, 221

E

ElBaradei, Mohamed, 3, 133–40, 140, 142, 144, 146, 238
Elhadj, Ailele, 24

F

Farino, Renato, 173–74
Federal Bureau of Investigation (FBI), 141, 199–202. *See also* US Intelligence Community

Feith, Douglas, 51, 53, 56–59, 63–64, 225
Fitzgerald, Patrick, 149, 151, 154, 235
Fleischer, Ari, 104, 160
Fleitz, Fred, 237
Foley, Alan, 113, 118–21, 124–26, 155
Ford, Carl Jr., 14, 40–41, 83, 120, 126, 132, 147, 223–24
Ford, Gerald, 57–58
Franklin, Lawrence, 32
Free Iraqi Forces, 60–61
French intelligence. *See also* General Directorate for External Security (DGSE)
 CIA and, 175–79
 Italian letter and, 3–4, 75, 172–82
 Marseille report and, 81
 SISMI and, 172–76, 179, 182
 Wilkerson's view of, 176
French Ministry of Foreign Affairs, 180
Frum, David, 233–34, 236
Fukuyama, Francis, 52
Fulford, Carleton, 78

G

Gadhafi, Muammar, 85
Gannon, John, 70–71, 218–19
Gates, Robert, 119
GCHQ, 139
General Directorate for External Security (DGSE), 75, 81, 172–77, 179–82. *See also* French intelligence
German intelligence, 5, 212
Gerson, Michael, 100, 106–7, 115, 155–56
Ghorbanifar, Manucher, 32–33
Gilligan, Andrew, 161–62
Goodman, Melvin, 69, 71, 119, 121, 125
Gordon, Michael, 101
Government Communications Headquarters (GCHQ), 139
Grossman, Marc, 147–48
Groupthink, 204–5
Gulf of Tonkin resolution, 5
Gulf War (1991), 12, 67, 70, 76
Gwozdecky, Mark, 140, 143

H

Habibou, Allele Elhadj, 188
Hadley, Stephen J. ("Steve"), 59, 98,
    106–7, 114–15, 154
Hagel, Chuck, 204
Hannah, John F., 62, 129
Harith, Mohammed, 55–56
Hastert, John Dennis, 1–2
Hersh, Seymour, 143, 183
Hitchens, Christopher, 92–94
Hoagland, Jim, 132
Houdek, Robert, 216
House Intelligence Committee, 237
Hussein, Qusai, 91
Hussein, Saddam. *See also* Iraq
    Italian letter and, addressee of, 4,
        20
    Middle East instability and, report
        on, 53
    nuclear weapons labs of,
        speculation about, 93, 95–96
    Scarlett's claims about, 161–62
    terrorism link of, alleged, 2, 5–9,
        50, 57, 61, 71, 99, 211, 238
    Wilson and, 76
    Wolfowitz and overthrow of, 51
Hussein, Udai, 91
Hutton, Law Lord (Baron), 161
Hutton inquiry, 161–62

I

IAEA, 3, 81, 89–91, 133, 135–38,
    140–44, 217, 238
Il Giornale, 194–95
INC, 8, 54–56, 60–62
Inge, Field Marshal Lord, 164
INR, 39–40, 76, 113, 121. *See also*
    US Intelligence Community
International Atomic Energy Agency
    (IAEA), 3, 81, 89–91, 133,
    135–38, 140–44, 217, 238
Ionta, Franco, 193–94, 196, 198
Iran, 138, 208, 211, 230, 237–38
Iraq. *See also* Hussein, Saddam
    aluminum tubes purchase of, 50–51,
        101, 121–22, 131–32, 217
    declaration to UN Security Council
        of, 112–14
    nuclear buildup of, alleged, 13,
        91–92, 101–2

reconstruction policy, 204
    September 11, 2001, terrorist
        attacks link and, alleged, 6,
        8–9, 56–57
    UN sanctions on, 85
    UN weapons inspectors and, 12
    uranium purchase of, alleged, 3, 6,
        16, 20, 27–28, 39–40, 65–68,
        73–74, 100–104, 106, 108,
        114–15, 123, 232
    weapons of mass destruction of,
        alleged, 2–3, 10–11, 13, 16,
        38–39, 50, 91–92, 100–105,
        109, 112, 148–49, 157,
        162–63, 167–69, 220, 231–33,
        232
Iraqi National Congress (INC), 8,
    54–56, 60–62
Iraq invasion (2003)
    Baghdad's fall (April 9, 2003), 145
    Berlusconi's position on, 192
    British support for, 170–71
    Bush administration and, 98–99,
        233
    Bush (George Herbert Walker) and,
        240
    Bush (George Walker) and, 13, 15,
        145, 221, 229
    Cheney ("Dick") and, 100, 221
    CIA and inevitability of, 130
    Cirincione and, 230–31
    Congressional authorization of,
        110
    fourth anniversary of, 220–21
    investigations of intelligence
        failures after, 203–9, 235
    Iraq's weapons of mass destruction
        and, lack of, 91–92, 203
    Italian letter and, 5, 38, 239
    Kwiatkowski and, 224–25
    Libby and, 52
    Newbold's view of, 64
    outcome of, to date, 5
    prewar intelligence and, 10–11, 160
    public support for, 3, 5, 10, 98–101,
        111
    rationale for, 3–4, 7, 15, 220
    questions surrounding, 238–39
    resolutions and protests against,
        111–12, 224–26
    Rumsfeld and, 7
    Scowcroft and, 231

L

LaFeber, Walter, 240
Lang, Patrick W., 10, 60–61, 221–23
La Repubblica
  Blix's comment in, 142
  Chouet interview in, 178–79
  Italian letter article, 183–84,
    186–88, 190, 192
"La Signora." *See* Montini, Laura
Lawrence Livermore National
    Laboratory, 121
League of Nations, 239
Ledeen, Michael Arthur, 31–33, 53
Levin, Carl, 106, 115, 136, 205–6
Libby, I. Lewis ("Scooter")
  challenges of intelligence analysts
    and, 71–72
  Cheney ("Dick") and, 57, 148,
    152–53
  Cooper and, 153
  Grossman and, 147–48
  Iraqi National Congress and, 62
  Iraq invasion and, 52
  Miller and, 101, 152
  Plame leak and, alleged, 147–48,
    151–53, 202
  Powell (Colin) speech draft and,
    129
  Team B and, 59
  trial of, 222, 235
  White House Iraq Group and, 98–99
Libya embargo, 85
London Times, 197
Los Angeles Times, 13
Luti, William, 58, 62

M

Mainassara, Ibrahim Bare, 88
Maine explosion (1898), 5
Malabarba, Luigi, 174
Maloof, F. Michael, 56–57
Manenti, Alberto, 192
Marseille report, 80–81
Martinez, Serge, 74
Martino, Antonio, 142
Martino, Rocco
  background information about,
    17–18
  Burba (Elisabetta) and, 15–22,
    25–26, 34, 36, 43–45, 68

deception of, 197–98
  Italian letter and, 20–22, 34–35,
    38, 66, 68, 172–73, 192, 194,
    196–97
  London Times interview of, 197
  Montini and, 34–36, 195–97
  motivation of, 17–19
  Nadal and, 179
  Niger secret codebook and, 21–22,
    188
  "outing" of, 201
  Panorama and, 21
  reputation of, 15
  SISMI and, 184, 192–94
  60 Minutes interview of, 197
Mayaki, Ibrahim, 84, 92, 152–54
McCain, John, 207–8
McGovern, Ray, 119–20
McLaughlin, John, 130, 213
Medusa rocket, 122
MI6, 159, 164–66, 170, 183, 209. *See
  also* British intelligence
Miller, Judith, 101, 148, 152–54
Miscik, Jami, 6, 116
Montini, Laura ("La Signora"),
    34–36, 73, 194–97
Mulé, Giorgio, 19, 26, 43, 45
Muller, Robert S., 201
Murray, Bill, 34
Myers, Richard, 114
Mylroie, Laurie, 9

N

Nadal, Jacques, 179
Nascetti, Dina, 187
Nasr, Hassan Mustafa Osama,
    200
Nasser 81 rocket, 122
National Counterproliferation
    Center, 140
National Defense University, 125
National Intelligence Estimate (NIE)
    (2002), 54, 105, 149, 163–64,
    181, 204, 213–14
National Intelligence Estimate (NIE)
    (2006), 230
National Military Command Center,
    7
National Military Joint Intelligence
    Center, 102
National Security Act (1947), 63

White, Wayne, 71, 95, 226
White House Iraq Group (WHIG), 11, 98–101, 106, 109–10, 112–14
White paper, 104–5, 125, 157–62, 164. *See also* British dossier
Wilkerson, Lawrence
  Armitage and, 236
  Bush administration and, vocal criticism of after leaving State Department, 226–28
  "cabal" of intelligence and, 51, 227
  Cheney ("Dick") and, 63, 227–28, 232
  Joseph and, 124
  Marseille report and, 80–81
  Powell (Colin) and, 127–29, 132–33, 226
  Rice and, 227
  Rumsfeld and, 227
Wilson, Joseph
  CIA and, 76
  Hitchens and, 92–93
  Hussein (Saddam) and, 76
  Italian letter, verifying, 41, 75–78
  Kristof's *New York Times* article and, 146–47
  lawsuit against government officials and, 235
  Mayaki and, 92
  New Republic article about, 147
  New York Times article by, 150
  regret of, 96–97
  report of, 78–79, 83–85, 146, 150–51, 180

Senate Select Committee on Intelligence report criticizing, 205
  Washington Post article about, 147
  White House motives for leaks about wife of, 155–56
Wilson, Woodrow, 239–40
WINPAC, 51, 74, 76, 94, 105, 112, 116, 120–24, 126, 144, 152
Wolf, John, 139
Wolfowitz, Paul Dundes, 8–10, 51–53, 56, 58, 63, 99, 216
Woodward, Bob, 149–50
Woolsey, James, 7–8, 31–32, 38, 55
World Economic Forum (Davos, Switzerland), 114–15
World Trade Center bombing (1993), 8–9
World War I, 5
Wurmser, David, 56–57

Y

Yellowcake, 4, 17, 33, 39, 41, 66–67, 84. *See also* Iraq, uranium purchase of, alleged
York, Byron, 204

Z

Zimmermann, Arthur, 239–40
Zimmermann Telegram, 1, 5, 239–41
Zinni, Anthony, 111–12